Some People Prefer Hotels

SOME PEOPLE PREFER HOTELS

Motorhome Novices Tour Cornwall

Nigel Rowland Hicks

Matador
9 Priory Business Park,
Wistow Road, Kibworth Beauchamp,
Leicestershire. LE8 0RX
Tel: (+44) 116 279 2299
Fax: (+44) 116 279 2277
Email: books@troubador.co.uk
Web: www.troubador.co.uk/matador

ISBN 978 178306 143 3

British Library Cataloguing in Publication Data.
A catalogue record for this book is available from the British Library.

Printed and bound in the UK by TJ International, Padstow, Cornwall
Typeset by Troubador Publishing Ltd, Leicester, UK

Matador is an imprint of Troubador Publishing Ltd

MIX
Paper from
responsible sources
FSC www.fsc.org FSC® C013056

To Ray…
…who much prefers hotels!

CONTENTS

PROLOGUE

We rudely awoke to the deafening RAT-A-TAT-TAT of giant raindrops smashing down on our flimsy roof, and felt as though we were incarcerated inside a giant drum. It was cold and damp inside our drum, and the wet patches on the floor beneath the soaking coats we'd hung up to dry the night before, along with our muddy boots spread out on soggy newspaper, did nothing to dispel our dismal moods.

We lifted the blind and peered out at the dreary view which was distorted by torrents of water cascading down the outside of the window. Whopping great raindrops were falling like stair rods from the dark overcast sky, and we were momentarily mesmerised by the concentric circles radiating out from where they splattered into the ever deepening, ever widening puddles in the gravel pathways.

It wasn't meant to be like this. What with the relatively long spell of hot dry weather, which we foolishly thought would last forever, we hadn't experienced such lousy conditions for some considerable time. And as we stared out into the gloom, we began to have serious doubts about our combined states of mind when deciding to invest virtually all our savings in the motorhome dream. Still, there was nothing we could do about the weather and it seemed stupid to even contemplate packing up and going home. Although, if truth be told, we were both tempted to do so. We just had to weather the storm, as it were, and hope it soon brightened up. After all, we hadn't been away from home for twenty-four hours yet, and surely the relentless rain would soon blow over. Wouldn't it?

★ ★ ★

It all started just a few weeks before when, virtually on the spur of the moment, we decided to look at motorhomes. My wife, Emm, hated flying and we usually holidayed by coach. However, we'd been to most of the European tourist traps and somewhere deep in the back of my mind I had a vague notion to buy a motorhome when we retired in a few years' time.

Emm had hankered after a holiday home abroad and a few years previously we'd been tempted with a property in the south of France. Finance didn't seem to be an immediate problem, as in the days before the credit crunch the building society generously offered to give us – or rather loan us – enough money to buy it. However, it would have meant increasing our existing mortgage by £80,000 and extending it for another twenty-five years. So, after much agonising, we decided against it. If flying was out of the question, it was a long way away and I, for one, didn't think we'd have got much use out of it. In any case, we'd only get to see the south of France.

But, with a motorhome, I reasoned, once we'd both retired, we'd be able to travel to loads of new UK and European destinations, as well as revisit some of our favourite haunts. We'd have the freedom to go where we wanted, when we wanted and stay as long as we wanted and we could take Monty, our beloved Border Terrier, with us, rather than always feeling guilty when we left him behind in kennels looking sad and forlorn with his tail between his legs.

Furthermore, I didn't think it would be wise to burden ourselves with a massive mortgage until we were well into our eighties!

And so it was, that, one sunny August afternoon, we found ourselves looking at scores of different motorhomes at a large dealer's premises in north Somerset. The salesman put us under no pressure whatsoever and was perfectly happy for us to browse around on our own for a couple of hours. In fact, if he'd been at all pushy we'd probably have gone home again with our bank balance still intact. However, even though we were surprised at the high cost of most of them, we were so impressed by what we saw that I suddenly found myself test driving a used motorhome along the roads around

Wellington. And, before we knew it, we'd agreed to part with almost all our savings and become first time motorhome owners!

By necessity, we'd always been careful with money and usually carried out loads of research before spending large sums. This time, however, we must have been seduced by the hot, sunny weather which lulled us into thinking motorhome holidays always enjoyed such glorious sunshine. We only went to get some idea of what we could get for our money, and even in our wildest dreams never thought we'd end up buying one that very afternoon. But we did. And, although we didn't like to admit as much to each other, we were both in a bit of a daze during our drive back home.

Even though it was one of the cheapest models they had, it still cost far more hard earned cash than we'd ever spent on any single item (apart from our bungalow of course). But we could see that motorhomes held their value much better than cars, so persuaded ourselves that, if it didn't work out, we could always sell it again and recoup most of our money. After all, we reckoned, how many thousands could we spend on numerous holidays in hotels and never get anything back?

Having looked at all the different layouts we both liked this one the best,[1] and that in itself appeared to be a good omen as we often disagreed on many things. The rear facing kitchen had more work surface than most; a gas cooker, with an oven, grill and hob; a large refrigerator that worked off electricity or gas, plus plenty of cupboard space. A washroom with hand basin, shower and toilet was situated to one side at the back, next to which was a gas heater with a spacious wardrobe above.

In the central lounge area there were two bench seats with masses of storage space beneath them, and these pulled together to form a double bed – duvets and pillows being stored in a large locker above the driving cab during the daytime – and there were loads of cupboards along both sides. A table could be placed between the bench

---

1   Two and a half-year-old, two berth, coach built, Fiat based, Ace Capri.

seats for mealtimes, but folded flat to be stowed away in the wardrobe when not in use, and a bicycle rack which could hold two bikes, plus a sophisticated awning to provide shade from the anticipated hot sun, were fitted as extras.

All in all, it seemed comfortable enough, as well as functional, and I think the deciding factor was the bright and airy interior colour scheme which, with its light wood veneer and pale yellow and orange seat fabric, somehow gave an illusion of permanently warm sunshine. So we were hooked!

My hand trembled as I wrote out a cheque to pay a deposit and we went away fully prepared to empty our savings account before returning the following weekend. Mind you, when we drove back to pay the balance and take delivery, although we didn't like to say as much to each other, I think we'd both started to have second thoughts. I know I did! We'd never even stepped inside a motorhome before, let alone knew anything about them, and had virtually acted on a whim.

However, once we saw our motorhome again gleaming in the sunshine, all negative thoughts were forgotten and we gladly signed the paperwork and handed over our large building society cheque.

As part of the deal we were grateful to receive a mini-course on how to manage our new acquisition and John, our instructor, took several hours patiently showing us motorhome novices everything we needed to know. For example, how to connect to the electricity supply, how to use the leisure battery, how to connect and operate the gas bottle, how to operate the water heater and how to put up the awning. Also, how to operate the fridge, how to fill the water tank, how to empty the waste water tank and how to fill and empty the toilet. When I say *fill the toilet,* I mean fill it with the special chemical – not fill it in its literal sense…

Anyhow, you get the picture. But it was all very confusing at first. And by the time John left us to it, we wondered how on earth we'd ever remember everything he'd so carefully explained. However, the next part of our course was to put everything into practice by spending the night in the dealer's car park. It may not have been all that salubrious camping on tarmac adjacent to a main road, especially as we felt a bit vulnerable being the only people there, but we were connected to electricity, had our own cooking facilities and toilet and, with the help of the handbooks, were able to go over everything again in our own time. After all, if we were to experience any problems, it was far better to sort them out now rather than on our first motorhome holiday – when we could make total idiots of ourselves…

Emm cooked our first motorhome meal which, as we weren't driving, we washed down with a celebratory bottle of wine. Technically, I suppose, we were still in charge of a vehicle and I was a bit concerned as to where we would have stood if some overzealous policeman decided to drop in on us with his breathalyser kit. But, after a couple of glasses, I no longer gave it a thought.

After finishing our meal, Emm washed everything up in the sink and I took Monty for a walk which, I must admit, wasn't all that enjoyable. Whereas we were more used to quiet country lanes and fields, we had to walk alongside a very busy road with noisy traffic thundering past. But, no matter, camping here for one night was a means to an end, and on our future motorhome holidays I knew we'd experience the peace and tranquillity of some of the best countryside and coastal locations in the UK, as well as Europe.

When we got back, Monty settled down and seemed happy enough in his new environment, whilst we studied the manuals once more and finished the wine. Eventually my head started to spin, not so much through drinking too much wine, I hasten to add, but more as a result of reading all the intricate and confusing motorhome technicalities. Well, that's my story and I'm sticking to it!

Eventually we could read no more and called it a day. Then, having stowed the table away, converted the bench seats into our bed for the night and made it up with the duvets and pillows we'd brought from home, we snuggled down beside each other. And very comfortable we were too.

After our breakfast cereal the following morning, John returned to see how we'd got on and we thought he was going to test us on everything he'd told us the previous day. He didn't, but we had loads of questions and points of clarification to ask him. Eventually, when we felt we'd gleaned as much information from him as possible, we thanked him and let him go home for his Sunday lunch.

Now we thought we had a pretty good idea of what we were doing, we prepared to pack up and drive home, Emm in the car and me in the motorhome. We switched off the electricity supply, disconnected the cable and coiled it up, turned off the gas cylinder, made sure the windows and skylight were closed and sorted out all the other essential things John had told us to do.

After Emm had gone on ahead in the car with Monty, I felt very alone. I nervously started the engine, slowly made my way out of the car park and apprehensively negotiated a busy roundabout before filtering onto the M5. Driving on the motorway was particularly daunting with all the Sunday afternoon traffic thundering past and causing the motorhome to wobble in their slipstreams. But, luckily, I didn't have to go too far before turning off at Taunton, where I picked up the A358 which took me back to our bungalow in the small village of Chiselborough, between Yeovil and Crewkerne.

When I arrived home and made my way up our narrow, twisty driveway, Emm was waiting for me, obviously worried about her large investment. As I turned into our parking area between a very mature conifer and our car, I worried how I'd ever manage to reverse out again and point the motorhome back down the driveway. It had never been a problem with the car, but with the wider, longer, taller motorhome I could see it was going to be rather tricky.

I didn't really have to worry about that at the moment though; I just wanted a cup of tea. However, I knew that in order to turn around in the confined space and head back down the driveway again, I'd have to move the car out of the way, then shunt backwards and forwards several times whilst taking great care not to hit any large shrubs or overhanging branches.

Anyhow, we both applied for annual leave and at the beginning of September 2006 were about to drive off to Cornwall for our very first motorhome holiday. This is how we got on. Or didn't, as the case may be.

1

PACKING UP

Packing up hadn't been quite as straightforward as I thought it would be. To my simple mind, preparing for a motorhome holiday should have been relatively easy. After all, it's not like going on a package tour by coach, train or aircraft where everything has to be carefully placed in suitcases and then unpacked at the final destination.

Nor is it like going in a car on a camping trip, as we used to do, when the tent, sleeping bags, cooking equipment and everything else had to be carefully crammed into every available space in our tiny Fiat 850 and then erected and sorted out at the campsite. Trying to pitch our tent in foul weather and sort out cooking equipment, sleeping bags and all the other essential stuff we had to take with us was always a bit of a nightmare, especially when we went away with our very young daughters.

It should have been so much easier with a motorhome – or so I thought. After all, we just had to take our clothes, complete with hangers, out of the wardrobe in the bungalow and transfer them to the spacious wardrobe in the motorhome. Fair enough, not all clothes are usually hung on hangers, so underwear, T-shirts, socks and suchlike could be placed in plastic baskets and either put on the shelf at the top of the wardrobe or in one of the many cupboards. Also, all food could be simply transferred straight from the bungalow fridge and kitchen cupboards to the motorhome fridge and kitchen cupboards. In other words, it should only be necessary to move everything from its usual place in the bungalow to its corresponding space in the motorhome – and then drive off.

However, for us, it wasn't that easy. For some unknown reason, Emm wasn't happy about travelling with clothes hanging on coat hangers in the wardrobe and wanted to pack them in a suitcase. I'd already hung my stuff up and told her it was crazy to crease up our clothes by cramming them in a case, and then have to unpack it when we arrived at our destination. After all, I reasoned, there was nowhere in the motorhome we could logically keep a suitcase, and the only place Emm could think of was in the wardrobe, which I thought was barking mad!

The last thing I wanted to do before we set off was have an argument. So I had two choices, either to just give in and take the case with us, or try to calmly cajole her round to my point of view. I took a deep breath, chose the latter and had three points to make. Firstly, I reasoned that touring in the motorhome wasn't like staying in a hotel where we could unpack, put all our clothes away (even iron them, if necessary) and then have plenty of room for an empty suitcase. Secondly, the built-in wardrobe in the motorhome really was designed for clothes to be hung up in whilst travelling along. Thirdly, the probability of our clothes falling off their hangers was very slight and, even if they did, the consequences would be insignificant. However, she wasn't convinced and still wanted to take the suitcase.

We also had words about what we could put in the top cupboards. Emm was worried that the cupboard doors could fly open and their contents would be hurled out and get damaged or cause an accident. I reiterated that the motorhome was meant to be driven along at reasonable speeds with everyday items put away in the numerous purpose built cupboards, all of which had special catches to stop the doors from inadvertently opening. Fair enough, we were warned that heavy objects, like televisions, microwaves and suchlike, shouldn't be transported in the top cupboards. But, in my view, Emm's knickers and my Y-fronts didn't really come into that category.

She was particularly concerned about her oval-shaped vanity case, which is about ten inches long by eight inches wide by ten inches high and filled with all manner of mysterious bottles, sachets and other *can't-do-without* items, all of which she argued were breakable or needed to be kept upright. I don't really know what they all were, or why she couldn't go on holiday without them, but every time we've been away the vanity case with its mysterious contents has always come with us. I've long ceased to ask the reason why, but whether we've travelled by car, coach or train, it's always been by her side and never out of reach.

Anyhow, I was forbidden to put the vanity case in a top cupboard, lest the door did come open. I was getting more frustrated by the minute; time was getting on and, what with our silly disagreements, I'm afraid I started to lose my patience and get ever so slightly irritable. And we hadn't even driven off our driveway yet!

Emm was still hung up over her suitcase, but there was no way I wanted to be tripping over it all week and positively refused to take it. I was about to give in by suggesting it could be stored under the motorhome when we pitched up for the night (so I could *accidently* drive off without it in the morning), when Emm saw the sense in what I'd been saying. But I had to compromise somewhere. So in the end, my trousers, shirts, fleeces and coats stayed on the hangers; Emm's clothes lay flat in a box in the bottom of the wardrobe; her vanity case, with all its strange contents, stayed on the floor in the washroom carefully covered in towels to cushion any violent movements, and the suitcase stayed at home.

That wasn't the end of it though, as we also had conflicting opinions about the bicycle I insisted on taking. Emm didn't want me to, but as there was a purpose built bicycle rack fitted to the motorhome my view was that it just had to be used. The problem was that my bike was nothing like a modern lightweight machine.

It was undeniably heavy and had belonged to my aunt who was a midwife back in the 1950s and 60s when home-births were the norm, and she used it to visit all the expectant mothers and deliver their babies. She has now passed her ninetieth birthday, and she probably had her bicycle when she was a very young lady, so you can imagine how old it was. I have to admit that it may have looked a bit odd with

3

its old-fashioned calliper brakes, rusty metal mudguards, and a basket strapped to its handlebars. But as I envisaged myself pedalling back from the local shops with everyday essential items like milk, bread, a newspaper and bottles of wine balanced in the basket, I didn't care what it looked like.

My aunt had kindly given it to our eldest daughter, Joscelin, some years previously when she was a teenager. But she refused to use it. At that age, she only ever wanted the very latest model bicycle, what they call these days a *mountain bike*, with twenty-five gears and no mudguards. And even though the chain would frequently come off when she changed gear, and mud and water would spray up all over her front and back, she would have been mortified to be seen riding Aunt's much older, but far more practical model, which only had two gears – *stop* and *go*.

I just can't understand how modern manufacturers have got away with selling bicycles minus mudguards for so long. I recently looked in at a large branch of a well-known bicycle stockist and couldn't see a single model fitted with them. I'm pretty sure that if I'd enquired of the spotty youth in charge about a bicycle with mudguards, or even for some mudguard accessories that could be fitted to a new bike, he wouldn't have had a clue what I was talking about and would have regarded me as some kind of geriatric old fart, which in today's mad modern world I suppose I am.

Rather than admit to my aunt that Joscelin wasn't actually using her faithful old machine, we might have given her the impression that she used it on a daily basis to go backwards and forwards to college and then took it with her to university. In reality, I took it to my place of work at the Royal Naval Air Station at Yeovilton, where I left it in the bike sheds and used it to cycle over to the squash courts at lunchtimes.

Now, I have to admit that when some of my squash opponents saw me arrive on this *Mary Poppins* style bicycle with my sports bag firmly secured on the ancient spring loaded metal carrier behind me and my squash racquet carefully balanced in the basket, they often had a huge laugh at my expense. However, the smile would be wiped off their faces after I'd given them a good beating which, even though most of them had the advantage of being decades younger than me, did happen fairly often.

Anyhow, I'd brought the bike home from work and, whilst waiting for Emm to finally decide what clothes to take, I gave it a good oiling and a quick once-over. Realising that the brakes weren't that good, I adjusted them as best I could before fixing it to the bike rack with the special clamp supplied with the motorhome. As I was checking it was absolutely secure, Emm reappeared to tell me in no uncertain terms that I'd been wasting my time and that we should leave it behind. However, I ignored her comments, and even though the antiquated relic might have looked a bit wacky strapped on the back of the modern motorhome, I stubbornly left it with a steely determination to prove her wrong and make sure I put it to good use on our trip.

Anyhow, it was getting on for ten o'clock and I was anxious to get going. We'd intended to leave much earlier, but after a hard week at work were both too tired to pack everything into the motorhome on the Friday night. If we'd done so, we'd have been halfway to Cornwall by then. But, having faffed about with suitcases, vanity cases and bicycles, etc., it had taken far longer to pack up than it should have. So when we were finally ready to leave I felt quite fraught, and the thought of all the Saturday holiday traffic we were bound to meet up ahead didn't help my mood one little bit.

Even though it hadn't been the best of starts to our motorhome holiday we'd hopefully learnt some important lessons and I was sure that packing up for our next trip would be much less stressful. For a start, we'd put as much as possible into the motorhome the day before we set off, thus enabling us to leave much earlier in a better state of mind. Also, especially after we'd retired in a few years' time, we'd travel off-peak when less traffic would be on the road.

2

DRIVING IN THE RAIN

Whilst waiting for Emm to finish her last minute packing, I decided to back out of our parking area and point the motorhome in the right direction facing down the drive. This was just as tricky as I thought it would be, and when reversing with only the wing mirrors to go by I found it impossible to judge distances between the rear of the vehicle and any obstacles behind it.

The rear of the motorhome was particularly fragile, so there was no room for error, and I wondered why the manufacturers didn't provide more protection for the flimsy plastic panels and rear light clusters. I know good old-fashioned metal bumpers would provide additional weight, but cynically thought that the motorhome industry would welcome a certain amount of damage so they could sell loads of spare body parts at highly inflated prices. Anyhow, I was lucky to get away with it that time, but decided that when reversing in the future I'd *always* get Emm to stand behind and guide me. Either that or I'd have to invest in reversing sensors or a rear view camera.

Anyhow, after all our faffing about, we really were ready to get going and Emm locked up the bungalow. Monty had already jumped aboard and was sat down between the front seats, seemingly just as anxious as me to get moving. However, before we could do so, we had to complete our pre-start checks. Having worked with aircraft, I knew all about the importance of pre-flight inspections and, based on what John had so diligently told us on our course, we'd typed up a list of essential checks to be carried out before setting off in the motorhome.

For example, we checked the gas bottle was turned off, and that all windows and the skylight were securely shut; we checked everything was stowed away, and that all cupboards were closed and locked; we checked the steps had been retracted; that the glass cover over the hob was in the down position, and that the fridge door was closed and locked. Knowing that we needed to fill up with diesel at the garage a few miles up the road, we then double checked which side of the vehicle the fuel cap was located so I'd be sure of pulling up at the pump with the filler cap close to the nozzle.

Having satisfied ourselves that everything was in order, we then made sure Monty was firmly attached to his travelling harness, which we'd secured to the base of one of the bench seats. This allowed him to be able to sit or lie down between us at the front of the vehicle, but not run amok or get in my way when driving. We then checked everything once more and when we were both happy I started the engine and selected first gear. I automatically reached for the hand brake with my left hand and was mystified why I felt nothing but thin air. Then, remembering the handbrake was on the opposite side to the car, I reached down with my right hand, but again only grasped a handful of fresh air.

For a split second, I was totally bemused and thought the handbrake must have become detached. I then came to my senses and remembered it was a lot lower down than in a conventional car, so reached down and bent forward at the same time. Much to my relief, my right hand met the handbrake this time, and regaining my composure I managed to release it before gently easing my foot off the clutch and slowly pulling away.

However, after travelling six feet or so, I stopped, slipped the gear lever back into neutral, pulled the handbrake back on and switched off the ignition. I then got out of the vehicle and went back to recheck the bicycle was still firmly secured – which of course it was!

Before finally agreeing we really were ready to set off on our first motorhome holiday, we then felt compelled to double check everything yet again. At the bottom of our driveway I strained my neck in both directions to ensure nothing was coming down the narrow lane, and then very slowly and very carefully I pulled away. At the end of the village we turned right at the crossroads, again taking an enormous amount of care, and were soon ready to join the A356 where I pulled up and prepared to turn right onto this fairly busy road.

This was always a rather daunting manoeuvre; the junction was at an acute angle to the main road, largely hidden from view by tall hedges and very close to a sharp bend immediately to our right. Consequently, traffic tended to whiz round the bend completely oblivious to other vehicles trying to pull out from the junction – just like we needed to do.

Every time we had to turn right at this junction – which was every day on the way to work – it almost felt as though we were risking our lives. This time it was even worse as I realised I could have positioned the motorhome better, and with the vehicle angled as it was, even though I had a good view of the bend to our right, I couldn't clearly see the road to our left through the passenger window.

Consequently, I had to rely on Emm to assure me that the road on her side was clear and it was safe to proceed. However, I knew from experience that it was never a good idea to just take her word for it and pull out without first double checking myself. The big problem is that she can't always tell right from left. So when, for example, she might warn me that a car was coming towards us from our left, it could be possible for me to look left, see absolutely nothing coming and then pull out into a potentially lethal situation with a car steaming towards us from the right hand side!

Anyhow, two heads are always better than one, and between us we apprehensively looked out for traffic in both directions and when, and only when, I was absolutely certain it was safe to do so, prepared to pull out and turn right. Again, I instinctively reached down with my left hand to release the handbrake, but quickly remembered it was on the opposite side. Hoping I would soon get used to this, I put my left hand back on the steering wheel and leant forward to release the handbrake correctly. However, my delay had allowed another car to speed around the bend towards us, so we had to wait once more until the road was clear. Eventually, it was safe to proceed and we were on our way, albeit much later than I'd initially hoped.

About half a mile up the road, I turned left onto the slip road and tentatively filtered into the west bound traffic on the busy A303 dual carriageway. Less than five minutes later I nervously negotiated the known accident black spot which is the South Petherton roundabout, and then very gingerly pulled into the Esso filling station. We both kept our eyes peeled for the nearest diesel pump as the last thing we wanted to do was overrun this pump and have to reverse back. In fact, I would have been perfectly happy if I never had to reverse this vehicle at all.

Almost with a spontaneous cry of relief, we both spotted the unfamiliar but distinctive black diesel pump and were pleased no other vehicles were queuing to use it. So, allowing plenty of room for me to open the large door, I pulled up alongside and managed to engage the handbrake correctly this time, just like I'd been driving the motorhome for years. I switched off the engine, climbed down from the cab, picked up the diesel nozzle and silently cursed to myself as the fuel cap was nowhere to be found!

Despite all our previous checking and double checking, I'd inexplicably pulled up with the pump on our right hand side, rather than the left hand side, and not wanting to look a wally I pulled the nozzle as hard as I could in the vain hope that it would reach around to the opposite side of the vehicle. This was never a problem in the car, but no amount of pulling and tugging would make it stretch far enough to reach the motorhome's diesel filler cap. I cursed to myself again, more audibly this time, before admitting to Emm that I'd have to reverse back and approach the pump from the other side.

She suggested we should just carry on to the next garage, but knowing we were low on fuel and there was no other filling station for miles ahead, I was anxious to fill up whilst we could. After replacing the nozzle, I walked around to the back of the vehicle to ensure nothing was behind. There wasn't, so I climbed back up into the driver's seat, restarted the engine and proceeded to reverse very slowly whilst frantically alternating my gaze from the right hand wing mirror, to the left hand wing mirror, and then back again. As I did so, I was immediately aware of many pairs of eyes homing in on us, which put me under even more pressure not to screw up this scary manoeuvre – lest I demolished a petrol pump or reversed into a car!

Emm then insisted on getting out and standing behind to make sure I didn't hit anything, which was precisely what we'd agreed she must do *every* time I had to reverse. Unfortunately though, she stood virtually in the middle of my blind spot and was mostly hidden from view in either of the wing mirrors. I could make out the end of her arms frantically waving about, but wasn't entirely sure what she was trying to signal me to do. Was she waving and pointing to tell me to keep moving? Or did she mean stop? Turn to the right? Or turn to the left?

I didn't really have a clue. But at least she stopped other vehicles from pulling up behind and blocking us in. And despite all this pandemonium, I somehow managed to reverse back far enough to allow me to drive forward again and pull up on the other side of the diesel pump without damaging anything, other than my pride, or running over my darling wife!

After fulfilling this essential task we finally set off again, just as it started to drizzle and the clouds ahead got very dark. Whilst we pushed on at a steady fifty miles an hour trying to be optimistic it would soon brighten up, we both noticed that whenever we met another motorhome driving toward us, either the driver or passenger would give us a wave. It seemed as though all us motorhomers were members of some exclusive club, and a friendly wave was some sort of obligatory salute. We soon found ourselves infectiously waving back, and after a while, when we saw another motorhome travelling towards us, we would try to make the first wave. Then, if someone didn't wave back, we thought they were a miserable lot and wondered what their problem was.

I was impressed with the excellent view the extra height of the driving position gave me, and sort of began to understand why so many normal motorists had been tempted to invest in those great big, gas guzzling 4X4 vehicles which constantly overtake my Volvo estate, then pull over in front of me to continually obscure my view of the road ahead – the ones with the blacked out windows being the worst!

I just can't comprehend why their owners don't want anyone to see inside their vehicle, or drivers travelling immediately behind them not to be able to see through their rear window and windscreen to get the clearest, safest view of the road ahead. They can't all be famous celebrities trying to retain their privacy. So what have they got to hide? Or do they honestly believe that everyone will be massively impressed, or even intimidated by them, and think that the driver of the 4X4 who has just overtaken them and immediately pulled over again to block their view, is some really important person and not just some idiot driver with more money than road sense and a huge ego to match!

I fully appreciate that not all drivers of these vehicles are egotistical and deserve such a bad reputation. After all, it's a free market and we live in a free country. So if someone wants to buy one of these blacked out 4X4s to use for the school run and clog up the town and city roads, notwithstanding careering down narrow country lanes with no regard to oncoming pedestrians, horses, tractors or whatever, it's their choice. There's no law against owning one and it's not for me to argue about. Only if it was up to me, I'd vastly increase their road fund licence fee and ban blacked out windows!

Of course, I can just imagine 4X4 drivers wondering who am I to criticise, having just bought a motorhome which takes up even more road space. They would have a valid point. But I would counter argue that motorhomes are generally on the road during off-peak hours, only travel a relatively small number of miles each year and are driven by more mature drivers, as reflected by relatively low insurance premiums. So, having got that off my chest, I'd better step down from my soapbox and continue on our journey.

Continue on we did, and the drizzle turned to heavy rain alternating with torrential rain. We dared not say so aloud, but we both wondered why on earth we were leaving the comfort of our spacious, centrally heated home to spend a week cooped up in this confined space during the first spell of miserable wet weather we'd had for months on end.

I'd started with the windscreen washers switched to their intermittent position, but soon had to have them on all the time. Then, as the rain became more of a monsoon, even the fastest speed wasn't fast enough to keep the windscreen completely clear of water. As we slowed down to thirty miles an hour at times with both wiper blades swishing hypnotically from side to side in double quick time, but still not sweeping all the water away, we started to have serious doubts about carrying on towards one of England's wettest counties during the worst weather we'd had for months. At least I seemed to have got more used to driving the motorhome, and apart from the weather everything else was going relatively smoothly. That is, up to the point where my driver's wiper blade suddenly started to travel too far to the right across the windscreen.

Or to put it more precisely, accompanied by a loud clicking noise, the top quarter of the blade swept past the windscreen before clicking again as it came back the other way. This was rather disconcerting to say the least, but not wishing to alarm Emm, and more importantly not wishing to stop and get out in the pouring rain, I cautiously continued and prayed that the rain would stop. However, it seemed I'd neglected my prayers for so long that they weren't listened to. Or if they were listened to, they were given a good ignoring to punish me for all my bad tempered grumpiness and cussing over the years!

So, apart from the noise of the rain beating down on the motorhome and the loud clicking from the windscreen wiper, we carried on in relative silence along the A303 and then the A30 beyond Honiton and Exeter. Then, as we proceeded up a fairly steep hill in heavy traffic, my dodgy windscreen wiper swept over to the right and went beyond the extent of the windscreen with a loud click once more. But this time didn't come back!

Faced with this rather worrying dilemma, whereby I was driving

12

along in considerable traffic during a substantial rainstorm with the passenger windscreen wiper swishing from side to side as it was designed to do, but with the driver's wiper blade stuck out to the side of the windscreen like a cat's whisker twitching in the slipstream, I couldn't help thinking our trip was jinxed. And that buying a motorhome was the most stupid thing we'd ever done.

I started to inwardly panic, but resolved to appear calm lest Emm panicked even more. However, my attempted calmness was somewhat hampered by a sudden urge to empty my bladder, a feeling made worse by the sight of all the water running across the windscreen in front of me. Gritting my teeth, and not daring to take my eyes off my limited view of the road ahead, I groped around for the electric window switch. Then, having pressed what I thought was my switch, Emm's window wound all the way down and allowed a deluge of rain water to blow into the cab and give her a good soaking, which rather wound her up!

Having realised this unfortunate mistake, and straining my eyes to see the road through the rain running in torrents down the windscreen in front of me, I finally managed to press the correct switch to open my window. Then, with both windows wide open and a fifty mile an hour gale and rain lashing into the cab, more in hope than expectation that it would start wiping once more, I reached out with my right hand and attempted to push the wiper blade back onto the windscreen where it belonged. Unfortunately, as I tried to do this the motorhome veered slightly, but very alarmingly, towards the kerb, Emm let out an audible cry and I realised I had to stop!

However, having rather belatedly reached this conclusion, it certainly wasn't practical or safe to do so on that particular stretch of road. Consequently, I had to carry on until we came to the next lay-by. Luckily the A30 heading west is more abundant in lay-bys than most roads, and we knew we wouldn't have to drive far in that dangerous, semi-blind condition.

I slowed to a crawling pace whilst we fumbled with the window switches and got them both closed again. Then, with the upper half of my torso unnaturally twisted and distorted and my neck strained to its limit, I leant across as far as humanly possible to enable me to just about see through the clear passenger side of the windscreen. And by half crossing my outstretched legs to fight off the increasing pressure in my bladder, I somehow still managed to operate the pedals and stretch my arms to their fullest extent to turn the steering wheel.

After a few minutes, which seemed like hours, with all the other traffic thundering impatiently past, we made out a lay-by in the gloom ahead where I thankfully pulled in, switched off the engine and wiped the sweat off my brow. Then, as fast as my legs would carry me, I rushed to the back of the motorhome and the on-board toilet where, with a huge sigh of relief, I blissfully released the pressure in my bladder. As I did so, I thought that this was far more civilised, not to mention convenient, than having to rush out in the rain to pee behind a hedge in the long wet grass. Meanwhile, Emm took Monty outside so he could cock his leg and then she also went to avail herself of the facilities.

I then had no choice but to go outside and see if I could sort out the wiper blade. Although it was still raining, it wasn't quite as bad as it had been and I stayed reasonably dry in the waterproof hat, trousers and jacket I'd put on. Luckily, I quickly discovered that the nut which was supposed to hold the wiper arm onto the spigot had become loose, and it just needed to be tightened up after correctly repositioning the wiper arm. However, I knew I didn't have any tools with us so wasn't at all sure what I could do about it.

Initially there seemed to be just two options: do nothing and wait until it stopped raining, or call out the breakdown service. Having concluded that the first option just wasn't viable, as the sky was still full of dark, threatening rain clouds, and that the second option would inevitably result in a frustrating delay, I suddenly remembered I had a mole wrench, which in the absence of a proper spanner I'd used to adjust the calliper brakes on the bicycle and was too lazy to put back in the garage.

I found the wrench and tried to lock its jaws around the offending nut, but quickly realised it was impossible to do so without first lifting the bonnet. I swore to myself as I searched in vain for the elusive bonnet release catch, which I naively thought must be in an idiot proof and prominent position. I groped around underneath the steering column, twisting and contorting my body in a vain effort to seek it out. I laid upside down on the driver's seat and poked around under the passenger side of the dashboard, but still couldn't find the damn thing.

My search was made more difficult by the varifocal lenses in my glasses, as lying in such an unnatural and uncomfortable position it was virtually impossible to move my head and focus through the correct part of the lens. Also, the sound of Emm's voice constantly suggesting we should either call out the breakdown service or give up and go home didn't help my concentration, and I had to force myself to tune my ears to *selective hearing mode* and filter out such unhelpful comments. Eventually, I had to squirm my way back out from under the dashboard, virtually admit defeat and dig out the vehicle's manual. I then looked up *'bonnet catch'* in the index and discovered it was under the steering column where I'd just been looking for it!

Mind you, being the same colour black as its surrounding plastic it might as well have been invisible, and I wondered why on earth vehicle manufacturers couldn't do something to make these catches more obvious. They just need to be a different colour, say bright red or yellow, so they would instantly stand out in the gloom under the steering column. I had the same frustrating problem whenever I had to drive a hire car at work. We were supposed to always check the oil level before we set off, but as I could rarely open the bonnet on unfamiliar cars I hardly ever did so. In my opinion, it should have been the car hire firm's responsibility to check the oil, not ours. After all, who checks their own car's dipstick *every* morning before they set off for work?

I don't really know why I let all that annoy me just then. Maybe it was because it started to rain more heavily again and I still had an unserviceable windscreen wiper to sort out. So, having lifted the bonnet and struggling to keep the rain off my glasses, I repositioned the wiper arm to where it should have been and attempted to lock the mole wrench onto the nut. However, it wasn't that easy. The nut was slightly recessed and designed to be adjusted with a socket, and it was only just possible to grip the top half of it with the wrench. I knew that irreparable damage could be caused by over tightening, but had to improvise somehow, and gave it just enough of a tweak to lock the dysfunctional wiper arm back into its rightful position.

Emm was still muttering about calling out the breakdown service or waiting until the rain stopped and going back home, but I ignored her unhelpful comments and asked her – she would say *told* her – to turn the wipers on, which she did with no conviction whatsoever. Mercifully the offending wiper blade swished back and forth across the windscreen in perfect harmony with the one on the passenger side and I hoped it wouldn't work loose again. I was fearful of over-tightening and damaging the thread so decided to leave it be. After all, even though I didn't relish the thought, if it did work loose again I could always give it another tweak. In any case, the motorhome was under warranty and I had every intention of getting the dealer to have a proper look at it when we got back from Cornwall.

So, having satisfied myself that all was now well (for the time being at least), I did my best to inject as much confidence as I could into my voice and told Emm we'd be OK to carry on. She still wasn't sure whether she wanted to or not, especially as she accused me of shouting at her, and as it had just started to rain heavily again I agreed to have a cup of coffee, fresh from the flask we'd made up at home, and wait to see if it stopped. By the time we'd finished our drink, it had eased up a fair bit and was now more of a steady drizzle. So we checked everything yet again, including the fridge which didn't seem to be all that cold. Maybe it needed much longer to cool down – especially the freezer compartment?

However, not wishing to waste any more time, I insisted we rejoin the ever increasing traffic and get going again. At least with both wiper blades now working I had an unobstructed view of the road ahead, which was just as well as the drizzle continued to alternate with heavy rain. I mainly kept to the inside lane at a steady fifty miles an hour, which I felt was a safe and acceptable speed for the conditions I was driving in. So I got rather alarmed when several cars towing caravans, which swayed alarmingly from side to side in the wind, overtook us in what I thought were most unsuitable places. Did these caravan owners have a death wish or something?

Occasionally though, I did move over to the outside lane to overtake the odd slower moving caravan. However, this was a bit off-putting, as after carefully checking my mirrors to confirm it was safe to do so, each time I signalled to pull out Emm would tense up into the bracing position in anticipation of a collision. It's always been like that and I've become used to it over the years. Emm is the world's worst passenger-come-back-seat-driver whose foot has always been, and I guess always will be, permanently positioned over an imaginary brake. My answer to this has been to ask her if she wants to drive, but she invariably declines. However, on the occasions when she does, I usually go to sleep and I can't understand why she can't do the same when I'm driving. She thinks that because I can happily snooze in the passenger seat I must be much more confident about her driving than she is about mine. That isn't really true – it's just that when I die, as indeed we all must, I want to die in my sleep!

Unfortunately, the traffic got heavier and heavier and eventually we began to slow down, ending up crawling along in a huge traffic jam at not much more than a snail's pace. We thought there must have been an accident ahead and wondered how long we'd be held up for. I got more and more frustrated with all the delays and kept complaining that we should have left home much earlier. Emm pointed out that if there had been an accident other peoples' journeys would have been ruined far more than ours, which slightly consoled me and I forced myself to calm down and be more patient.

But then, ahead of us in the distance, we saw the dreaded road works signs and I realised it wasn't an unfortunate accident that was forcing the traffic to a virtual standstill, but the local council who'd decided this major holiday route needed to be dug up on the very weekend we were travelling on it.

Emm kept reminding me there was nothing we could do about it, which was right of course, but I couldn't help my smouldering frustration and had to fight back the road rage rising up inside me. The fact that there was a *'Sorry for the Delay'* sign made no difference whatsoever to my worsening mood, and I knew that whoever put the sign there was nowhere near as sorry as me and everyone else who was stuck in this monumental tailback. It then crossed my mind that not so long ago we'd managed to have a pee, and I suspected that half the stationary drivers and passengers were possibly bursting to do the same – but couldn't. And I think that irrational and selfish thought cheered me a little!

As we gradually approached the dreaded forest of cones, the long queue of slow moving traffic virtually ceased to move at all. We barely crept along in first gear stopping and starting, then stopping and starting again, for what must have been a couple of exasperating miles. Then, the closer we got to the point where the two lanes converged into one, we stopped far more than we started. In spite of all the mass frustration, most of the drivers did their best to resign themselves to the situation and crawled along as patiently as possible.

However, I couldn't help myself from getting rather irate when flashy cars and 4X4s, especially those towing caravans, and more especially 4X4s with blacked out windows, whether towing caravans or not, insisted on moving over to the outside lane and overtaking all the more tolerant drivers who'd pulled over in anticipation of the single lane just ahead of us. I found this especially infuriating, as with their indicators flashing hypnotically like Belisha beacons, they would wait until the very last moment when they'd run out of road before even attempting to pull back over to the inside lane.

I'm ashamed to admit that when these idiots tried to pull in in front of me with their smug looks on their faces, I rather lost my rag, kept as close as possible to the car in front and denied them any space to pull into. I stared blankly ahead as though I hadn't seen them and avoided all eye contact. Almost without exception, unless it was a pretty young lady, especially one showing a bit of leg, I just focussed on the small gap between the motorhome and the rear of the car in front. I concentrated on keeping it as small as possible, never gave an inch and offered little chance for any high and mighty 4X4 drivers, or drivers of any other vehicles for that matter, to be able to squeeze in in front of me!

They'd overtaken all us more sensible drivers, who'd moved over to the inside lane in plenty of time and formed an orderly queue so we could all funnel into the single lane in a fair and efficient manner. They'd taken advantage of what they probably perceived as a weakness in us more considerate motorists and stayed in the outside lane until there was no road left. So let them stay in the disappearing outside lane now, I thought to myself – the arrogant bastards!

We must have been held up for almost an hour, but once we'd eventually passed the road works I more or less regained my composure and felt much better – especially after it stopped raining and we were cruising along the dual carriageway making reasonable progress once more. After a while we started to feel peckish and pulled into a layby for a leg-stretch and a bit of lunch. Emm took Monty outside on his lead so he could have a wee, whilst I got the table out of its special stowage point in the locker and quickly put it up.

Then, as I made up a couple of fresh ham, cheese and salad rolls, I realised that one of the beauties of this motorhome lark was that we didn't have to make up sandwiches or rolls at home and eat them hours later when they'd all gone soggy. By just taking the bread out of the cupboard and the margarine and fillings out of the fridge, we could now make up fresh rolls whenever we felt like it and sit down at the table to enjoy them, which was far more civilised. I also pointed out to Emm that we didn't have to make up flasks of tea or coffee at home either, as we could just turn on the gas cylinder, light the gas ring, boil the kettle and make a fresh brew any time we wanted.

It was at this point I realised why the fridge wasn't very cool. There are four switch positions on the high-tech fridge: one marked *'Gas'* for operating from the gas bottle, which we were not doing and it's certainly not recommended to have the gas supply switched on whilst travelling; another marked '240V' for operating from the mains, when connected to an electric hook-up on a campsite; and yet another marked '12V' for operating from the vehicle battery whilst driving along – just like we'd been doing for the last few hours.

The other possible position is 'Off', which was precisely what our fridge was switched to, so no wonder it didn't seem cold! I rectified this by turning the switch to the '12V' position before sitting down to a leisurely lunch. Then, having finished our meal, we packed everything away and set off once more full of renewed enthusiasm, especially as a few patches of blue sky had appeared from nowhere amongst the grey clouds.

Without further event of note, we arrived on the outskirts of Helston and started to follow the directions we'd been given to the 3 star campsite we were booked into for the first two nights. We were familiar with this area as, more years ago than we cared to remember, we'd spent a couple of enjoyable family holidays there with our small daughters, Joscelin and her younger sister Rowena, in a very basic static caravan.

Mortgage rates seemed to rise every other month in those days, peaking at an unbelievable 15½ percent, and we never had a great deal of spare money for expensive holidays. Like most mothers at the time, Emm didn't go to work. She'd voluntarily given up her job to stay at home to bring up the children and we only had my meagre salary coming in. However, I wouldn't like to give the impression we were hard done by – that's just what mothers did in those days when present-day childcare was unheard of.

We'd been living on the south coast near Lee-on-the-Solent, where I was working at the old HMS *Daedalus* naval air base, and after I gained promotion in 1983 I took up a new post in London. We then moved inland to Farnham, Surrey to be within reasonable commuting distance. However, we missed living by the coast so much that we somehow or another managed to scrape together enough money to buy a second hand static caravan at Durdle Door in Dorset. After a bit of a spruce up, it became our second home by the sea and we certainly never had a foreign holiday until sometime later.

This caravan was very basic and didn't have electricity or running water. The lights ran off Calor gas, and we had to pump water up from a large plastic container which constantly had to be refilled. There was a comfortable lounge area, where the girls also slept, plus a separate bedroom for us. Although there was no toilet, the caravan had a very small room where we put a chemical Porta Potti which we used at night time, when it was pouring with rain or when we were really desperate. In the main we used the nearby campsite washrooms which were always clean.

This simple caravan was our weekend retreat and holiday home for the next eight years, and during the summer months I would leave the office early on a Friday afternoon, rush for the train and get home as quickly as I could. Emm would have got everything ready and packed into our minute Fiat 850 car, and we'd hit the road for the hundred mile journey to Dorset.

We all loved that caravan and the freedom it gave us, and we spent some of the happiest times imaginable down in deepest Dorset. I may be looking back now with rose-coloured glasses, but the sun always seemed to shine and we spent many an enjoyable hour down on the sun-trapped beach, swimming or searching the rock pools for sea creatures. We bought a small rubber dinghy which could just about take three of us – or two of us plus Dudley, our first Border Terrier – out onto the sheltered waters of Man o' War Cove. We walked countless miles along the spectacular coast path and visited all the many attractions that Weymouth, Swanage, Wareham, Dorchester and Portland had to offer. We also explored a multitude of delightful Dorset villages and frequented a few pubs that welcomed children, which was quite rare in those days.

Dear reader, you are probably wondering what all this has got to do with our motorhome trip. The answer is nothing really, except that near the end of our Durdle Door caravan period around about 1990 we had a bit more money coming in after my promotion, and for two successive years we decided to spend a separate week's holiday somewhere other than Durdle Door. Emm managed to find a cheap caravan park, which in truth was more like a farmer's field, near Kennack Sands on the Lizard Peninsula, and it was that familiar area we were now driving through. By the time we'd turned off at Helston and passed the busy Royal Naval Air Station *Culdrose*, the memories came flooding back of those economical but happy Cornish holidays when the girls were about ten and thirteen years old.

The static caravans we stayed in then were still pretty basic, and by today's standards not at all luxurious. Unlike our Durdle Door caravan, they did have mains electricity and running water, but still no inside WC or shower. So, whilst staying at Kennack Sands, irrespective of whether it was the middle of the night, pouring with rain or we were really desperate, we always had to go outside to use the toilet. It was located just a short distance away in a rusty, cobweb infested corrugated iron shed, which seemed to house the vast majority of Cornwall's spider and daddy-long-legs population. The alternative was to cross one's legs extremely hard! There was also a very basic shower in an adjacent corrugated iron structure, and standing naked in the draughty enclosure under a dribble of lukewarm water was always a bit of an endurance test. So, it wasn't used all that much.

Anyhow, we used to go down to the beach which, with a constant easterly wind blowing, was usually too cold for swimming, but still a wonderful place to explore. As I drove along in the motorhome I vividly remembered young Rowena's passion for rock pool exploration and Dudley digging in the sand, as all terriers do, and sending vast clouds of the gritty stuff cascading all over our picnics. I also remembered the old inn at Kuggar, not far from the caravan park, where we enjoyed several meals out. Children weren't allowed in pubs in those days, or more specifically not allowed in bars where alcoholic drinks were served. But the landlord obviously knew he couldn't afford to turn away holiday custom, and had set aside a separate room where families could enjoy a reasonably priced meal with the drinks they'd bought in the bar.

We used to sit by a bay window overlooking a field where there were several horses grazing, and I recalled sitting there all those years ago. Emm and I had our backs to the window, whilst the girls sat opposite. In a rather loud and innocent voice, young Rowena suddenly asked me what the two horses in the field were doing. I nostalgically recalled looking up from my pasty and chips, turning my head and seeing a very virile stallion mounting a very willing mare.

I smiled to myself as I also recalled other parents with young children looking at me, suppressing bouts of laughter and waiting in total silence for my reply. I also remembered the agonising look of embarrassment on Joscelin's face as I explained, as quietly as I could, that *'they were just playing.'* Well, as Emm and I tried to change the subject, I secretly admired that stallion's stamina as they continued their horseplay for an extraordinary length of time!

Anyhow, as we now continued past the huge satellite dishes on Goonhilly Down and I took in the barren heather covered landscape, another motorhome came towards us. I slowed down and raised my hand to wave, but its driver never reduced speed, never waved back and forced me to sharply pull over towards the kerb to let it pass. After this wake up call, rather than carry on reminiscing and admiring the scenery, I realised we were now very close to our campsite and it wasn't the time to lose my concentration and risk losing our way.

Following our directions, we turned off down a narrow lane on our left hand side, but couldn't help worrying when it turned into an even narrower and muddier unmade track. The blue patches of sky which teased us earlier had completely disappeared, and as we proceeded through a very shady and much wooded area it suddenly seemed very dark and we thought we must have taken the wrong turning.

There would have been hardly any room for two vehicles to pass each other, and when overhanging branches started to brush against the sides and roof of the motorhome we couldn't help panicking. If we were going the wrong way, it would have been impossible to turn around, and I certainly didn't relish the thought of being forced to reverse all the way back to the main road.

So, we did what we normally do in such situations. We kept going and hoped for the best. I had visions of meeting a 4X4 towing a caravan coming the other way, probably one I'd refused to let filter in front of me in the traffic a couple of hours earlier! However, this didn't prove to be the case and, with a feeling of intense relief, we finally saw the *Silver Sands Holiday Park* in the gloom up ahead.

3

THE FIRST NIGHT

After our long and frustrating journey we were grateful to have finally arrived without getting lost, which was quite an achievement as far as we were concerned. Emm stepped down from the cab straight into a large puddle, which we hoped wasn't a bad omen, and then squelched into reception to book us in. She came back out with two wet feet, a selection of tourist pamphlets and directions to our designated pitch, which was just up the track on the right hand side.

We'd largely chosen this site as David Bellamy had given it a *Gold Award for Conservation*, which seemed like a good recommendation to us. Mind you, with the rain water dripping off the trees and splashing into the deep puddles on the gravel driveway, I must admit it didn't look particularly welcoming. However, we knew the weather was invariably changeable in this part of the world, and tried to convince ourselves that better days were ahead.

Unfortunately our pitch was on grass, which as it had been dry and sunny for most of the summer was of no great concern when we booked. But after the day's heavy rain, it was now very soggy. For one thing, I didn't want us to keep going in and out of the motorhome with wet feet treading mud all over the carpet, and for another I was concerned that if it carried on raining for much longer we could end up with our tyres sinking into the greasy West Country mud. However, we were stuck with the grass pitch for the next two nights as there were no hard standings to be had on this green site, where concrete and gravel was obviously outlawed.

Luckily, it was dead easy to manoeuvre onto with no need for reversing; I just needed to drive in at one end, park parallel to the track and, when it was time to leave, simply drive forward and turn back onto the track. It was also pretty secluded, with a fair amount of privacy provided between the generous pitches by informal shrub hedges and mature trees, which seemed to be sheltering numerous birds and possibly other wildlife.

So taking great care, I turned onto the grass and brought the motorhome to rest in the middle of the pitch, applied the hand brake and turned off the ignition. Considering our irksome journey, I felt rather pleased with myself that I'd driven all that way in such awful conditions and arrived safely. However, Emm spoiled my smug moment somewhat by querying why I'd stopped and pulled up where I had. I think she wanted me to park nearer the hedge although, as I didn't really listen, she may have meant further from the hedge or possibly more parallel to the hedge. However, I knew she wanted me to move the motorhome within the boundaries of our pitch to an *ever-so-slightly* different position from where I'd actually parked it.

I wasn't really surprised. Every time I park the car she will invariably ask me why I parked in that particular space and then, for example, want me to move nearer the entrance, further from the entrance or further away from the car with the big dog in it. The best thing that can happen when parking is to be confronted with just one space and one space only. No matter where that vacant space is, provided no one else beats me to it, I will then be happy in the knowledge that Emm will consider us lucky to have found anywhere to park. And I won't have to move.

But, if confronted with a virtually empty car park, I know that wherever I bring the car to rest, I'll be questioned as to why I picked that particular space and be asked (more like told) to move elsewhere. Parking the motorhome on our large pitch proved to be just as tiresome, and although I didn't want to move it and risk churning up the wet muddy grass, rather than provoke a quarrel I casually gave Emm the keys, told her I was going to inspect the toilet block and left her to it.

I came back to find that she'd shunted the motorhome back and forth a few times, and brought it to rest about eighteen inches away from where I'd originally parked. My fears were realised when I noticed the churned up grass and exposed patches of pure mud beneath the front tyres. However, being too tired to argue, I forced myself to say nothing about it and got on with turning on the gas bottle and connecting the cable to the electric hook-up. After remembering to switch the fridge to the '240V' position, I then confirmed that since I'd switched it to '12V' several hours previously, the fridge – and especially the freezer compartment – had now reached the correct operating temperature. And almost lost some skin off my fingers in the process!

Despite that, we managed to get everything sorted out and were soon enjoying a fresh cup of tea. As we were hungry, we thought we'd eat before going for a walk. Nothing adventurous I'm afraid, just supermarket pizza, a tin of sweet corn and some potatoes from our garden. At least it was quick and easy to prepare and went down well enough. Next was the washing up, which at home is dead easy. We just have to stack everything in the dishwasher, switch it on when full, remove the sparkling crockery, saucepans and cutlery when ready, and then put it all away. Unfortunately, the motorhome's excellent kitchen wasn't fitted with this essential modern day appliance, so this tedious task had to be completed the old fashioned way.

Rather than use the basin and water supply in the motorhome, I put all our dirty crocks, etc. into our plastic bowl and took it all over to the campsite washing up facilities along with washing up liquid, dish cloth and a tea towel. There was an abundant supply of scalding hot water, the basins and draining boards were clean and, even though I was out of practice at washing and wiping up by hand, I quickly completed this essential task.

As I slowly made my way back to the motorhome, precariously balancing the gleaming crockery, saucepans and cutlery in the bowl lest something dropped onto the wet muddy ground, the dark clouds, greasy grass and deep puddles reminded me of numerous camping experiences with Emm when we were courting more than thirty years previously. In those days, after pitching our small tent in a quagmire of a field somewhere during a rainstorm and then eating something as unappetising as corned beef, baked beans and semi-raw onions, we were more than content to snuggle up together in our sleeping bags for hours on end, not caring whether the rain stopped or not. Even though recalling such blissful times when we were so wrapped up in each other brought a smile to my face, I now expected a great deal more comfort during our motorhome excursions and hoped we'd seen the last of the rain.

Anyhow, having been cooped up in the motorhome all day, unlike us Monty was full of energy and needed a good walk before settling down for the night. We knew there was a track that led from the campsite, through a wood and down to the beach at Kennack Sands, which was where we decided to take him.

Unfortunately though, it looked like it was going to rain again at any moment, so we put on our wet weather gear and, doing our best to avoid the numerous puddles, started off along the muddy path. Monty led the way pulling on his long flexi-lead, the other end of which was attached to Emm's outstretched arm, and soon did what he had to do in the woods. And as we try to be responsible dog owners at all times I picked up his deposit in one of the small plastic bags I always carry with me. In fact, I usually have so many plastic bags stuffed in so many pockets that I've lost count of the times I've gone to pull out a handkerchief and almost blown my nose on a plastic bag – albeit a clean and empty one.

It didn't take us long to reach the large exposed and deserted beach, with Emm still being dragged along by a very energetic Monty and me carrying a knotted plastic bag full of dog poo. Then it started to rain again. Not much at first, but enough to dampen our spirits and, with the strong wind driving the rain and salty spray right onto our glasses, make it difficult to see. All the time we were looking out for a dog bin to get rid of the full and smelly plastic bag, and eventually Emm thought she saw one further along the beach. I must admit that through squinting screwed up eyes in the driving rain, this red box did indeed resemble a dog bin. But, when I got closer, I thought it would be rather unpleasant for the local lifesaving team to unwittingly come across this unsavoury deposit the next time they had reason to open the Kennack Sand's lifesaving equipment box!

As the tide was rushing in, and the rain and wind showed no sign of abating, we decided not to hang around any longer in such exposed conditions. So, still carrying the bag of Monty's poo, we made our way back to the campsite via the road which we joined at the end of the beach. As we then huffed and puffed our way up the rather steep hill, sweating profusely under all our wet weather clothing, we remembered ambling along the same road many years before with Dudley and our exited young daughters.

We recalled them carrying their buckets and spades and chattering excitedly as we all made our way down the very same hill in glorious sunshine. Then, having thoroughly enjoyed themselves on the beach all day, paddling and exploring the rock pools, they'd be tired out and have to be cajoled back up the hill again. Now, as we tried to take our minds off the cold, the wind and the rain, we picked out landmarks we recognised from those long ago happy family holidays.

We soon reached the larger more *'up-market'* caravan park near to the one where we previously stayed, and noticed that all the caravans were relatively new and that the site was now even more *'up-market'* then it was back then. There was even an electronically operated security barrier across the entrance, which we were sure wasn't there before, and we both began to feel our respective ages as we realised just how many years had passed since we were last there with our little girls. Just a bit further on, we were pleased to see the old inn which didn't appear to have changed one bit. The bay window was still there and even the menu seemed to be the same, with pasty, chips and peas still being available. The only differences were the increased prices, and that there were no amorous horses playing with each other in the field opposite!

We were tempted to go inside and have a drink for old times' sake, and wondered whether we'd be able to take Monty in with us. I assumed that if they allowed children all those years ago, they'd probably welcome a small well behaved dog. However, the light was fading and we didn't relish the idea of having to find our way back across the fields in the dark, so we reluctantly agreed to give it a miss.

The footpath back to the campsite was right next to the inn, but we couldn't go back until we'd looked to see if the nearby pottery, with its small gift shop, was still there. It was, and had hardly changed at all. In fact, it looked as though the very same clay pots, plates, worms and Cornish pasties were still in the window covered in at least twenty years accumulation of dust. For a reasonable sum, the owners provided the opportunity for children and adults alike to have a go at making their own pottery, which they could then paint, have fired and take home as a unique holiday souvenir.

My mind went back to when our little girls had had a go with fairly mixed results. I don't recall them making fancy pots or plates; the clay worms and pasties were more their style, and I was sure we still had a couple of their efforts at home somewhere. The do-it-yourself pottery was still available, and was an ideal activity where parents could leave their children for an hour or so whilst they went for a quiet drink at the inn, or back to their caravan for an afternoon 'siesta.'

Having come this far, we couldn't resist making our way a little further up the road in the hope of seeing the cheap caravan site where we'd stayed in the farmer's field. It was no longer there, but at least we found a bin to dispose of Monty's poo. We thought we recognised the old rusty iron gate that led to the field where the caravans used to be, but that was about all. The caravans had obviously met their demise and, in the face of competition from the more up-to-date facilities on offer at the nearby modern caravan park, we imagined it hadn't been financially viable for the farmer to replace them.

Anyhow, although it had thankfully stopped raining for the moment the light really was fading fast, so we hurried back to the inn where we joined the footpath that would take us back to the campsite.

We had to cross a couple of unusual stiles, which were made from large, flat slabs of ancient looking rock that bridged a gap in the hedge. Over the years, countless pairs of feet must have passed over these slabs and worn them down to a very smooth glass like surface. What with the rain and the fine layer of algae which now covered them, they were now virtually frictionless and I had to take great care not to lose my footing whilst crossing over.

I was worried about Emm though, who was a bit wary to say the least, and offered to hold on to her. However, she insisted she didn't need any help and was perfectly capable of managing by herself – which she did by sliding across the damp and frictionless slabs on her backside. And, apart from a wet bum, she suffered no mishap.

Not like a couple of years previously when we'd walked up Great Gable in the Lake District with Joscelin and Lee, her husband. Bearing in mind that Great Gable is the tenth highest mountain in England at 2930 feet, this had proved to be a long and tiring day for us oldies. Having descended some very steep and precarious tracks, we were walking along a completely flat path within a few hundred yards of the pub where we anticipated a well-deserved drink. Joscelin and Lee had raced on ahead of us, no doubt in their haste to get to the pub, when Emm lost her footing, tripped over a prominent stone and hurt her arm. I'm ashamed to admit that when she got to her feet I tried to hurry her along to catch up with the others, and didn't offer much sympathy.

Several days later her arm was still hurting, so we went to a chemist to get some advice and possibly some pain killers. The pharmacist took one look at her swollen arm and told her to go immediately to Keswick Hospital for an X-ray. Of course I drove her there straight away, and when we were told she'd suffered a hairline fracture in her arm, which would need to be encased in plaster for a couple of weeks, I felt extremely guilty regarding my initial unsympathetic attitude towards her.

Rather than admit she just carelessly tripped over a stone because she was tired, and even though I still feel guilty about not offering her more compassion at the time, we always refer to this as her *'mountaineering accident.'* However, this incident made her even more wary when traversing those very slippery Cornish rock stiles and I was very nervous for her. In this day and age, they should have had health and safety warnings adjacent to them!

As we carried on following the path back to our campsite, we came across the sad remains of an old static caravan which had been scrapped and abandoned. One of its sides had been ripped away to expose its rusting cooker, a saturated mattress, cupboards with their doors either missing or hanging off, decayed seating and torn curtains. It reminded us of our beloved Durdle Door caravan, and we couldn't help thinking it may have also provided a family with a cosy weekend and holiday retreat for many a happy year. Either that or maybe it had come from the old Kennack Sands caravan park, and was possibly one of the actual caravans we'd stayed in.

Anyhow, wrecked and abandoned in the drizzle and the dwindling light, it was now a very sad sight. Having been broken up and vandalised, with most of its fittings ripped out, all of its windows smashed, bits of aluminium flapping wildly in the wind and unsightly chunks of environmentally unfriendly glass fibre insulation strewn all around, it was also a blot on the landscape.

It reminded us of when we had to abandon our highly prized caravan. As far as we were concerned there was nothing wrong with it, but a rule had been imposed whereby caravans over twelve years old could no longer remain at Durdle Door. We'd been lucky enough to get a couple of reprieves, but the site owners sensed rich pickings at the time and had gradually ordered all the older vans like ours off the site. They then replaced them with brand new ones for which highly profitable commissions could be obtained, as well as increased ground rents.

Of course, the modern caravans were far more luxurious, being firmly fixed down onto new concrete bases and connected to mains water, sewage and electricity. Consequently, they were fitted with all mod-cons such as hot and cold running water, flush toilets, hot showers, central heating and all the other luxuries everyone expects to have at home these days. Sadly, loyal caravan owners like us with their older, but much loved and much used models had to confine them to the scrapheap, just like this sad old van we'd unexpectedly stumbled across.

On the very last weekend of the caravan season in October 1991, we'd packed up our cherished caravan for the final time and set off for home with heavy hearts and a few tears knowing full well that our caravan, where we'd spent so many happy weekends and holidays, was going to be towed over to the back of the caravan park, broken up and set fire to. And, if that wasn't bad enough, we actually had to pay the site owners to do so.

We consoled ourselves with the thought that, as the girls were growing up and no longer so keen to come away with us, we couldn't have carried on using it as often as we had done. Joscelin had reached an age whereby she had more homework to do, as well as wanting to be more independent by spending time at weekends with her friends. However, it was still a sad occasion and a wrench to know that, after eight years, we'd no longer be able to go and stay in our very own caravan at beautiful Durdle Door whenever we wanted to do so.

We thought we'd still manage to go there for the odd weekend, or even a week, and rent another owner's caravan. But, of course, we never quite got around to it. We did get to go for just one long hot and sunny weekend the following year when we camped in our old tent. But it wasn't the same, especially as another elderly caravan had been moved to our pitch and we could see no logical reason why ours couldn't have stayed there. We used to go back for the occasional day trip and meet some friends who'd rented the caravan from us when their children were young. We'd walk through the campsite and along the cliffs before having a meal in the local pub, where we'd reminisce about the *good old Durdle Door days*.

We always made a point of walking past our old pitch, and it seemed that the new caravan bubble had burst. The elderly caravan, which appeared to be in no better condition than ours (albeit probably a few years younger) remained for many years and the same caravan that used to be next to ours, also stayed. However, when we went back in October 2006 we saw that every older caravan had finally been replaced by a modern top-of-the-range mobile home, with all mod-cons and a price tag to match.

By then our girls were all grown up, had flown the nest and happily settled down leading lives of their own. Joscelin had married and was living far away in Cumbria, whilst Rowena had finally come through her rebellious teenage years, which extended well into her twenties, and astounded us by buying a house with her boyfriend in Bristol. Although we missed them and don't see them as often as we'd like, we are very pleased and proud that they are both happy and independent. It's also very pleasing that they both enjoy camping and caravan holidays, and especially gratifying that Rowena recently told us she'd camped at Durdle Door several times, which 'was magical.'

Even though Emm sometimes says she'd still enjoy camping, no more tents for us. Call me a miserable old sod if you like, but there's no way I will now be persuaded to pitch a tent in a howling gale in a muddy field, cook a meal on a small burner in the rain or sleep on hard, damp ground. And I certainly don't relish the thought of having to crawl out of a tent during the middle of the night and make my way in a half-awake state through the pitch dark, the mud and the rain to a spider infested corrugated iron toilet for a pee. Or, alternatively, do it against a hedge outside the tent. That was OK when we were courting and camping was about the only way we could spend the night together. Now I expect much more luxury, and with my weak bladder insist on having the use of a clean and comfortable indoor toilet.

Likewise, no more static caravans (or mobile homes) on caravan parks where, no matter what their condition, all caravans have a shelf-life and can only stay for a certain number of years. No, we now had the freedom of our own two-berth motorhome, which could take us to virtually anywhere we might wish to go. And here we were in Cornwall, just about ready to settle down for the evening in our truly mobile home.

Whilst we were at Durdle Door we had a portable black and white television set which, as well as operating from mains electricity, also worked off 12 volts direct current. When we wanted to watch a programme, I would pass a long cable out of a window and connect it to the car battery with a couple of crocodile clips. However, we had to limit the amount of time we could watch, lest we flattened the battery and the car wouldn't start. But at least we were able to enjoy the odd programme when we felt like it. After being forced to give up the caravan we'd hung on to the television for many years, but never used it again. It went from loft to loft as we moved house several times and eventually, I reluctantly took it to the tip and dumped it.

Now of course, until such time that we invested in a new portable colour set, it would have been useful to have had with us on our motorhome trips. It's always the same. We both hate throwing things away. But as soon as we do have a clear out, I will urgently need a length of wood exactly like the off-cut I'd kept in garage for years and Emm, for example, will have an immediate use for a piece of curtain material that's followed us from loft to loft during all of our house moves and only just got rid of.

No matter, we could manage without television for this holiday at least, and whilst enjoying a glass of wine we read a bit and planned what to do the following day. We then made up the bed and settled down to enjoy an excellent night's sleep. I didn't even have to get up in the night for a pee, which for me was a momentous occasion and a good sign we were going to enjoy our new motorhome way of life. That is, as long as it didn't rain all the time!

4

RAIN, TOILETS AND SHOWERS

We were woken too early for our liking by the sound of more heavy rain hammering down on the roof and thought that surely it couldn't rain all week. When we first saw our motorhome glimmering in the strong sunshine at the dealers we foolishly assumed that, as we leisurely travelled around to all sorts of interesting and exotic places, the sun would always be shining and we'd eat every meal *al fresco* with a bottle of wine whilst watching magnificent sunsets, just like all the smiling couples featured in the motorhome magazines we'd read.

But, ever since we'd left home, the reality had been dark clouds and relentless rain with only a fleeting glimpse of blue sky, let alone sunshine. Now, parked up on a waterlogged patch of grass in the middle of nowhere, surrounded by wet coats and muddy boots, the confined space of our motorhome seemed far less appealing than that portrayed in the glossy magazines. We cursed our luck that the superb summer we'd enjoyed had ended so abruptly and that we hadn't set off just a couple of weeks earlier.

Although we'd been warm enough during the night, when I got out of bed it was cold – the sort of damp cold that goes right through to the bone – so I decided to light the gas heater. We lived in a village with no mains gas supply and weren't used to gas appliances, but it seemed simple enough. All I had to do was turn the knob to the *'On'* position, hold it down to turn on the gas supply, and then press a button to provide the spark to light the gas. I then had to keep the knob held down for a few seconds otherwise the flame would immediately go out again. Which is exactly what it did. So I had to start again by turning the knob, holding it down, simultaneously pressing the button to provide the spark, keep holding the knob down and hope the gas ignited. And, more importantly, stayed ignited.

However, when I have to follow such simple instructions, they never seem to be quite so straightforward and it took me a number of attempts before the darn thing decided to turn itself on and provide any heat. It wasn't easy to see if the gas had actually ignited or not and the last thing I wanted to do was turn the gas on, go out with Monty and come back to find Emm had been asphyxiated.

Finally satisfied that the heater was operating correctly and also that the bed clothes were far enough away so they wouldn't catch fire, I slipped on some clothes in preparation to take Monty out for his early morning wee. I tried to put on an outward show of optimism to reassure Emm that the weather was bound to improve soon and told her that, by mid-morning, the sun was sure to be shining and we'd enjoy fine sunny weather for the rest of the week. However, knowing she was forever the pessimist and even more fed up than me, I knew I was wasting my breath and that she'd never be convinced, no matter what I said.

I laboriously put on my waterproof jacket, trousers, hat and boots, put Monty's wet weather coat on him and took him outside on his lead onto the sodden, muddy grass in the pouring rain. Almost wishing I was back in our spacious, centrally heated bungalow in the warm and dry, I sincerely hoped I'd be proved right and that it would indeed stop raining soon. If not, we were in for a thoroughly miserable time!

I led Monty just a short way around the campsite and, after I let him cock his leg and relieve himself against a tyre on someone's 4X4, quickly took him back to the motorhome. I sat down on the steps by the rear door, picked up a bemused, wet and muddy Monty, turned him upside down on my lap with his legs sticking up in the air and, using one of his old towels, cleaned him up and dried off his underparts as best I could. Satisfied he was as clean and dry as I was ever going to get him, I carried him inside and removed his doggy coat, which dripped water all over the floor. This coat was made of a waterproof material and held in place on his back by Velcro straps which fastened beneath him. It may have done a pretty good job of keeping the top half of him dry, but it was now sopping wet and the Velcro was covered in slimy mud.

At home, I always hung it in the cupboard with the oil fired central heating boiler, where it soon dried off and didn't really matter too much about making a mess on the floor. However, in the confines of the motorhome, there was nowhere that suitable to hang it. So, for the time being, I left it on a piece of newspaper just inside the door. I then removed my muddy boots and spread them out on the same newspaper, which quickly became sopping wet, took off my dripping wet weather gear and shook it outside the door before hanging it up on the hooks above the warmth of the gas heater. Having sorted myself out, I resolved to remain as cheerful and optimistic as I could which, within the cramped space with water dripping all over the floor, wasn't easy.

Emm was still in bed, obviously intending to stay there until the sun came out, and seemingly prepared for a very long lie-in. Sensing her continuing mood of gloom and despondency, I thought I'd butter her up by making a cup of tea. I put the kettle on, gave Monty his breakfast, made two cups of steaming hot tea, took my trousers off and slid back under the duvet beside her. I still wasn't sure whether she was sufficiently buttered up or not but, despite the continuous rain, we found the bed to be warm and comfortable.

After a while, I needed to go to the toilet and thought I might as well get dressed, go and sort myself out and have a shower. I grabbed my wash bag and towel, put on my sopping coat and, dodging the puddles, hurried across in the rain to the toilet block where I entered a WC cubicle. I hung the towel up on a rusty nail, put the bag on top of the cistern and intuitively checked there was enough toilet tissue for the business in hand. Having been caught out in such places before, I didn't want to be caught out again! Satisfied that there was, I took a few sheets and wiped some water, which had dripped off my wet coat, from the seat. At least, I hoped it was rain water that had dripped off my coat. Then, under the watchful gaze of a couple of very large spiders and various assorted insects, I carefully lowered my trousers and eased my bare backside down onto the cold plastic toilet seat.

As I did so, I received a most disconcerting shock as I felt the whole toilet pan tilt to one side beneath me. Quickly springing upright again, I instinctively held up my trousers so they didn't drag on the damp floor and then inspected the pan very closely. The problem was that it was only secured to the floor by two loose screws on one side of the pan, with the corresponding screws on the other side both being missing. Now, I am of rather slim build and don't carry excess weight, but goodness knows what the consequences could have been if a more portly person had plonked themselves down on this unstable toilet seat. The mind boggles!

However, in spite of having to sit with my weight very evenly distributed, lest I caused the pan to topple sideways again, and at the same time being put off by the farmyard like noises coming from another camper in the adjacent cubicle, not to mention some very unpleasant odours, I successfully finished what I had to do. Like most Englishmen, I prefer to carry out this essential daily ritual in privacy and comfort, preferably with a good book or the sports pages, and couldn't help wondering what the heck I was doing in this draughty toilet block, precariously balanced on a cold, clammy, unstable toilet seat, with an extremely thin and certainly not sound or smell proof partition between me and a total stranger. With the din of the rain beating down on the roof, the cold, damp concrete floor, the spiders' webs, and having to share the impolite noises and nose-twitching odours emanating from the adjacent cubicle, I felt as though I was in a farm building, rather than on holiday at a 3 star campsite and seriously started to think we should just give up on a bad job and go home.[2]

---

2 According to their website, since our visit the Silver Sands Holiday Park has refurbished their toilet block. There are now free hot showers, individual wash cubicles, plus a family shower/wash room.

However, I supposed it could have been worse. I could have been staying on a French campsite, for example, and sitting on a toilet with a woman in the adjacent cubicle, which was a regular occurrence on another family holiday some years previously. It wasn't too bad if the lady was *française* as, after all, *la madame ou mademoiselle* would probably be used to such arrangements; but if I knew she was English I found it doubly embarrassing, especially if there were lots of noise or unpleasant smells coming from either party.

Even more so if my female English companion and I both emerged from our respective cubicles at the same time. I was never sure whether she'd think I was stuck up, rather than bunged up, if I ignored her and failed to wish her good morning and ask after her health. After the first few embarrassing encounters I tried to get over to the WC before the rush, as it were, and then get out again as quickly as I could. However, whilst living on a basic holiday diet of *baguette avec fromage*, which well and truly blocked up my system, I found it impossible to be *that* quick!

It was far, far worse though, on a particular French campsite we stayed at which had *Turkish* toilets. For anyone lucky enough not to be familiar with these – *avoid them like the plague*. In fact, it's a wonder these types of toilets haven't caused a great modern plague epidemic. They just consist of a ceramic base with a hole in it, either side of which are a couple of distinctive marks where the unfortunate user is supposed to place their feet. Then, with trousers and underpants round their ankles, they have to crouch down and try to aim into the hole.

When I was forced to use one of these *comfort stations* (or more precisely, extreme *discomfort stations*,) I concentrated solely on getting on with the business in hand without losing my balance. However, whilst squatting in this unnatural position, what with the constant strain on my leg muscles plus the very real fear of toppling arse over elbow into the nauseating mess which had accumulated around the hideous hole in the ground, it was not a pleasant experience. And there was certainly no question of lingering for a while, savouring the moment or reading the paper!

It seemed to me that these toilets were never, ever cleaned and that they solely relied on fast flowing, warm urine to wash the worst of the encrusted excreta away. In order to survive the noxious odours emanating from the bowels of the earth up through this hellish hole, I had no choice but to limit my breathing. Now, holding one's breath for any length of time can result in a fainting feeling and, believe me, a Turkish toilet on a French campsite – or anywhere else for that matter – is the very last place to pass out! Not surprisingly, I was more or less constantly constipated on that holiday!

Unbelievably, at that same campsite, the men's urinals were on the *outside* of the toilet block in full view of everyone. Many of the men who used them must have splashed over the edge of the porcelain, and in order to get inside the main block where the WCs and washing facilities were everyone had to walk along the permanently wet and smelly path alongside lines of revolting *Français* relieving themselves. I could personally never bring myself to stand there and pee with women and children walking past, so I always went inside to a cubicle, which is what I'm sure most of the more reserved Englishmen did. I wondered whether the majority of French people are actually happy to use facilities such as these. Or did they just expect tourists, especially English tourists, to put up with them?

It was only afterwards, when looking at the brochures for French campsites, we realised that civilised campsites specifically stated that they had *English toilets*. So be warned, if this important statement is missing from your French campsite holiday brochure, then it's a disgusting hole in the ground, constant constipation and men peeing up against the outside wall lavatorial experience to look forward to on your hard earned continental camping holiday. As far as we could see no brochure mentioned *Turkish toilets*, that all important fact not being something the agents would want to point out. No, toilet wise, even though it wasn't up to hotel standards, this Cornish campsite toilet, although far from warm and comfortable, was ultimately superior to the repulsive and foul facilities on offer at that particular *français terrain de camping* where we once stayed – but would never, ever go back to.

Anyhow, having completed my business, as it were, I then had a quick shave followed by a shower, which also proved to be a bit of a pantomime. For a start, I looked for some hooks, or even a rusty nail, where I could hang my towel and clothes. But there weren't any. So, even though I thought they might get slightly dusty, I hung my towel and my coat over the top of the door. However, the only place I could put my clothes was in the corner of the cubicle on top of a slippery plastic chair, and it was only after I'd covered my hair in shampoo that I realised my clothes were still within range of the strong shower spray. By then they were getting wet and, when I tried to move the chair out of the firing line, I only just managed to stop them sliding off onto the sopping wet floor. However, the challenge of keeping my clothes dry went away when the fierce shower spray suddenly halved in intensity.

The man who'd occupied the WC next to me had by now entered the adjacent shower and it immediately became apparent that the plumbing was such that, if just one shower was in use, a good flow of water spouted forth. But, because my shower was at the end of a long pipe run, as soon as my neighbour turned his on, the flow from mine considerably reduced. I was grateful my clothes were no longer sharing my shower. But, at the same time, I now needed a more powerful jet of water to rinse the luxuriant foaming shampoo lather, which because of the extra soft south west water was far more luxuriant and foaming than usual, from my longish curly hair.

Again I couldn't help wishing I was back in our cosy warm bathroom at home, rather than sharing this woeful washroom with my as yet unseen, but well and truly heard, flatulent friend, who was now singing lustily to himself just a few feet from me on the other side of the wafer thin shower partition. I eventually succeeded in washing away the shampoo and, when I finally turned the shower off, the singing was abruptly replaced by a loud expletive as my neighbour's shower spray would have suddenly doubled in intensity and almost certainly given his clothes a good soaking!

I then had the problem of trying to get myself dried and dressed in the tiny shower cubicle. I towelled myself as much as possible, but as the whole of the floor was sopping wet it was impossible to keep the soles of my feet dry. I picked up my pants, sat on the chair on top of the rest of my damp clothes and did my utmost to dry my feet without dragging the towel on the wet floor. After drying them off as best I could, I slipped them through my underpants, but in order to pull them up around my backside I then had to stand up again. Of course, as soon as my feet touched the floor, they got wet again. I swore out loud to myself, snatched my trousers off the chair and sat down once more to re-dry my feet. Then, with them both raised off the floor, but still not entirely dry, I strove to slide each foot in turn through its corresponding trouser leg.

However, as I grappled with my trousers in carrying out this simple everyday task, I really got annoyed with myself when I inadvertently dropped one of the trouser legs on the wet floor. Then, after finally forcing both feet into their respective trouser legs, in order to pull them up properly I had no choice but to stand up again on the cold, wet floor, which once more made the soles of my feet wet through. I then got even more exasperated when I had to sit down again to dry my feet for what I hoped would be the last time.

Anyhow, even though I just about managed to get my first foot reasonably dry, I then had to pull on one of my socks which, having momentarily received the full force of the shower, were both damp. Then, once I'd got a clammy sock on a foot, I couldn't allow myself to put that foot back down on the floor, so had to straight away slide it into its corresponding shoe. That shouldn't have been too difficult, but when I did so I discovered that enough water had been sprayed inside my shoe to make my sock even wetter. Anyhow, knowing full well I was now going to have to change into a dry pair of socks the moment I got back to the motorhome, I then made a futile attempt to dry my other foot for the final time, pulled on its sock and tetchily forced it inside its shoe.

Mind you, I suppose I was pretty grateful the chair was provided, as I remembered some of the times I'd got dressed in campsite showers in the past, especially spartan corrugated iron ones which were even worse than these. They usually had cold bare concrete floors, which were always wringing wet after being slopped out each day with a dirty old mop and bucket, just like I'd imagined these had. Also, they were often provided with a rancid wooden duck-board, which if trodden on could potentially cause all sorts of fetid foot fungus to take hold. So I used to lean them against the wall and never dared put my bare feet anywhere near them.

I recalled that getting myself dried and dressed was an even more exasperating experience than the one I'd just gone through. With nowhere to sit, I'd end up hopping about on one leg hoping to remain balanced, with the opposite knee bent and raised high enough to enable me to lean forward and dry my foot. Once I'd got that foot dryish (I could never get them completely dry whilst in that position) and then poked it through a leg hole in my pants, as soon as I put that foot back down on the floor it immediately got wet again. I would then have to carry out a repeat performance balancing on the opposite foot which, with one leg already through my underpants, would be an even more tricky operation. On one occasion, I remember ending up with my pants on back to front, so had to repeat the whole crazy routine again!

Then, of course, I'd have to go through another pantomime performance, balancing once more on each wet foot in turn and, at the same time, trying to force the other one into a trouser leg without toppling over or dropping the towel, a trouser leg or both on the wet floor. And once I'd got that sorted out, I'd still have the same problem with my socks and shoes. Anyhow, you get the picture…

For now though, after putting on the rest of my clothes, I stood outside the shower cubicle on the relatively dry floor towelling my hair when my friend emerged from his shower and wished me a habitual good morning. As I replied in kind, it was difficult to suppress a laugh as his trousers and shirt were pretty well soaked. Not only that, but they would have been size XXL as well and goodness knows what injury he could have done to himself if he'd got out of bed just that little bit earlier and beaten me to the WC cubicle with the wobbly toilet pan!

Still, at least I now felt clean, thoroughly freshened up and was in a slightly better mood, and as I walked the short distance back to the motorhome carefully negotiating the puddles I wondered what to do with the rest of the day. The rain had eased off for the moment, but the sky was still full of depressing dark rain clouds, and I didn't need a degree in meteorology to know that even more rain was on its way. When I got back, I removed my wet shoes, carefully placed them on the even soggier sheet of newspaper and put on a dry pair of socks. With hindsight, I decided that the next time I went for a shower in a campsite washroom I'd go over wearing the absolute minimum of clothes; just a T-shirt, shorts, slip-on shoes and definitely, no socks. Also, that on future motorhome trips I would bring my flip-flops with me and wear them to walk to and from the washroom, as well as in the shower itself.[3]

Emm surprised me by being up and dressed and had already started to revert the bed back into daytime seating. This wasn't as easy as it should have been as, for some unknown reason, one of the bed bases required a fair bit of force to make it go back under the seat. However, after some pushing and pulling, heaving and shoving, not to mention a bit of effing and blinding, I eventually managed this tricky and frustrating task without damaging anything. There was obviously a knack to this and I hoped I would conquer it before the end of the week.

Having sorted that out and put the bedding back in the locker above the cab, the next challenge was to get the table out of its storage position in the wardrobe and erect it ready for breakfast. Although we'd done this before, we still found it to be a somewhat awkward

---

3 We decided not to use our motorhome shower. It's very small; water would splash onto the WC, toilet paper, & washbasin; I'd always be topping up the water tank, as well as emptying the grey water; and I'm sure that water would inevitably find a crack in the sealant and end up causing the wooden floor to rot, eventually resulting in a very expensive repair being required.

and tricky operation. This was because the legs are held in the flat position by fairly strong springs, which makes the table resemble a very large and sensitive, double ended mousetrap. *(Or should it be man-trap?)*

Consequently, unless great care was taken, there seemed to be a very real risk of the legs springing back and trapping fingers or even an arm! However, we eventually managed it between us and proceeded to get everything set up for breakfast.

5

WALKING IN THE WET

I'd love to say we prepared a full English breakfast in our small but efficient kitchen. In theory, we could have done. After all, the motorhome magazines we'd read with such interest seemed to be full of glossy photographs of cheesy couples sitting in their vehicles with satisfied and contented grins on their faces tucking into huge plates of bacon, eggs, sausages, mushrooms, fried bread, baked beans plus all the rest of the trimmings. The sun would always be shining and it almost looked like they were dining in luxury hotels, rather than self-catering in motorhomes.

However, we decided on a simple breakfast of cereal, fruit and yoghurt, not so much because of wanting to choose the healthy option but more to do with taking things easy and ensuring the washing up was kept to a bare minimum, notwithstanding a strong desire to avoid pungent cooking smells lingering in the confined space of our living and sleeping quarters. We also had far too many memories of bad camping and caravanning experiences when our disastrous non-culinary fry-ups resulted in unappetising, lukewarm food floating in pools of congealed grease, as well as burnt pans needing loads of effort to wash up. Consequently, we'd decided to stick to basics and take the easy option. Maybe another time we might be more adventurous, but then again, maybe not.

Breakfast over, Emm volunteered to do the washing up. This was fine by me, but meant that, by default, I would have to take Monty out for his morning walk. I didn't mind too much, but was wary of the ominous black rain clouds overhead. Suitably clad in a waterproof peaked cap, an essential item to keep the rain off my glasses; a waterproof anorak over a warm fleece; waterproof trousers over the top of my every day trousers; and my walking boots, I set off with Monty who was likewise clad in his own waterproof coat.

With water dripping down on us from the trees, we made our way towards the beach along the woodland path which, after the heavy overnight rain, was like a quagmire underfoot. I trod carefully through the thick mud but, annoyingly, it was impossible to prevent Monty from getting it all over his feet, legs and underbelly. Although I tried not to think about it too much at the time, I wondered how I'd ever manage to get him cleaned up again before letting him back into the motorhome. It wasn't going to be easy, that's for sure. Perhaps I'd end up taking him over for a shower?

Soon after we reached the beach and passed the lifesaving equipment, the heavens opened and I started to get well and truly saturated. Or I would have, if I'd not been wearing all my wet weather gear to keep me dry. Even so, once again I had little protection from the strong horizontal wind which blew straight in off the sea and, irritatingly, deposited salty spray under my peaked cap and onto my glasses.

In spite of this, once I'd accepted that there was absolutely nothing I could do about the weather, it was perversely exhilarating to be walking in the wet along this deserted beach with the rain hammering down and the waves crashing onto the rocks. This made me think about the power of the sea and all the poor sailors who'd lost their lives in the many shipwrecks which I knew had occurred along this rugged Cornish coast. And I wondered how many times the lifesaving equipment, which Emm had mistaken for a dog poo bin the night before, had been used in earnest. With those grim thoughts in my mind and my head bowed to try and limit the amount of spray on my glasses, a drenched and windswept Monty and I made our way to the far end of the deserted beach.

I decided to walk back via the same circular route we'd walked the previous evening and proceeded to climb the fairly long and steep hill up the lane. I hadn't gone that far when my exertions caused my body heat to rise rapidly underneath my fleece and wet weather gear, and I began to perspire profusely. Consequently, as well as feeling exceedingly hot underneath all my warm and waterproof clothing, I started to feel just as wet and clammy as I would have done if I hadn't been wearing it at all.

However, in spite of my sweaty discomfort I plodded on, stopping every so often to let Monty have a good sniff of whatever it is that dogs sniff at. It's always irrationally intrigued me as to what domesticated dogs find so compelling about sniffing all the various smells that other dogs leave behind, for example, in grass verges, up gate posts or on car tyres. Mind you, this unsavoury to human, but pleasurable canine habit is nothing compared to their socially accepted greeting. By this, I refer to when dogs of either sex meet and their good mannered habit of circling around each other, sticking their noses well and truly between the other's hind legs and having a really good snuffle.

It's said that dogs often look and act like their owners and vice versa, and there's no doubt there's some truth in this. After all, I did once win first prize at the Lower Bourne village fair for the owner who looked most like his dog.[4] But can you imagine if people were even more like their pets and actually greeted total strangers, even ones we hadn't been introduced to, by crouching down on all fours and sticking one's nose right alongside the other's genitals? Even more bizarrely, what if royal protocol meant that, instead of bowing and curtsying to Charles and Camilla et al., both you and they got down on all fours and went through this same bizarre and smelly ritual? The mind boggles, but that's what our darling dogs do and no one seems to think it's that weird.

Anyhow, as I struggled up the hill with these stupid thoughts, interwoven with memories of our young daughters walking excitedly along the same lane to and from the beach, I paused for breath as I

---

4   Dudley our first Border Terrier at Lower Bourne near Farnham, Surrey

recognised a clearing at the top of the cliff overlooking the sea. I certainly didn't want to get too close to the edge, but the view was spectacular as I watched the rough sea below, smashing against the rocks with such ferocious force. I remembered standing on the same spot on a much better day many years previously, and holding both girls' hands very tightly to make sure they didn't stray too near the edge.

I then thought that a vehicle could easily be parked there, and that it would have been interesting to have spent the night there in the motorhome overlooking the sea. That would have been true wild camping, something which is certainly not encouraged in most places in this country. But on a foul night like we'd just experienced, if we'd just parked up for the night in this remote spot, I doubted if anyone would have been any the wiser and, in any case, didn't see what harm it could have done.

I was suddenly aware and disgusted by the amount of litter that was strewn all around me. It was obvious that someone had indeed parked there, possibly even wild camped for several nights in a motorhome or similar vehicle, and then just thrown all their rubbish, including used disposable nappies, out onto the grass! What sort of people can go out into our beautiful countryside and travel along our spectacular coastline such as this, without being inspired by its sheer wildness and beauty, then defile it by leaving such a despicable mess behind?

Surely, it's not too much to expect everyone, without exception, to put all their rubbish in a plastic bag until an opportunity arises to dispose of it properly, even if it meant taking it home. Such selfishness by a minority of morons is probably why responsible wild camping is mostly prohibited. It's totally beyond my comprehension how such low life litter louts can live with themselves and I wondered what their own homes are like. Mind you, these culprits may well have been travellers who didn't have a home as such to go to, but whose selfish behaviour spoils it for responsible campers and council tax payers alike.

Shaking my head in disbelief and wondering who would

eventually clear up the mess, I carried on in the rain and left the spectacular and disgusting view behind me. I stopped again a couple of hundred yards up the lane in yet another clearing, where there was a couple in a car looking at a map. It then dawned on me that since we'd arrived, apart from the lady Emm met in reception and the man I bumped into in the toilet block, we hadn't seen another soul. Then, as I approached to look at the view again, the man got out and asked me something or other – I can't remember what. But the conversation then centred on the weather, like it usually does, and he told me that, according to the forecast, the sun would soon be shining.

He said he'd just driven over from the north coast, which had been basking in glorious sunshine, and that the southern Cornish coast, where we were, would be likewise by lunchtime. I admired his optimism and remembered my first visits to Cornwall, when we seemed to spend most of the time driving backwards and forwards from the south coast to the north coast in the belief that the sun would be shining on the other side of the county. For now though, the rain was still teeming down, albeit not quite so heavily, and it was difficult not to believe it would be raining all week.

Having exchanged further pleasantries with this weather guru, I bade him farewell and set off once more. The lane soon levelled out, and when I reached the large caravan park on the left hand side I wandered inside its entrance and tied Monty up outside the campsite shop, where I bought some milk and, more importantly, a Sunday paper so I could get the football results. Luckily the rain had suddenly eased off, which allowed me to have a quick look at the sports page without it disintegrating in my hands.

I was cynically overjoyed to see that England had overcome the might of the Andorran national team in a vital European Championship qualifying match by five goals to nil. I'd heard the half time score when I dared turn the radio on in the motorhome for a short time on the way down, but as Emm hates football I didn't listen to the match or the final scores. The result, which wasn't unexpected, cheered me slightly after all the rain. England remained top of their group and surely nothing could now stop them from easily qualifying for this prestigious football tournament or even winning it in the summer of 2008![5]

I was also pleased to see that my team, Aldershot Town, who I'd supported since I was ten years old, had beaten Halifax Town in the Conference league with a single goal scored one minute from the end. Unfortunately, back in 1992, Aldershot had had huge debts and a poor team, whose wages they couldn't afford to pay, and were forced to wind up and resign from the football league. A new club was immediately formed and they'd steadily worked themselves back up the lower leagues to the Conference, where they were one of the favourites to become champions this season and gain automatic promotion back to where they belonged.

This was their fourth season in the Conference and they'd twice come within a cat's whisker of gaining promotion back to the football league proper via the play-offs. Surely they wouldn't disappoint again this season – would they?[6] After this result, the early signs were good and they were now fourth in the league, only three points behind Oxford United, another former league club fallen on hard times.

Ironically, Oxford were managed by the much travelled and respected Jim Smith, known as the bald eagle who, when he had a full head of hair, was an Aldershot star in the old 4th division (where they spent the majority of their league career). He was a key member of the glorious Aldershot team which, in January 1964, beat mighty first division Aston Villa by two goals to one in front of 13,556 spectators at a packed Recreation Ground in an FA cup 3rd round replay. Villa were the first big team I ever had the opportunity to watch, and after the Shots valiantly held them in the first match to a goal-less draw at Villa Park, with our goalkeeper heroically saving a penalty, there was no way I was going to miss the replay.

---

5   Humiliatingly, England failed to qualify let alone win the championship!

6   Aldershot Town finished in a disappointing 9th position and had to wait until the following season when they were glorious champions and deservedly regained their football league status.

I caught the first bus after school and, with a mate and my brother, stood behind the High Street end goal for a couple of hours before the match even started. They were not all ticket matches in those days and spectators just queued up at the gate, paid their money, walked in and found somewhere to stand. I can still visualise both Aldershot's goals, which were scored right in front of our eyes, one from a curling free kick by big Jim Towers and the other direct from a bizarre corner kick taken by Chris Palethorpe. What a match and what a result!

Better even than when fourth division Aldershot beat another first division team, i.e. Oxford United (I did mention they'd fallen on hard times) by a walloping three goals to nil in an FA cup match in 1987, a match which, regrettably, I didn't attend. This time the crowd was less than 2000 as fans stayed away, partly because no one gave them a hope in hell of winning, but mostly because the debt-ridden club greedily trebled admission prices.

Anyhow, enough of me boring any non-football fans, who can't, or just won't understand the passion our national sport stirs in most of us red blooded males. A man's love and passion for his particular football club is similar to his first love and passion for a woman – it's never forgotten. But unlike with a woman, no matter how our team treats us, we can never fall out of love with our chosen football team – even unglamorous ones like Aldershot!

Despite the weather, I was happy in the knowledge that both England and Aldershot[7] had been victorious, and made my way back as quickly as I could, with the milk and newspaper tucked away in my rucksack to keep them dry. I'd been away for a fair amount of time and was aware that Emm would probably be worried about me, or if not about me, about Monty. The rain, which had eased off for a short while, had again turned to a steady drizzle, and by the time we got back I was soaking wet and so hot and sticky under my waterproofs that I needed another shower.

Even though he's a tough little dog and didn't seem to mind too

---

7   To complete my weekend footballing joy, Yeovil Town had drawn 1-1 with Swansea City the previous Friday evening.

much, Monty was thoroughly bedraggled, with water dripping off his top half and his underneath parts covered in dark, sticky mud, and in the state he was in there was no way I could let him go back into the motorhome to get mud all over our carpet and seat covers. Just inside the back door at home we had a large sink in the utility room, and if he was muddy after his walk (which was quite a frequent occurrence in our part of Somerset) it was relatively easy to plonk him in the sink and give him a thorough wash before drying him and allowing him further inside the bungalow. But how on earth was I going to clean him up now before letting him back into the cramped motorhome?

I was seriously tempted to take him over to the shower block, but although I was pretty sure no one would see me I thought I'd better not. Instead, I sat on the steps in the rain and with cold fingers unfastened the muddy Velcro straps on his saturated coat, took it off and shook it out as best I could. Before setting off for our walk I'd put a couple of his old towels within easy reach just inside the door, and having these to hand I turned Monty upside down on my lap and carefully wiped as much muck from his feet and underbelly as I could. When he was as clean as he was ever going to be, I swapped towels and did my best to dry every square inch of him before allowing him inside.

I then took off my muddy boots, placed them on the remains of the disintegrated newspaper just inside the door along with Monty's coat, removed my wet clothes, shook them out and again hung them up above the gas heater to dry. When we'd camped out at the dealers, living in this confined space didn't seem to be too much of a problem. But what with the continuous lousy weather and surrounded by wet clothes, towels and boots dripping all over the floor, the first twenty-four hours away from home on this holiday hadn't been much to write home about.

After a lousy journey we were parked up miles from anywhere on wet muddy grass, with relentless rain beating down on our roof and barely enough room to swing a cat. It felt like we were on an endurance exercise, rather than a relaxing holiday, and even though I did my best to convince Emm, as well as myself, that the weather would soon improve, it wasn't easy to remain upbeat.

We'd paid for this site for another two nights and had also paid in advance for another more expensive one in St Ives for the following two nights. After that, we'd planned to take pot luck and see where our journey took us. However, if it was still raining by then, I thought we might go home via Wellington to see if the dealer would buy the motorhome back for not much less than we'd paid for it!

6

DOG MESS & LOST IN THE TWILIGHT ZONE

Trying to put such negative thoughts behind me, I absorbed myself in the paper to catch up on all the football action and the rest of the news, whilst Emm carried on reading the book she'd been engrossed in all morning It must have been really interesting as she didn't appear to have worried about me being out with Monty in the rain for so long. She hardly said a word and seemed utterly resigned to sitting in the dry in the motorhome all day. Monty was curled up on the floor in a deep sleep, and we all relaxed for an hour or so in total silence with the sound of the rain washing over us.

Meanwhile it looked as though the man I met on my walk was going to be proved right as the weather miraculously improved. Whilst we'd been absorbed in our reading, the dark rain clouds had gradually dispersed to leave behind the most wonderful clear blue sky and bright sunshine, the like of which we'd almost given up hope of seeing on this holiday. We both thought we'd be cooped up inside the motorhome all day, if not all week, but now it had stopped raining we wondered what to do with the rest of the day.

We both wanted to go to Trebah Gardens, which wasn't that far away on the Helford estuary. We'd seen this garden several times on television and were particularly impressed with its collection of gunnera (or *giant rhubarb*) and large tree ferns. Ever since we'd lived in our bungalow, aptly named *The Ferns,* we'd been interested in ferns of all kinds, and had been gradually increasing our own collection in the shady parts of the garden. Consequently, we were especially keen to check out Trebah's fern species as well as all the other exotic plants which thrived in the sheltered valley. We knew that dogs on leads were welcomed and didn't want to waste any more time before getting to Trebah.

It can be very frustrating, but understandable I suppose, when dogs are barred from some public gardens and suchlike. It's not possible to leave them in cars, so we either don't go to such places or have to take it in turns whilst the other one of us stays in the car park with Monty. Unfortunately, some irresponsible dog owners spoil it for everyone else by not keeping their dogs under control and not clearing any mess. It's something that really annoys me and gets all us dog owners a bad name.

Notwithstanding the fact that it's extremely unpleasant for anyone who accidentally treads in dog excrement, it's a totally unacceptable health hazard. Smelly deposits from big dogs can be much larger than human waste matter, and it just defies belief that a minority of dog owners think it's acceptable to allow their animals to just do it wherever they feel like – and then just leave it there. Of course, it's not the dogs' fault, but their ignorant owners who don't give a damn about leaving dog crap trailing in their wake.

They wouldn't drop their trousers and defecate in a public place, so why on earth do they allow their dogs to do so without clearing up after them? Such objectionable action (or should it be *inaction?*) spoils it for the vast majority of us blameless dog owners who abhor such antisocial behaviour and, as far as many non-dog owners are concerned, we are all tarred with the same brush.

Strong plastic bags, which are even scented, are sold these days specifically for picking up poo, and a dog bin where it can be deposited responsibly is never that far away. A hundred bags can be bought for a pound so when their dogs are caught out, so to speak, there's no excuse whatsoever for dog owners to be caught out without a bag to pick it up with. As well as buying these scented bags I never throw a small plastic bag away and, as I've said before, I always have loads of them in my pockets. The small supermarket bags used for fruit and vegetables are ideal, although extra care has to be taken if they have holes in them!

In this day and age it's completely unacceptable for anyone not to clear up after their pet, tie a knot in the bag and dispose of it properly. Even if there isn't a purpose-made dog bin close by, surely it's not too much to expect *all* dog owners, without exception, to accept responsibility for their own dog's mess and pick it up, take it home and put it in the wheelie bin.

What I find even more incredulously disgusting, and it happens more often than I care to mention, is when I see plastic bags full of dog dirt just thrown in a hedge. This can be even worse than not picking up in the first place, as wrapped in a bag it will take much longer to break down naturally. It really makes my blood boil and I wonder what sort of ignoramus does such a thing. I mean, if they pick it up in a bag and tie a knot in it in the first place, how on earth can they then think it's OK to just chuck it in a hedge and leave it dangling from a blackberry bush or wherever?

Very recently, I saw literally dozens of plastic bags of the stuff incredulously dumped together in a huge pile on the cliff tops at Burton Bradstock. It was almost as though a bin used to be at that very spot and, for some reason or another, had been removed. Maybe dog walkers who regularly used that path took umbrage that their bin had been taken away, and just carried on dumping their bags of dog poo where the bin used to be.

That's just my theory and I have no evidence to back it up. But it wouldn't be, nor could it be, any excuse and I just can't understand how any dog owner would feel it was acceptable behaviour to add their bag of dog dirt to the pile. Maybe those particular people considered themselves far too superior to carry a bag of poo to the next available bin, and have got their noses so far up in the air that they wouldn't even consider taking it home with them to put in their wheelie bin? And who did they think was going to clear up all the collective crap on the cliff top? Some poor minion from the local council I suppose?

Anyhow, as I said, I can understand why some public gardens don't allow dogs. It must be horrendous for any gardener to accidentally grab a handful of smelly brown stuff whilst weeding the flower bed. Or, as once happened to a man tidying the verge by our village church, get sprayed with it whilst strimming the grass.

I've ~~hardly ever heard of anyone being pro~~secuted and fined for allowing their dogs to foul without picking up after them, so there doesn't seem to be a serious deterrent. If only the irresponsible dog owners could be rounded up and sprayed with their own dog's mess or have their noses rubbed in it, they might have second thoughts in future and be ready with the plastic bag!

I felt so annoyed when I kept seeing dog mess in our beautiful village that it prompted me to write the following, which I sent to the parish magazine. However, for some reason or another, the editor didn't think it suitable reading for the local parishioners and didn't publish it. Maybe he was one of the culprits?

It's not very nice, when you're walkin' along,
And you get a whiff of a terrible pong.
As you feel your foot slip, you like it much less,
When you know you've trod in a pile of dog mess!
Some selfish person's let their dog perform,
And then just left it, as though it's the norm.
But when dogs defecate, it's a very bad sin
Not to scoop up in a bag, and put it in the red bin.
There's one on the common, and one by the church.
Always carry a poop bag, don't be left in the lurch.
Save bags from Asda, just like what I do,
Or Tesco or Morrisons, to pick up dog's poo.
Keep our village smellin' beautiful,
Safe to tread where your dog went,
By never, ever failing to pick up its excrement.
Scoop it up and bag it and you'll always be a hit
With everyone who live here,
When you pick up your dog's dirt.

Now I've got that off my chest, which metaphorically speaking is far better than scraping it off your foot, back to the motorhome. As I said, the gloomy wet weather had blown over, leaving behind an incredibly clear Cornish blue sky with bright sunshine. We actually saw steam rising from the damp grass, and as our combined moods increased in direct proportion to the rising temperature we began to think that our holiday might not be such a mitigating disaster after all.

So, deciding not to waste any more of the day, we quickly made some lunch and plotted our route to Trebah. The tourist leaflet we'd picked up somewhere suggested that, if approaching from the west, which we were, the recommended route was to take the main A394 towards Falmouth and then follow the brown and white tourism signs. It all sounded simple enough, but when I looked at our road atlas it appeared to be an unnecessarily long and roundabout way to get there. On the other hand, a much shorter more direct route seemed to be via Gweek, which is famous for its seal sanctuary on the river estuary.

Even though the leaflet also stated that *'the route via narrow lanes east of Gweek is not recommended,'* I didn't think it would present much of a problem to make our way there via quiet country lanes. Emm wasn't so keen though and thought we ought to stick to the suggested route. However, I managed to win her round by arguing that they only encouraged people to go that way in order to keep most of the traffic on the main roads. In any case, I was quite used to driving on minor roads around Chiselborough and it would be far more picturesque and relaxing than driving straight down a dual carriageway. Or so I thought…

Anyhow, anxious to get going before it rained again, I turned the gas bottle off and disconnected the electric hook-up. Sorting out heavy cable turned out to be a mucky and frustrating job; it was wet and covered with mud from worm casts, and when I coiled the writhing mass of slippery and heavy cable around my arm it became heavier and heavier, made my arm ache and my hands and sleeve dirty. It was also very twisted in places and even had a few knots in it, which made this *simple* task much more difficult than it should have been. When

I'd eventually manhandled it into a reasonable coil, it was a struggle to force into the canvas bag I'd acquired for it, and after I'd done so my hands were wet through and covered in mud.

I went over to the washroom to clean myself up, and when I came back Emm was sat in the passenger seat impatiently waiting to set off. So it was just as well I saw our wet coats and dog towels hanging over the bicycle rack on the back of the motorhome, where we'd hung them up to dry in the sun. I gave them to Emm to put away whilst I removed my wet and muddy boots and changed into my indoor driving shoes. Then as I sat down in the driving seat and she started to go through our pre-start check-list, I told her to add *'check nothing hanging on bicycle rack'* to the list. Then, after double checking everything once more, Emm finally gave me the go-ahead to get going.

Luckily, I didn't have to reverse or perform any tricky manoeuvres to drive off our pitch, and I was very thankful for that. All I had to do was ease forward and turn through the gap in the hedge onto the gravel road. Even so, after all the rain, I was acutely aware the grass was exceptionally wet and greasy. Knowing our luck, I had visions of the front wheel driven tyres spinning and slowly sinking into an ever deepening hole in the soft ground. So keeping my fears to myself, I gently let out the clutch and slowly inched forward. Thankfully the tyres gripped and I carefully turned the steering wheel to take us onto the solidity of the gravel track, just like I'd been driving the motorhome for years.

I made our way out of the campsite and cautiously headed back up the shady narrow lane, all the time negotiating deep puddles and hoping we wouldn't meet another vehicle coming towards us. Thankfully, we didn't and soon joined the B3293, turned off to our right towards Gweek and went past the seal sanctuary. So far all was well and I thought we'd soon see a sign for Trebah. We didn't and from here on the journey became increasingly problematic.

All might have been well if we'd brought our Ordnance Survey map of the area with us – but stupidly we'd left it behind. We were navigating by means of a ring bound road atlas which, although it had a scale of 2½ miles to the inch, showed no indication of gradient. Also, to frustrate and confuse our map reading even further, the wire binder divided the pages precisely through the area where we were trying to navigate.

We realised that the roads weren't very wide; but the reality was that they weren't really roads at all, just very minor country lanes that became more twisty, more hilly and, alarmingly, more narrow the further we went. I was quite used to driving along the narrow country lanes around Chiselborough, but that was in my Volvo. The motorhome was a much wider and much taller vehicle, and its sides and roof constantly brushed against the hedges and low overhanging branches. Because of the weight of the rainwater saturating all the leaves, the branches were possibly lower than usual and I hoped the roof and fragile body panels wouldn't get damaged or scratched too much. There were very few passing places and it was just as well we never met another vehicle coming the other way. It would have been an absolute nightmare if I'd been forced to back up the way we'd come and steer around the bends in reverse gear.

Emm kept telling me to turn around and go back. But, even if I'd wanted to, it just wasn't possible. Unless the lane considerably widened, or we came to a junction, there was no turning back and nothing I could do to get us out of this mess. Hoping for the best, but fearing the worst, I did my utmost to give the impression I knew precisely where we were and was confident we'd soon arrive at Trebah. However, although I wouldn't admit as much to Emm, the further on we went, the more worried I became – as did Emm, only more so.

We hadn't seen a single signpost and, by this time, we hadn't a clue where we were on the map and were in a right state. We were hopelessly lost with Emm blaming me, saying we should have gone via the main road and that we would have been there by now if we'd done so. Of course she was right, although I couldn't admit as much, but her constantly telling me so didn't help the situation at all.

We eventually found ourselves at the top of a hill where, through a gap in the trees, there was a magnificent view of the sunny estuary down on our right hand side. I told Emm, in a more confident manner than I felt, that Trebah was on the estuary so we must be going in the right direction and it couldn't be that far away. Hoping against hope I was right, we carried on and reached a point where the road veered sharply round to the left and the estuary disappeared from sight. My misplaced confidence immediately nose-dived, but being unable to do otherwise we carried on in an awkward silence and, as always, just hoped for the best.

Eventually the lane widened slightly by a turning off to the left, where there was a signpost pointing towards a place called *Constantine*, and we were both relieved to be able to pull up and try to work out where we were. We found Constantine on our map and after a bit of joint map reading and discussion, or more truthfully a minor argument, we more or less worked out where we were. Or rather, where we thought we were.

Unfortunately, we both thought we were in totally different places. So, after even more discussion and argument, plus a fair proportion of pig-headedness, we agreed to differ. Emm wanted me to either turn around and give up as a bad job or take the left turning, whereas I was convinced we should carry on, believing that if we followed the lane to our left we'd be led even further away from Trebah. Anyhow, as I was in the driving seat I made the executive decision to ignore the lane to Constantine – which, much to Emm's displeasure, is what I did.

I stubbornly carried on for about fifty yards or so, but even to an obstinate idiot like me it became blindingly obvious that the lane was getting even narrower. And to make matters worse, we were about to descend down a very steep and winding hill. It was impossible to avoid the hedges and extensive overhanging branches on either side of us and they constantly scraped the sides and roof of the motorhome. It almost seemed as though the trees were about to engulf us and that we would end up in some unknown Cornish parallel universe or *twilight zone*, like in some scary science fiction fantasy or ghost story.

Any remaining optimism I might have had completely drained away when we saw the *'Road Unsuitable for Large Vehicles'* sign. This made me realise that, if I bloody-mindedly carried on, we'd almost certainly end up getting stuck in the middle of nowhere, hopelessly lost and unable to proceed either forwards or backwards, which was definitely not a situation I wanted us to be in. I therefore prepared to reverse back to the turning I'd stupidly ignored in the first place.

Emm climbed down from the cab to guide me as I anxiously backed up, and after several scary minutes zigzagging blindly back the way we came, I managed to pull up again by the junction. Thankful to have managed this tricky manoeuvre without any mishaps, we remarked it was just as well we hadn't met any other vehicles. It then dawned on us that, ever since we'd passed the seal sanctuary, we'd not seen a single vehicle apart from our own.

We jointly consulted our road atlas once more, but no matter how hard we looked we still couldn't pinpoint with any certainty as to where we actually were. So, not wanting to give up and go back to the campsite defeated, I conceded that Emm had been right all along and I agreed to follow the sign to Constantine and hope for the best.

At least the lane gradually widened and we soon found ourselves in the centre of the small village of Constantine, where I drove as slowly as possible as we both strained our eyes for a signpost to Trebah Gardens. But there didn't appear to be one. We would have asked someone for directions, but it was eerily quiet and we didn't see a single soul. We might as well have been in *Constantinople* rather than Constantine and, for all the help with our directions we were going to get here, I couldn't help thinking we'd already entered the *twilight zone* after all.

I began to realise how difficult it would have been for enemy spies, parachuted into this part of the world during World War Two, to have found their way about when all the signposts had been deliberately removed. For all we knew, there could have been the odd geriatric German agent still holed up in this part of Cornwall, living off the land and completely unaware that Britain and Germany are now partners in the European Union.

Anyhow, more in hope than expectation (we'd almost given up by this time), we decided to follow a signpost to a place called *Mawnan Smith* which appeared to be in the general direction we thought we needed to go. Then, much to our immense relief, we finally saw an elusive brown and white tourism signpost to *Trebah Gardens*, which we followed with silent prayers of deliverance, and before long we triumphantly arrived at the elusive gardens.

The car park was virtually empty, which made us wonder just how many other lost souls were still driving round in circles trying to find their way there. Even though we'd finally arrived, we now had to make a major decision and agree exactly where to park the motorhome. We spent an inordinate amount of time looking around at the vast choice of spaces and decided, or should I say Emm decided, that we'd park in a shady spot right at the far end of the car park. I would have parked right bang next to the garden entrance, but what the hell? After insisting we go there via the scenic route, I didn't want to start another argument so conceded quietly and, as carefully as I could and with Emm's help, backed into the enormous space.

At long last we were ready to go. The sun was shining even more brightly and the sky was a glorious blue colour with not a cloud to be seen. After all the rain we'd experienced, the contrast in the weather didn't seem at all possible. Indeed, it did almost seem as though we must have indeed passed through some magical *twilight zone* and arrived in a parallel, sub-tropical universe. We both felt really warm for the first time and, after the miserable start to our holiday and our frustrating journey, everything started to seem right with the world.

7

TREBAH GARDENS

The name *Trebah* is derived from the Celtic *Tre-Baya*, which means *House on the Bay*, and is first recorded in the Domesday Book of 1086 when it was the property of the Bishop of Exeter. It never ceases to amaze me that, throughout the centuries, the Church owned so much land and were so rich and powerful, whilst the vast majority of people were extremely poor and beholden to the Church and rich landowners. It seems to fly in the face of most of the religious prophets who led simple lives, and does not sit comfortably with me. However, I digress.

Over the next seven hundred years or so Trebah passed through many owners until, in 1831, it was acquired by Robert Fox of Falmouth, who later passed it on to his son, Charles. As well as being Quakers, the Fox family were very successful and wealthy businessmen who had substantial interests in shipping, tin mines and pilchard fishing. They also had an expensive hobby, i.e. horticulture, and created at least six exceptional Cornish gardens including Penjerrick, Glendurgan, Rosehill and, of course, Trebah, all of which still survive today. Being very rich, and in the shipping business, the family were well placed to stock their Cornish gardens with all sorts of exotic plants, many of which had never been grown in Britain before.

During the late 1830s and early 1840s, Charles Fox first laid out the original twenty-six acre pleasure garden at Trebah in readiness for the first of his ships to arrive laden with plants from around the world. He planted numerous species of pines and deciduous trees to provide windbreaks and shelter the garden from the worst of the elements, many of which are still thriving today.

Charles had a tremendous creative energy and a gift for meticulous detail and planning. For example, after giving full consideration to the best possible view from his house when each individual tree eventually reached its full height, he worked out precisely where each tree was to be planted. After all, it's a bit late to move that little shrub when it's grown fifty or sixty feet tall, so best get it right first time. Which is exactly what he did!

On the precise spot where he thought a tree might be planted, he had his gardeners build a temporary scaffold tower of the exact height each tree would eventually grow to. From his attic window he would then survey the scene through his telescope, and after ordering one of his youngest staff to climb the tower and wave a white flag he would bark out his orders through a megaphone. If, after bawling out a few 'left a bit' and 'right a bit' instructions, he still wasn't entirely satisfied, the scaffold would have to be moved somewhere else, quite often more than once, until he was totally convinced in his own mind that, in the fullness of time, the fully grown tree wouldn't obstruct the best of the views over the estuary. When surveying the magnificent mature trees today, visitors will surely appreciate his thoroughness, as well as the efforts of his many staff who continually erected, moved, and dismantled the scaffolds before planting each specimen. I know we did.

As well as being a highly successful businessman and horticulturist, Charles Fox was described as having a wide knowledge of many different subjects. For example, he was President of the *Royal Geological Society of Cornwall* and contributed a number of articles to scientific journals. He co-founded the *Miners' Association of Cornwall and Devon,* which helped improve miners' skills and education, and was also active in prison reform. All in all, he must have been a bit of an all-round clever dick in his day, albeit a kind and benevolent one who gladly gave his money and energy to any project that helped the people of Falmouth and the surrounding districts.

When Charles died in 1876, his son-in-law, one Edmund Backhouse MP, inherited Trebah and, as was the wont of so many Victorian plant hunters and land owners, made it his life's work to gather a huge collection of exotic plants and trees from all over the world. One of the many species he had shipped back from Australia were several thousand tree ferns, which were shared out between the best gardens in Cornwall where they thrived in the ideal conditions. During the Backhouse years paths were constructed, pools were dug out along the stream which ran down the valley and hundreds of rare plants were gathered from all over the world and planted out.

The Victorians were great lovers of rhododendrons and huge numbers were taken from Asia and the Mediterranean and introduced to all the great estates across Britain. Cornwall was often the first port of call for these rhododendrons and Edward Backhouse had his fair share of these non-native specimens planted out at Trebah. Unfortunately, during our visit, they'd long since flowered and were nowhere near their colourful best. However, as lovely as the flowers are, for Emm and me they don't last long enough, and when not in flower the plants are rather boring. Also, they are a thuggish horticultural tyrant.

Or rather the variety *Rhododendron ponticum* and its hybrids are. Since they were brought to these shores by the unsuspecting Victorians, they have rapidly expanded and eliminated the majority of native plant species within their vicinity. Their branches grow out laterally and, where they touch the ground, easily take root and continually extend the rhododendron's cover. Each flower head can produce thousands of seeds of which, given the right conditions, a good number will germinate. Light cannot penetrate to the soil below them and, coupled with the fact that they produce a chemical which inhibits the growth of all other plants in their surrounding area, nothing much can grow near them. Additionally, their leaves are poisonous to animals so can't be controlled by grazing, and fallen leaves which don't rot down smother the ground, acidify the soil and significantly reduce the earthworm population.

Consequently, they have invaded vast swathes of British countryside completely killing off many native British plants. Animals and insects which rely on indigenous plants for their food supplies have died out and the highly invasive plant can even cover streams so that fish, such as trout, which largely depend on invertebrates falling off native riverside plants for food, have also suffered.

So, it really is no exaggeration to describe this plant as a *thuggish horticultural tyrant* and it definitely needs taking down a peg or two. Fortunately, that is exactly what is now happening all over the country as huge overgrown and overbearing *Rhododendron ponticum* plants are being cut down to allow indigenous British plants to re-establish. However, it's a never ending battle as new shoots rapidly grow on their roots. Also, their leaves are waxy and any herbicidal treatment has to include a chemical additive to break down the wax before the herbicide can take effect. Even then, such treatment has to be repeated over a number of years.

Furthermore, once the plant has been removed, a toxic humus layer remains and has to be removed before natural regeneration can take place. All in all, it's a rather depressing legacy that the Victorian plant hunters left us with. However, on the other hand and much more positively, they also left future generations with many magnificent gardens to enjoy and I suppose they can be forgiven for a few mistakes. After all, at the time they never appreciated the thuggishness of this tyrannical plant with the lovely flowers – did they?

Even though there are loads of different varieties and hundreds of rhododendron specimens, some of which are over 150 years old, still thriving at Trebah, I'm not aware that any tyrannical *Rhododendron ponticum* or their hybrids still grow there. If there were, then surely they would have spread out far across their borders and wiped out many of their much more passive neighbouring plants by now?

Anyhow, in 1907 the vastly improved gardens were then acquired by a Mr Charles Hawkins, who was obviously a very keen gardener, to say the least, as was Alice, his wife. For the next thirty years and more, the gardens continued to flourish under the Hawkins' custodianship. The pond was improved and stocked with pretty pink flamingos, which are still there today. Well, maybe not the same birds, but rather their offspring or their relations' offspring, which all made a fantastic sight with their pink feathers gleaming in the bright sunlight and being reflected in the clear water. A boathouse was built, as was a thatched summerhouse, and huge numbers of tender plants including countless varieties of bamboo were planted. These were indeed magnificent and we found it difficult to believe there could be so many different varieties of mature bamboo growing in one place in Britain.

Likewise Trebah's huge collection of ferns which were growing in the dampness of the valley, especially the very tall prehistoric tree ferns, particularly interested us. As previously mentioned, we'd been planting out many different varieties of ferns in our garden, but all our efforts paled into insignificance compared with Trebah. Mind you, they'd been at it for more than 170 years or so and started off with a far bigger budget than we could ever imagine. On one hand, Trebah's ferns almost made us feel as though we were wasting our time, but on the other hand inspired us to do more and try to cultivate a tree fern in the near future.

Similarly, their extraordinary collection of gigantic gunnera plants, which towered above me like huge umbrellas in the wet areas by the ponds, were particularly spectacular and put the specimens I'd planted to shame. Emm, who knows more about these things than me, had insisted they wouldn't do well, saying it was too hot and dry where I'd planted them. However, I'd stubbornly gone ahead and, even though I'd dug in vast amounts of moisture retaining organic matter and kept them well watered, they were obviously not that happy and only grew to about three feet in height before their leaves dried out and got scorched during the long hot summer we'd just enjoyed.

I couldn't imagine many failures at Trebah though and, judging by what we saw, being sheltered from the worst of the elements, their gunnera, ferns, bamboos and all the other plants enjoyed perfect growing conditions, with moist, fertile soil, plenty of sunlight, as well as shade where it was needed, and a mild, frost free climate. Consequently, every single plant seemed to have flourished brilliantly. There probably were some that failed to do so, but no doubt a few failures would have been accepted as part of the grand experiment.

Trebah became more and more famous during Alice's time (Charles had died in 1917) and the aristocracy and many distinguished visitors came from all over the country to see for themselves the splendid gardens which had been created in the unique coastal micro-climate in far off Cornwall. Amongst the eminent visitors were Edward the Prince of Wales with a certain Mr and Mrs Simpson in 1935, presumably before Mr Simpson was aware his wife was the Prince's mistress and certainly before the world knew of the events that would lead to the abdication crisis in 1936!

A few years later, in 1939, two important events took place which further shaped Trebah. Firstly, Alice died and secondly, World War Two broke out. After Alice's death the substantial estate was sold off in many small packages and, consequently, the garden was deprived of any income to maintain it in all its glory. This was a tragedy for the garden, but in the overall scheme of things, not such a great global tragedy as the war against Hitler. The war left its mark on Trebah, insomuch as most of the gardeners and servants, who were still working there, would have been called up to fight or undertake other war work. The loss of this labour further hastened the garden's decline, and when peace eventually broke out again, it's doubtful whether many of the surviving staff returned to work on the estate.

However, Trebah itself did its bit for the war effort. The secret preparations for D-Day drastically destroyed the tranquillity of the gardens as in 1944, in order to prepare for the Allied invasion to liberate Europe, its small beach leading onto the Helford estuary was completely covered in concrete. Large rocks on the beach were dynamited so that tanks and other military vehicles would have easier access to the water when being loaded onto landing craft, slit trenches were dug all over the old gardens and a huge ammunition dump was constructed. It certainly wouldn't have been such a peaceful and tranquil place during that historic time, especially as enemy fighter bombers periodically attacked these invasion preparations, albeit without too much success.

Similar preparations happened in total secrecy all over southern England and, after a delay due to appalling weather, on 1st June 1944, seven thousand five hundred nervous young American infantrymen crossed the concrete beach at Trebah to board ten 150-foot long flat-bottomed landing craft, which were loaded with tanks, guns, ammunition and other military equipment. Then, for five extremely long and miserable days they slowly battled through exceptionally high seas to the Isle of Wight and on to Normandy where, on 6th June, they landed on Omaha beach along with around 30,000 fellow American troops.

When the invasion was planned it was assumed the weather would be reasonable with calm seas. After all, it was mid-summer. However, there was unseasonably stormy weather which threatened the whole operation. Then, after much deliberation by the Allied leaders, when the invasion was finally given the go-ahead the weather inexplicably worsened yet again. When crossing the English Channel in the unstable flat bottomed boats, the brave young soldiers must have suffered terribly from sea sickness and surely couldn't have been in the best condition to fight their way onto the exposed beachhead. Indeed, as they landed on the heavily defended shore, they must have been scared witless and it's not surprising they suffered tremendous losses. In fact, the landings on Omaha beach were very nearly a total disaster. Most of the tanks couldn't be landed in the stormy seas and many casualties were suffered, much more than on any of the other D-Day landing beaches.

There is now a poignant little plaque by the beach at Trebah commemorating the American troops, who gave so much to free Europe from the evil Nazi occupation. Indeed, everyone who was born after that terrible time, me included, have so much to be thankful for. We all owe a huge debt to the generation before us, which we can never hope to repay. They gave everything they could and much more, including the ultimate sacrifice, so that their children and future generations could live in relative peace and prosperity. Having meandered slowly down through the beautiful gardens to the small concrete beach, where we ate a delicious Cornish ice cream in the warm sunshine and watched the pleasure boats in the estuary, I found it very humbling as I tried to imagine the scene here on that very spot in 1944 and what followed shortly afterwards across the Channel.

As I said, compared to those brave young Americans, who were so far away from home and never knew what lay ahead or whether they'd make it back home again (which of course thousands of them never did), we have so much to be grateful for today and so very little to complain about. And yet these days, we hear of immature, over-privileged university students, around the same age as those brave young soldiers, urinating on war memorials and callous, cowardly thieves stealing metal plaques off war memorials to sell for their scrap value. Many old timers would say such subhuman people should be given a rifle and sent to the front line in Afghanistan. I would say the same, but their very presence would put our brave present day professional soldiers at risk. In any case, such spoilt brats and cold-hearted criminals would probably piss their pants, or worse, just at the thought of it!

After the war Trebah was to change hands several times and was gradually restored in all its glory to what it is today. In 1981 it was bought as a *retirement project* by a Major Tony Hibbert (who was himself a distinguished war hero who was awarded the Military Cross) and his wife, and they began a major programme to restore the garden to its former glory. They opened to the public in 1987 to help pay towards its substantial cost and eventually gave it to a registered charity, the Trebah Garden Trust, so that it would be preserved for future generations to enjoy. Major Hibbert must be a very special man and one wonders what he would think of the mindless morons who deface war memorials and the like today.

Today Trebah is described as *a uniquely beautiful, twenty-six acre Cornish ravine garden – the wild and magical result of 160 years of inspired and dedicated creation*. It certainly didn't disappoint and it's definitely a place we will visit again, perhaps when the rhododendrons are in full bloom. Anyhow, it was all too soon time for us to leave and we started to make our way back up through the valley towards the exit. Of course, we had to go out through the gift shop, where we were tempted with all sorts of goodies, especially plants. I didn't really mind, however, as everything in the shop was good quality and reasonably priced. They had a fantastic selection of plants for sale and I would love to have bought some more ferns for our garden, but had to agree with Emm that it would be too much trouble to look after them in the motorhome for the next week before we got home. Therefore, somewhat reluctantly, we set off back to the car park.

Provided we stuck to the main roads this time and followed the signposts, we were confident we'd have no trouble finding our way back. However, we must have been over confident because, believe it or not, we were soon lost again! We'd successfully made our way back to Constantine, where we foolishly followed a sign back towards Gweek, which we never found and, just like before, ended up hopelessly disorientated and clueless as to where we were. It had been a long day and, by this time, we were both tired and hungry and not at our best. Eventually, we were saved from driving round in circles for an eternity when we saw a signpost to Helston. We knew that if we followed the sign we'd eventually end up joining the main A394 somewhere near Helston itself and end up going back the long way round. But at least we knew the way from there and it would be impossible to get lost – even for us! We really should have paid more attention to the note in the leaflet which advised that *the narrow lanes to the east of Gweek were not recommended.*[8]

Anyhow, rather later than expected, we arrived back, parked up, reconnected the electricity and turned on the gas supply. We then

---

8   There is now a warning in Trebah's website which states 'If you are using a SatNav, we recommend you do not go off into the countryside, some roads are difficult to navigate and not signposted. Stick to the main roads and specified routes, especially when travelling from Helston/West and The Lizard.' Although we didn't have SatNav, it still proved to be an absolute nightmare taking our short cut. So be warned and stick to the main route!

spotted that one of the rear wheels was parked right on top of our rubber doormat, which had been pushed into the muddy ground. It had proved to be a useful mat to have outside the door to wipe our feet on and I'd completely forgotten to take it inside when we set off for Trebah. In order to retrieve it from under the wheel, I had to move the motorhome forward a couple of feet and pull it up out of the ground. It was indented with so much mud that it would have been useless for wiping mud off the soles of our shoes, but perfect for transferring mud onto them. As I closed my ears to Emm, who kept telling me to be more careful in future and that it would have been all my fault if we'd moved on to a different site and left our doormat behind, I did my best to remove all the sticky mud from between the rubber indentations and made a note to add *'bring doormat inside'* to our pre-setting off check-list.

Once we got sorted out and settled down again, we cooked an easy meal of lasagne, potatoes and salad. I'm afraid the lasagne was an easy-to-cook ready meal from the supermarket and the potatoes were out of a tin, but the meal tasted good, especially when washed down with a whole bottle of wine. We had yoghurt and blueberries for dessert, but Emm somehow managed to drop most of her berries on the floor. Monty thought it was a great game as we scrambled around on all fours, frantically trying to pick them all up before they got trodden into the light coloured carpet, and I dared to tell Emm to be more careful in future!

Once we'd washed up and taken Monty out, we read for a bit and then had an early night. After eating too many mince pies one Christmas with her unique homemade brandy butter (which always had more brandy than butter), I remembered our sister-in-law telling us that, after being out in the fresh air all day when she stayed with her family in our Durdle Door caravan, she was always too tired for nooky.

I knew exactly what she meant. It had been another long day; we were both pretty much exhausted and were fast asleep before our heads hit the pillow!

8

CAMPING & COURTING
IN THE RAIN

After our hectic day at Trebah we'd both slept like logs and were still dead to the world at eight-thirty or thereabouts, only to be woken by Monty telling us he desperately needed a wee. Obviously it was me who drew the short straw and, after slipping on some trousers and shoes, I took him outside.

It was a misty start to the day, but warmish, and I was reasonably optimistic that the sun would soon burn through and the fine weather we'd enjoyed the previous afternoon would continue. The gravel pathways had mostly dried out with the large puddles considerably reduced in size, and we certainly didn't want any more rain; neither did we want a wet, muddy dog leaping about getting dirty paws all over our light coloured carpet and seat covers.

Motorhome life would be so much easier in the dry without having to take muddy shoes on and off as we went in and out, to hang up wet waterproofs in the confines of the relatively small living space, or having to keep wiping mud off Monty and dry him each time he came inside the motorhome. Now we were no longer in the flush of youth we were definitely fine weather campers, and if the rest of the week wasn't sunny and dry we could still have been tempted to return the motorhome to the dealers and sell it back to them at a loss.

I remembered when we were courting in the very early 1970s and, irrespective of the weather, we'd always look forward to camping in our small tent at every opportunity. We would drive down to the New Forest and camp in a field behind the *Red Shoot Inn* at weekends and go much further afield for longer summer holidays. Several times we went all the way to Cornwall, where our love affair with that beautiful county (as well as with each other?) blossomed. Another time we even drove all the way to the other end of the country to the Lake District, where we had a horrendously wet week. I'd been to the Lakes several times before, had absolutely loved it and was very keen to take Emm. Knowing she'd never been there I especially wanted to impress her by showing her Lake Windermere, the mountains and all the beautiful and romantic scenery the Victorian poets wrote about.

I first went there with a friend for a week's walking holiday in September 1966 when I was a very young eighteen-year-old. My friend had been there several times before with his family and had raved about the scenery and the mountains. He meticulously planned out our complete route for the week, including overnight stops in youth hostels which we booked in advance. Unfortunately, all the pre-planning counted for nothing as we enjoyed a tremendous amount of torrential and seemingly endless rain, the likes of which I'd never experienced before.

We had to be out of the hostels by a certain time in the morning, I think it was around ten o'clock, and were not allowed inside the next one we'd booked into until somewhere around five o'clock. However, in view of the awful weather we knew it would be far too dangerous and foolhardy to walk via spectacular mountain peaks as we'd planned. And instead of being exhilarated whilst enjoying magnificent views as we expected, we spent the days shuffling morosely along roads and muddy tracks with torrents of water streaming down them. The rain dripped off our hats and ran down our necks, poured off our rucksacks and streamed down our backs, then onto our legs and inside our boots. So, by the time we reached our next youth hostel, we were like two drowned rats.

We invariably had to wait around in the worst rain imaginable, longing to get into the warm and dry, before the hostel warden finally condescended to open the doors and allow us in. We would then change into our spare clothes which had somehow remained dry wrapped in plastic bags in our rucksacks, before hanging our sodden clothes in the steamy drying room, where they stood half a chance of drying before we were pushed out into the foul weather again the following morning.

It wasn't entirely all gloom, however, as we did have two fine days out of the seven. As we set off from Keswick on our first day and made our way south past Derwent Water towards the wilderness of Langdale Fell, it was fine and sunny. I can't remember where we stayed that night, but my friend and I were both full of optimism after a most enjoyable walk and I was itching to climb my first mountain. Then, next morning it rained. And it continued to rain like I never knew it could rain for almost all the remainder of our holiday.

It only brightened up for one more day when we actually managed to reach the summit of Great Gable, a mountain which was to be fairly significant to me and my family in the years to come. I'd never seen such a wild, rugged and rocky landscape before and the incredible views, particularly over Wastwater, which at 258 feet is the deepest lake in England, almost made the misery of the monsoon weather worthwhile. Many years later, it was after climbing Great Gable that Emm had her mountaineering accident, which I've already mentioned, and it also dominated the background to Joscelin's wedding photographs, which were taken by the side of Wastwater in glorious sunshine in August 2005.

Despite the rain, I must have enjoyed my youth hostelling holiday in the Lakes, because when I had the chance to go again for a week with the Air Cadets the following year, my name was the first to go on the list. This time it was during the month of May and we enjoyed some fantastic weather, which obviously made all the difference from my first Lake District experience. I stayed in a hostel, owned by the Air Training Corps, in Windermere with other cadets from all over Hampshire and thoroughly enjoyed it. We climbed Scafell Pike, the highest mountain in England, Great Gable, Helvellyn via the awesome Striding Edge, plus some other smaller mountains, and I found walking the fells and the views from the peaks to be quite intoxicating. We also managed some rock climbing and abseiling which, although a little nerve racking at first, gave me an adrenalin rush and was great fun.

As well as staying in the relative comfort of the hostel, we spent a couple of nights under canvas, which I must admit I didn't look forward to all that much. We had to carry all our gear, including tent, sleeping bag and food, for about ten miles or so across the rugged Langdale Pikes, ending up in a campsite somewhere in the Langdale Valley. I recall that we didn't enjoy clear skies and wall to wall sunshine for the whole of the week. That would have been just too much to expect in the Lake District, and on the first night we spent under canvas there was a very heavy downpour which did dampen our spirits somewhat.

As part of the exercise, we had to cook our own meal of tinned stew, peas and instant mash on a Primus stove outside in the open, whilst our officers went off to the Langdale Hotel for a slap up meal and a drink or two. However, it rained so hard that we ended up cooking and eating our dinner in the salubrious surroundings of the gents' toilet on the campsite. Not the nicest meal I've ever had and certainly not the best surroundings, but after our long trek on the fells we were all starving hungry. Anyhow, we survived and I must have enjoyed the mountains as I went back again the following May with the cadets, when the weather was also very good, being sunny and mostly dry.

As I said, I wanted to take Emm and impress her with the unique Lakeland scenery. At the time, I had a 1960 *Ford Classic* car, which was a poor imitation of an American style car, and I drove it up the relatively quiet M5 and M6 to Cumbria, or was it Cumberland and Westmorland back in 1971?[9] Anyhow, as impressive as the gleaming black and chrome car, with its great big bench seats, may have looked,

---

9   Local government boundaries were changed in 1974 and Cumbria was created out of Cumberland, Westmoreland, Lancashire-over-Sands and Sedbegh district (formerly in Yorkshire).

there was a problem with it, insomuch that it seriously lacked power. It would accelerate reasonably well up to about forty-five miles per hour and then, as I depressed my foot further down on the accelerator, it would inexplicably slow down again.[10] When trying to overtake a lorry on the motorway this was a bit disconcerting to say the least, and it certainly didn't bode well for driving around the mountainous Lake District.

To cut a long story short, this camping trip in the Lake District was not the total success I hoped it would be. Even though it was the end of May, when on both my previous trips with the Air Cadets the weather had been largely fine and sunny, it rained virtually non-stop and was just too wet and cold to get out much and explore.

We'd planned to do most of our cooking on a single burner camping gas stove, which was virtually impossible and no fun at all in the rain. But at least this time I didn't resort to cooking and eating in the gents; we cooked in the confines of our small tent which, as it was always soaking wet and would have been impossible to catch fire, we didn't consider to be that dangerous. Our favourite camping meal was paella and rice, which was quite an exotic meal at the time, and just had to be added to water and boiled. Other favourites were instant mashed potato, tinned stew and mushy peas or corned beef with fried onion and baked beans.

Another outstanding memory of that trip with Emm is of Hardknott Pass which, with 1 in 3 gradients, shares the honour of being the steepest road in England. It's a very narrow, single track road with treacherous hairpin bends and few passing places, which as it twists and turns through some of the most desolate terrain right in the middle of the Lake District reaches a height of around 1,300 feet above sea level. I'd walked along it during torrential rain on my first trip to the Lakes when I was youth hostelling and, wanting to impress

---

10 For the mechanically minded, I'd only just bought the car for a bargain price and the previous owner had rebuilt the engine. Unfortunately, he fitted the timing chain incorrectly and the valves never completely closed on the compression stroke. Hence, the lack of power.

Emm, decided that I just had to drive across this awesome route on our holiday.

Unfortunately, it was pelting down and Hardknott Pass was just as remote and desolate as before. I don't recall seeing any other cars and, bearing in mind there were no mobile phones in those days, goodness knows what would have happened if we'd broken down, which was a real possibility considering the car was extremely underpowered and embarrassingly slow on the hills. In fact it was so bad I literally had to stop at the beginning of the steepest gradients and change down into first gear before the car would begrudgingly move onwards and upwards. Indeed, it was always touch and go whether we'd move up or just slip backwards down the hill.

Needless to say, this was a very hairy drive indeed. However, we made it, but couldn't really appreciate the scenery or the wildness of the views (not that there was much to see through all the rain and thick clouds). We were just too worried as to whether we would eventually make it over the pass or not, and we were both very much relieved when we eventually found ourselves on the relatively flatter roads close to some sort of civilisation at Eskdale.

After four or five days of our Lake District endurance test waiting in vain for the rains to stop, we decided to pack up and go somewhere else. By this time we were absolutely sick of the foul weather and felt as though we needed a submarine rather than a car. The last straw was when I somehow locked the car keys in the boot. We'd just taken the tent down in pouring rain and packed everything up ready to move on, when I realised I didn't have the keys. After searching every nook and cranny in the car and all my pockets, I asked Emm if she had them.

She didn't, and after a thorough inquisition, we realised the only place we hadn't looked was in the boot which was locked. At first I had no idea what to do, then remembered it was possible to take the back seat out of the car. After struggling to remove it, I somehow managed to wriggle my arm through a small hole between the back of the car and the boot, and then grope around amongst all the wet camping gear for the missing keys. In some ways, it must have been our lucky day, and as I reached out with my arm as far as it would go I suddenly felt what I was searching for. Fearful I would push them further away, I stretched my fingertips as far as they would go and somehow succeeding in gripping them between two fingers before triumphantly pulling them back through the hole. How our relationship survived such near disasters, I'll never know. But somehow, it did.

When she was a child, Emm had been to Blackpool on holiday with her family and wanted to take the opportunity to show me the Golden Mile, which I had to admit was a bit of a contrast to the remoteness of the Lakes. Anyhow, now we'd found our keys and packed up, we headed south towards the M6 and on to Blackpool and hunted around for a campsite. We went into the first one we saw, which was in a quagmire of a farmer's field just outside the town and, needless to say, as we struggled to pitch our small tent, it was still pouring down and very, very windy.

Hoping it would still be there when we came back, we left the tent and drove into Blackpool where we parked the car somewhere and walked along the seafront. It was completely deserted and seemed almost as desolate as the Lake District; we could just about make out the famous sands but, as the tide was out, couldn't see the sea. What we could see though, was rain, rain and more rain blowing in horizontally off the Irish Sea at what felt like speeds approaching a hundred miles an hour. We literally had to bend double, lean into the wind and walk crab-like in a sideways direction lest we got swept away down the side roads.

I'd never previously known a wind like it, and the experience was only surpassed when I had to walk from central London to Waterloo during what became known as the Burns' Day storm on the 25th January 1990. I was alone in the office during the early afternoon when word spread that a violent storm was imminent and we should make our way home. The wind didn't seem *that* excessive until crossing Waterloo Bridge, where it was so strong that I literally had to cling to the railings to prevent myself being bowled over by the hurricane-like wind rushing down the Thames. It was a frightening situation with high sided vehicles blown over and lying on their sides across the bridge and shards of glass and other debris flying about in the air.

The station was cordoned off and I joined a crowd of anxious commuters trying to get information. A confused policeman told us to catch the tube to Wimbledon from where trains were still running, and a man who lived in Winchester and hadn't been to London for years, asked if he could go along with me. Of course I agreed and we then met two of my colleagues who had to get back to Fareham and Gosport. We made our way together to Wimbledon where a train then took us on to Woking, and we were shocked to see scores of houses with roof tiles being ripped off and flying around in the air.

At Woking I left my travelling companions and caught another train to Farnham, so I consider myself extremely lucky to get home that day. The storm raged all over southern England and Wales with gusts up to ninety-three miles an hour; massive devastation to property resulted, with three million trees damaged or uprooted and half a million homes left without electricity. The actor, Gordon Kaye, of 'Allo 'Allo fame, ended up in a coma after a piece of wood struck his head and was lucky to escape with his life. Hundreds, if not thousands, were stranded in the capital due to all the train cancellations, with forty-seven unfortunate people losing their lives and never making it home.[11]

My two colleagues got no further than Winchester and the stranger we met at Waterloo took them home with him, before driving them on to Fareham and Gosport. We never did find out if this Good Samaritan got back to Winchester safely through all the chaos caused by fallen trees and overturned vehicles. I certainly hope he did, as do my colleagues who were eternally grateful to him.

Anyhow, I digress. Back in Blackpool, soaked to the skin yet again

---

11   Most casualties were caused by falling debris and being crushed by collapsed buildings. There were more casualties in Europe.

and almost suffering from hypothermia, we gave up any idea of cooking a meal in the tent and went in a pub for a drink and something to eat. Refreshed and warmed up a bit, Emm wanted to show me Blackpool Tower, so we braved the howling wind and rain once more and struggled the short distance up the road to the famous landmark. We paid our entrance fee and made straight for the famous ballroom, which was an amazing experience. Outside, it was totally inhospitable with foul and miserable weather, but the scene inside couldn't have been more conflicting.

Blackpool Tower was inspired by the Paris Eiffel Tower and was opened to great acclaim in 1894. The whole place was like nothing I'd ever seen before, being more like the Palace of Versailles than a northern dance hall. Thinking about it now, when designing the ballroom, the architects may well have been influenced by the Palace of Versailles. After all, they probably hopped across the Channel in a steamer and on to Paris a few times to look at the Eiffel Tower and, whilst there, could well have taken a horse and carriage ride out to Versailles to see the palace. If that was the case, they just had to be inspired by what they saw when creating the magnificent ballroom we found ourselves standing in.

We were surrounded by sheer opulence and splendour. No expense had been spared to create the vast palatial building, with its resplendent gold leaf figurines, dazzling paintings and giant ritzy chandeliers. Apparently, it takes over a week to lower the chandeliers to the floor so they can be cleaned, which must be quite some cleaning job, and I imagine the ballroom has to be closed whilst this work is going on. The floor was made up of solid mahogany, walnut and oak blocks, which we were soon to discover was superb for dancing on. Everything just oozed with Victorian and Edwardian luxuriousness, splendidness, magnificence and grandioseness. The contrast to our previous surroundings in the Lake District and our little tent in the muddy farmer's field where we had to return to, couldn't have been more diametrically opposed!

I supposed that, with the coming of the railways, which opened up this remote part of England for tourism, and bearing in mind the unpredictable weather (or maybe because the Blackpool weather is entirely predictable with its wind and rain), the first wealthy tourists had to have somewhere exclusive where they could amuse themselves when it was wet. If that was the case, they certainly succeeded with the Blackpool Tower ballroom and all those rich toffs would have felt quite at home whiling away the hours surrounded by all this splendour. Now, it seemed they let anyone in – even us two wet and scruffy tent refugees!

A Wurlitzer organ was belting out loud old time dance music which, as we started to warm up a bit, we couldn't help tapping our feet to. From when I was a child, I remembered Reginald Dixon who was famous for playing the grand Wurlitzer[12] and was always on the wireless. Emm had seen him when she came to Blackpool as a young girl, but as he'd just retired I was slightly disappointed he wasn't playing then. I've no idea who was actually performing that day, but he sounded pretty good to us.

Anyhow, even though it was during the afternoon, there were loads of couples, mostly more elderly ones, dancing amongst all this grandeur, some of whom were excellent dancers and some not so good. We stood and watched for a while and eventually plucked up courage to join them on the floor. In those days, when we went dancing we always dressed up, girls in smart dresses and boys in suits and ties, and I couldn't help feeling out of place in our shabby clothes. However, although they didn't look quite as bedraggled as us, most of the couples were wearing casual clothes. So, having dried out a bit, we waltzed around the floor and didn't feel all that conspicuous amongst them. Even though I've got two left feet when it comes to ballroom dancing, or any other kind of dancing for that matter, we thoroughly enjoyed ourselves.

After a couple of hours, hoping that the weather might have

---

12   Reginald Dixon played the Wurlitzer at Blackpool Tower from 1930 to 1970, which was quite some run!

improved, we decided to make our way back to our tent. However, it was still pouring down and we struggled in the horrendously strong wind and heavy rain back to the car. In an attempt to dry us out I turned the heater on full blast, and we somehow managed to find the field where our windblown tent was miraculously still standing in splendid isolation, which wasn't all that surprising as not many people would be mad enough to camp out in such dreadful conditions. After getting another soaking whilst checking all the tent pegs and tightening the guy ropes, we both crawled into our tiny refuge and struggled in the tiny space to take off our wet clothes.

We then snuggled down and cuddled up in our sleeping bags and did everything we could to keep warm. The weather never improved for the next twenty-four hours or so and we stayed in the relative comfort of our sleeping bags for almost all of that time. So at least our trip to the Lakes and to Blackpool in appalling weather does hold some happy memories...

9

CADGWITH & THE LIKELY LADS

After our near disastrous drive to Trebah the previous day, we decided to leave the motorhome where it was and walk along the coastal path to the lovely fishing village of Cadgwith where we could treat ourselves to a pub lunch.

We'd always enjoyed walking along the South West Coast Path, whether in Dorset, Devon, Cornwall or North Somerset. Every step of the way, there's beautiful and unspoilt scenery to appreciate and, although I also love walking in the countryside, the spectacular views across the sea from a cliff top never fail to add an extra sparkle. Over the years we've walked along most of this outstanding coastal path in small sections, including this walk to Cadgwith, but could never tire of it. I'd love to take on the challenge of the whole 630 mile walk sometime, but that would involve a great deal of planning, as well as time. But maybe one day I will manage it.

Anyhow, as far as the weather was concerned our prayers had been answered. The sun soon burnt off the sea mist and it turned out to be a warm, dry and sunny morning, which we hoped would last for the rest of the week. We anticipated a pleasant walk to Cadgwith and were not disappointed. Every step of the way the sun shone ever brighter, with only a few fluffy white clouds drifting non-threateningly across the bright blue sky, the turquoise sea sparkled in the sunlight gently lapping against the rugged rocks below us, and to add to the peaceful scene a couple of fishing boats bobbed about, followed by greedy flocks of squawking seagulls. Out in the warm fresh air amongst such glorious scenery everything seemed to be right with the world, and it was a sharp contrast to the rough, wild seas and the soaking I'd received at Kennack Sands the previous morning. Even so, it was hard work walking up and down the gradients, and when we reached Poltesco Cove we decided to have a short rest.

At the top of the path that led down to the cove was a stone shed-like building with a pitched slate roof and, to its left, a mysterious circular stone wall with a gap in it, possibly so someone could stand inside and look out over the cove. At least from the coast path they looked like a shed and a wall, but when we walked down the steps to the beach both structures revealed themselves to be completely different and more imposing. For a start, the rectangular building was three stories high and had a plaque near its apex with the date 1866 set into it, which gave us a bit of a clue to its age. It was in amazing condition, and what we thought was a wall now revealed itself to be a round, windowless structure of similar height to the side wall of the rectangular building it adjoined.

On the opposite side wall (of the rectangular building), I could see a join where a sloping roof would have butted up against it as well as the remains of thick stone walls, and it was obvious that another building had once stood there. It all looked too solid to have naturally crumbled away, and in any case there were no fallen stone blocks to be seen. I suppose it was deliberately demolished at some point and the stone taken away to build another cottage close by, or even a wall. The remains of other, smaller buildings could also be seen in the dense undergrowth at the base of the cliff, and it was obvious they were all some sort of working buildings that had fallen into disuse.

The beach was made up of large smooth pebbles of various colours, and trickling across it was a small stream which continually filled up a small shallow pool of reasonably clear water before running out into the sea. Being alone on the beach with the deserted buildings, it was all rather eerie and I could almost visualise ghosts of people who worked there still toiling away. I initially thought they must have been tin miners, but later on I discovered it was an old Victorian serpentine factory, which closed down in 1890.

Serpentine is an attractive dark green stone with red and white veins running through it and can be highly polished to give an extremely smooth finish. It was very fashionable with the Victorians for the manufacture of large architectural interior items, such as pillars and fireplaces, and many examples can be seen in grand houses all over the country. However, it does have a tendency to dry out and crack with heat, so perhaps it wasn't all that suitable for fireplaces after all. That may have partly explained why it eventually fell out of favour and the Poltesco Cove Serpentine Factory closed down. Or maybe, as fewer grand houses began to be built, the bottom fell out of the market? Today, serpentine souvenirs such as lamp-holders, ash trays, paper weights, clocks and model lighthouses are still made and sold in many shops all over Cornwall, but especially on the Lizard Peninsula.

As we carried on towards Cadgwith we kept Monty on a tight lead as the footpath was very near the cliff edge in places. The views were breathtaking – some people might have said they were *'to die for'* – but it was rather terrifying looking almost vertically down on to the jagged rocks below us, and even I didn't want to get too close.

Eventually we turned the corner and the beautiful picturesque fishing village came into view. We'd been here before and it appeared to be just as we remembered – totally unspoilt, uniquely Cornish and very welcoming with its many varied and colourful, mostly pink or white, cottages. Just like many villages along this coast, Cadgwith once had a major fishing industry, and at one time in the 19th century held the record for the most pilchards caught in a single day. However, that was long ago and now the much smaller number of boats catch crabs, lobsters and small quantities of fish, some of which are served in the local pubs and restaurants.

We stood on *The Todden*, a rocky point of high ground jutting out into the sea, to admire the panoramic scenery. To our left, near the centre of the village, was a stony beach where the fishing boats operate from, and to our right, a smaller sandy beach. I suggested carrying on around the headland to see a spectacular feature, which was created when the roof of a sea cave collapsed to leave an arch of rock over the old cave entrance. In rough weather the sea crashes noisily under the arch far below the cliff top, and angrily swirls around the confined space where the old cave used to be. It's then said to appear as though it's boiling, hence its name – *The Devil's Frying Pan.*

It's certainly not a place for someone suffering from vertigo, and as Emm hates heights she didn't want to go there. She implied it would take too much time, and that we needed to get a table at the pub before it got too busy. I didn't protest too much as I'd already stood too close for comfort by a vertical cliff face, nervously looking down on to jagged rocks far below, and agreed to give it a miss this time. So, saying we'd go along that part of the cliff path the next time we came to the area, I dutifully followed Emm down to the Cadgwith Cove Inn where she insisted on sitting outside on the terrace.

It may have been sunny, but a slight sea mist was beginning to descend and a fair sea breeze was funnelling up through the natural harbour. I much prefer to eat my food whilst it's hot, and didn't particularly want to eat outside where I knew the wind would soon turn a hot meal into a tepid one. When I said as much and that it would be best to go inside, Emm was adamant and said that Monty wouldn't be allowed in the pub. I didn't want to start an argument I could never win (anything for a quiet life), and asked her where she wanted to sit. As all the tables were unoccupied we could have sat anywhere we liked, so deciding where to sit should have been a no-brainer. However, Emm can rarely make up her mind about anything and even making a simple decision like that was never going to be straightforward.

She says it's because she was born under the star sign *Libra* that she sees everything from all points of view and has difficulty making decisions. I was born under *Taurus* and can usually make up my mind about anything pretty much straight away, believing it's far better to actually make a decision, even if it's the wrong one, than it is to keep dithering around and forever changing one's mind. I don't believe in astrology and can't comprehend how being born at a certain time of the year can possibly map out people's lives for them. However, it does seem strange that Emm balances everything out, weighs up all the pros and cons and takes forever making the simplest of decisions, whereas, as she often points out, I can be like a bull in a china shop and charge straight in.

I just looked around at all the empty tables, eliminated all those in the shade and sat down at one which was in full sun and sheltered from the wind. Dead simple I thought. But Emm immediately queried why I'd chosen that particular table and suggested we sat at another one, then another, and another, until we eventually sat down again at the one I'd originally chosen. Choosing where to park our backsides on a table in a pub or restaurant is just like deciding where to park the car, or the motorhome, in an empty car park. As I've mentioned already, we have to try out quite a few of the available spaces before finally parking and it was just the same with the table at the pub.

Anyhow, a mutually agreed decision of sorts finally being made, we sat down, tied Monty's lead to the leg of the table, took his bowl out of my rucksack and gave him a drink. We then had two other decisions to make, that is, choosing what to eat and what to drink. The food choice was relatively easy. Being in a fishing village, we both wanted fish and chips which we expected to be freshly sourced from the adjacent cove (the fish that is, not the chips).

Without hesitation I decided to sample the local beer, and Emm initially chose a lager. She then changed her mind to a glass of wine, but couldn't decide whether to have white, red or rosé. As we were having fish, she eliminated the red, then ummed and ahhed whether to have white or rosé before saying she'd have an orange juice. Then, just as I was about to go into the pub, she shouted out that she'd have a lager after all, unless it was Carlsberg, which she doesn't like!

The pub was empty, but full of character with loads of memorabilia relating to Cadgwith's relationship with fishing and smuggling, and I wanted to have a good browse around to soak up the atmosphere and history of the place. However, it wouldn't have been fair to leave Emm on her own for too long, so I ordered our meals and bought our drinks. I told the barmaid we were sitting outside but asked if we could come in with our small well-behaved dog if we changed our minds, which she said would be fine. I took the drinks back out and casually mentioned to Emm that we could go inside with Monty if she started to feel cold, but she didn't, so we stayed where we were.

Considering we appeared to be the only customers, the food seemed to take ages to arrive. We must have got there a bit too early, possibly before the chef arrived, and I suppose we did get a bit impatient, especially me as I'd virtually finished my pint and was decidedly hungry. Also, after the sun disappeared behind a cloud and with the wind blowing in off the sea and swirling around our table it got decidedly cooler. However, even though I was grumpy because I wanted to sit inside, I didn't think it would be a good idea to raise the subject again.

Emm kept prompting me to find out where our food was and, thinking we'd have to wait for one of the trawlers to come in and land our cod, I'd just got up to go and ask when a smiling young lad brought out our order. Still feeling grumpy, I thought he'd been taking our food all around the pub looking for us, assuming that no one would be eating outside in the cool breeze, and that by now our meal would be stone cold.

However, I was wrong. Everything was served up piping hot and the portions had certainly not been skimped on either. I have to say it proved to be well worth the wait, especially as the sun came out again from behind the cloud to bathe us in warm sunshine. The fish was cooked to perfection, was coated in a beautiful crispy batter and tasted as though it had been caught first thing that very morning, which it probably had been, and the chips were amongst the best we'd ever eaten, crispy on the outside and soft and fluffy on the inside. As I write this now, my mouth is beginning to water with the thought of that meal and, even though I've just had my Sunday dinner, I'm tempted to go out and get some fish and chips. However, I will resist the temptation. Our local fish and chips are good, but not quite as good as the ones we enjoyed that day in Cadgwith.

Anyhow, as we tucked into our meals and the sun came out again, so did the wasps – which is another reason I prefer to eat inside. Every time we eat *al fresco*, it seems that one of the little perishers will inevitably join us and then invite all its mates over as well. When I was a child I was petrified of them and thought they would always give me a nasty sting. Nowadays it's not so much a fear of getting stung that bothers me, it's just that they're so bloody annoying. As long as I'm certain I'm not going to inadvertently put one in my mouth on my food or in my drink, I can ignore them to a large degree.

I might just gently wave them away with my knife, and if a particular wasp has been particularly annoying I might try and squash it if I get a chance. However, I rarely resort to jumping up and down, frantically waving my arms around in a blind panic, which is just what Emm started to do. Of course, the wasps then started to feel threatened and gave us the full treatment by buzzing around our heads in a mad rage. One landed on the table to feed off a crumb or something and I managed to trap it under my empty glass, where it stayed and drank a few drops of beer. (When we left, I mercifully released it and it drunkenly flew away.)

Despite the attentions of these black and yellow menaces, I managed to finish my meal, but Emm, as well as being a slower eater than me anyway, was much more distracted by the wasps and still struggling to clear her plate. She managed to eat all her fish and salad, but nowhere near all of her chips. Being brought up to eat all my food and always empty my plate, I did my best to finish them off for her, but by this time they were stone cold and didn't taste nearly as good as the delicious piping hot chips they'd been twenty minutes previously. However, with a little help from Monty, I still managed to polish most of them off.

By that time a few more customers had joined us and ordered food, including a couple with a small terrier-like mongrel which kept barking loudly at us. Monty barked back and strained on his lead in an effort to reach his canine cousin, who continued to bark even more loudly. It was just as well we'd finished our meal as, no matter what we tried to do, the two dogs just carried on barking. There was nothing for it but to exchange pleasantries with the terrier's owners and leave them to enjoy their meal in peace. As we made our way down the road the terrier quietened down, and when I looked back I noticed its owners were waving their arms around trying to shoo away the wasps.

It would have been good to go to the Cadgwith Cove Inn on a Friday night, when the bars resonate with the sounds of much merriment and loud traditional sea shanties. Apparently, many years ago on a particularly nasty Friday night, an Irish monk named *Inebriatus* was shipwrecked off Cadgwith. He miraculously made it ashore on a raft made from empty beer barrels lashed together with baler twine and virgins' hair *(not sure where he got that from!)* and he ended up at the Cadgwith Cove Inn. He liked the place so much that he stayed on to join the local population, and every Friday night since then this momentous occasion, known locally as *Saint Inebriatus Eve,* has been celebrated. Nowadays, a local group of fishermen, The Cadgwith Singers, lead the celebrations by singing their time-honoured sea shanties, which everyone in the pub joins in with. (No doubt they scrounge a drink or two off any tourists, and I wonder if that's where the expression *to cadge a drink* comes from?)

Anyhow, we made our way down to the main beach where, after taking care not to trip over various chains, cables, nets, lobster pots and other assorted fishermen's gear, I skimmed a few stones across the relatively calm sea. There was a fair amount of activity going on and we admired the weather-beaten fishermen who looked as though they'd just unloaded their morning's catch. We liked to think they were the same fishermen who'd caught the delicious cod we'd just enjoyed, and were very grateful to them for that. In these days of dwindling fish stocks, fish quotas and European bureaucracy, it must be an extremely difficult and uncertain way to earn a half decent wage. With all the odds stacked against them, there must be something in the blood to make men go out at all hours and in all weathers to make a living this way, and, although I admire them very much, I certainly wouldn't want to change places with them.

Having completed our inspection of the beach and the fishing boats, we walked off our lunch around the village and were impressed by all the idyllic looking cottages, which mostly looked as though they would grace the proverbial chocolate box lid. The majority had picturesque cottage gardens full of colourful flowers and plants, and it was obvious that everyone took a pride in their homes and their surroundings.

We knew that the actor, Rodney Bewes, had a cottage here and couldn't help wondering which one it might be. For anyone who doesn't know, Rodney Bewes is probably best known for starring with James Bolam in the brilliant 1960s television comedy series *The Likely Lads,* and its follow up series *Whatever Happened to the Likely Lads?* in the 1970s. They played two young Geordie working class *Jack-the-Lads,* who got into all sorts of scrapes and unlikely situations every week. Bolam played a character called Terry Collier, who was only interested in girls, beer, football and having a good time, whilst his best mate, Bob Ferris, played by Bewes, while also interested in the same things, ultimately aspired to more in life.

The original series ended with Bob wanting to join the army so he could get a better career for himself with prospects. Terry was happy just to carry on for the rest of his life living from week to week and having a good time, but was mortified by the prospect of being left without his mate and secretly signed on as well. In the final scene, Bob returned home after failing the medical but, of course, Terry was accepted and had no choice but to serve his time, which was something he never really wanted to do.

The follow up series, *Whatever Happened to the Likely Lads?,* which was set three years later, started with the two lads unexpectedly and hilariously meeting in a darkened railway carriage. Terry had just finished his stint in the army and was returning back north from London. In the meantime, Bob, who was on his way back from

London on a combined business and shopping trip, had worked his way up in the world and was now in management. He'd become engaged to Thelma, who both he and Terry had known from school. She was a bit stuck up, to say the least, and not the sort of good time girl they would have lusted over in the past.

Terry was alone in the railway carriage and, just as Bob opened the door to come in, all the lights went out. In the virtual darkness, even though Bob accidentally treads on Terry's foot and they get into conversation, they don't immediately recognise each other. Terry says he's just come out of the army and Bob replies that he nearly joined up once and that there was a funny story attached to it. He goes on to explain that he had a mate who just couldn't take the idea of him joining up and being left behind on his own. Laughing, he goes on to say that this old mate just couldn't function without him and signed on just to be with him, while he himself was immediately discharged because of flat feet!

Bob is now in full flow and rubs it in by stating that you've got to see the funny side of it, and that you should have seen the look on his mate's face when he realised. Terry slowly registers that, after three years away in the forces, he's just met up with Bob again and, as the truth dawns on him, the way his silhouetted head slowly moves up is priceless. Bob carries on laughing, Terry is absolutely silent and the lights come back on. Bob then realises he's just met his old mate who's not spoken to him since the day he joined up. It was a brilliant story line and that scene in particular struck a chord with me, as my mate, the one I first went to the Lake District with, joined the RAF when we left school and saw the world, whereas I stayed at home, completed an aircraft apprenticeship and ended up in management.

Throughout the series, Terry always managed to come between Bob and Thelma and deride him for his ambition. Whilst he'd been away in the army, he'd married a German girl, but it didn't work out as she couldn't speak English and he couldn't speak German. The last straw in their marriage was when West Germany beat England, the current football world champions, by three goals to two to knock them out of the 1970 World Cup quarter finals in Mexico. I remember that match as though it was yesterday. England had been cruising into the semi-finals having taken a two goal lead, but the Germans fought back and, with the help of the fumbling English reserve goalkeeper, England eventually lost after extra time. It was a cruel blow, and if I'd had any German friends at the time the relationship would have been doomed along with England's world cup aspirations ever since…

Anyhow, Terry and his German wife divorced and he constantly exaggerated the pitfalls of marriage to Bob who, despite almost changing his mind, went through with it in the end.

The two actors then starred together in the film version of *The Likely Lads*, which was also very funny and much better than most of the TV spin off films which were popular around that time. They went off for a short holiday in a caravan with Thelma and Terry's current girlfriend. There was a side-splitting scene where the girls were fast asleep in the caravan and, for some reason, the boys decided to hitch up the van and drive off with the girls still sleeping inside it. When they stopped at some traffic lights the girls woke up and stepped outside. Just as they realised they were inexplicably in the middle of a town, the boys drove off, completely oblivious to the fact that the girls were left stranded in their nighties!

The two television series were brilliantly funny and it was a shame when no more were made. James Bolam wanted to do other things, which he did brilliantly, starting with the drama *When the Boat Comes In*, also set in the north east. He's hardly been off our television screens since, having starred in a host of highly successful comedies and dramas. Despite all his success, he's always been an extremely private person who hates his privacy being invaded. As far as I'm aware he's never appeared on any chat shows and has very rarely given interviews.

Rodney Bewes, on the other hand, seems to be completely different and loves to talk about himself. However, his career doesn't seem to have been quite as spectacular as his old partner's. After *The Likely Lads* he created, co-wrote and starred in another TV comedy, *Dear Mother…Love Albert,* which I never really saw that much of. For a while he was *Mr Rodney* to *Basil Brush* on television and had a number of roles in the theatre. When I was working in London in the early 1980s I remember seeing him outside the Shaftesbury Theatre where I think he was starring in the Ray Cooney farce, *Run for Your Wife*.

In the 1990s he created two very good one man shows, *Three Men in a Boat* and *Diary of a Nobody*, both of which he performed to much acclaim at the Edinburgh festival and then at theatres all over the country. For *Three Men in a Boat* he tows a magnificent twenty-four foot highly polished wooden skiff in a trailer behind a Ford Mondeo from theatre to theatre. I saw both these shows in Yeovil and they were quite amazing. How he remembered all the lines is beyond me. He did make one or two gaffs, but that only added to the enjoyment. I suppose that if you are going to write, direct and produce all the scenery yourself, then you might just as well perform the shows single handedly like Rodney does. That way, he keeps *all* the money!

There was some talk of another series of *The Likely Lads* being written, with them now both being grandfathers. It's very unlikely to happen though, which is a real shame as there seemed to be a special chemistry between the two characters. It would have been brilliant to see how their respective lives panned out, hear them reminiscing and no doubt arguing about the past.

I'm a big fan of James Bolam and virtually every programme he's appeared in has been well worth watching. However, after they made *The Likely Lads* film, he apparently fell out with Bewes and it's been reported that he despises his old partner and hates talking about *The Likely Lads*. The problem was that Bewes unintentionally tipped off the press that Bolam's wife was pregnant, which really upset him. He considered it an unforgivable invasion of privacy and even after all these years has never forgiven him. Bewes would phone to apologise, but Bolam would always hang up on him and the two of them have never met or spoken to each other since.

For many years Bolam vetoed repeats of both *The Likely Lads* series, which would have affected all the other actors by depriving them of considerable repeat fees. At the time, it would seem that Bewes wasn't doing that well and any income from repeats would have been more than welcome. I'm sure Rodney Bewes never meant any harm by his supposed indiscretion and it's very sad that James Bolam still holds a grudge. It seems to be so easy for some people to fall out with a good friend or a loved one, but a darn sight harder for them to say sorry and make up again.[13] Anyhow, whilst strolling around the village we didn't bump into Rodney; he was probably towing his twenty-four foot skiff up a motorway on his way to perform another one man show at some provincial theatre.

Eventually we found ourselves at the top of the hill by the car park where we'd have ended up if we'd driven. However, we were pleased we'd left the motorhome behind, as we would have missed out on some great views along the coast path. As we made our way back towards the village centre, we followed an interesting wooded footpath and unexpectedly came across a tiny, freshly painted bright blue corrugated iron church, which had a large white wooden cross on its roof over the doorway. It wasn't much bigger than someone's front room and I would have loved to look inside, but sadly it was locked.

I later found out it was known as *St Mary's Church* and dated back to the 19th century when it was a Roman Catholic Mission for the fishermen of Cadgwith. I'm not sure when that changed, but it now belongs to the Church of England and services are held every month, mainly for worshippers who can't get to the larger church at nearby Ruan Minor. It was a beautiful tranquil spot for a church, and I couldn't help thinking that some particularly sad services must have taken place there over the years after fishermen, or other seafarers, had been lost at sea. Conversely, it must have been a great location for weddings, christenings and other happy family occasions and, knowing

---

13 See Rodney Bewes' excellent biography, *A Likely Story* published by Arrow Books, for the complete story in Rodney's own words.

the local fishermen's reputation for singing, I imagined their voices reverberating around the small interior and echoing down the valley.

After leaving this peaceful and interesting little church we couldn't help peering into people's cottage gardens, which were all well cared for. We also noticed that there were a fair number of cottages available to rent, and later we especially admired some holiday cottages by the harbour. We thought that, no matter what the weather was like, Cadgwith would be a splendid place to spend a romantic week in the comfort of a cosy cottage with a blazing log fire, especially with the coast path and the Cadgwith Cove Inn right on the door step.

On the other hand though, I couldn't help wondering how all these holiday homes, and presumably second homes, have affected the local economy. Sure enough, it would be great to own one and they do bring tourists into the area to spend their money in the shops and pubs, etc, but when property prices are so inflated by outsiders how on earth do the young locals ever manage to own a home of their own?

However, it was soon time to get back, and as we made our way slowly up the coast path we both glanced over our shoulders to take in our final view of Cadgwith, before continuing on our way back to the caravan site in the fading afternoon sunshine.

10

DOGS BEHAVING BADLY

Even though we were walking back along the same path, the fact that we were going in the opposite direction made the views look different and just as exhilarating as before. We met a few people coming the other way towards Cadgwith, with whom we exchanged pleasantries, and were thoroughly enjoying our peaceful walk.

In the far distance we saw a couple coming towards us who had a large Doberman dog, which bounded on ahead at great speed and, barking loudly, ran around us in circles. Emm threw a wobbly and, sensing her nervousness, Monty barked back. Before we knew it both dogs were making a right old racket and, as we were on the narrow coast path at the time and uncomfortably close to the cliff edge, it all started to get a bit hairy. Monty was on his long flexi-lead, which I'd immediately shortened, but the Doberman was loose and its legs started to get tangled in the lead, which made the situation worse as the two dogs started to become more aggressive towards each other.

Being aware I could get bitten, I managed to untangle the Doberman from the lead before quickly picking Monty up. Emm bravely positioned herself between me and our assailant, waving her arms around to shoo it away. However her efforts were to no avail as the Doberman kept barking even louder and started to jump up at me. Hanging on to a wriggling Monty for dear life I tried to lift him even higher and, keeping my back towards the huge dog, move further away from the cliff edge. Emm kept shooing it away, and the situation started to get out of control with both dogs barking more aggressively towards each other. We dreaded to think what could happen if the two dogs managed to get to each other. Nor did we want to find out.

The Doberman's owners ran up to us as fast as they could and the man ran around me grappling with his huge dog as he tried to get it on a lead. Eventually he did so, and much to our relief pulled it away. I put Monty down and, with both dogs straining on their respective leads and still raging at each other, the man apologised profusely in a breathless voice before we went our respective ways. I have to admit it was pretty scary seeing this big powerful dog rushing towards us. It was a young dog and I'm sure it only wanted to play, but once it started jumping up all over Monty and getting caught in his lead, Monty was bound to feel threatened and react accordingly, which I suppose triggered the Doberman off.

We both thought the Doberman's owners had been irresponsible and stupid not to have their dog on a lead in the first place, especially as the path was so close to the edge of a steep cliff. Even the most well-behaved and obedient animal can get into trouble, as had just been demonstrated, and we couldn't help feeling that some people just don't have that much common sense. We were shaken up a fair bit by this incident, and as we carried on past the old serpentine factory I recalled some other times we'd had a problem with dogs behaving badly because they were not under proper control.

The vast majority of dog owners are very responsible and do keep their pets under full control at all times, but there are always a few that let their dogs run wild. In our experience these dogs always seem to be of the large variety, like the Doberman we encountered near Cadgwith, and they make a real nuisance of themselves by invariably making a bee line for other peoples' dogs which are on leads. This has happened more than once when we've been out walking with Monty and minding our own business.

All of a sudden, some huge dog has come bounding up to us and, before we knew it, has jumped all over Monty, just like the Doberman on the cliff edge. Sometimes, just like the Doberman, they've even jumped up me and deposited muddy paw prints all over my clothes.

The owners usually told me their darling pet only wanted to play and would never hurt anyone, but that's no consolation when they get tangled up in Monty's lead and end up fighting with him. Then to make matters worse, I've been told by some patronising dog owners that their dogs don't like other dogs on leads and insinuated that it's all my fault their darling pooch gets excited and out of control.

Well, I don't like being ambushed by some big aggressive looking Alsatian or lollopy Labrador, for example. If these dogs were on a flexi-lead, which still gives them a fair amount of freedom, they would be controllable and, even if they do just want to play, wouldn't be able to come bounding up to other people in a seemingly threatening way! In such situations, the other dog has usually been much bigger than Monty and he's been known to become very defensive and start to growl. Then, of course, the other dog growls back and before we know it they can get caught up in Monty's long lead and start to take bites out of each other. Monty is usually so passive, but he's a brave little terrier and if he does get forced into a scrap he won't pull out.

A big problem started a few years ago with a particular male Golden Retriever in our village, when I was picking blackberries in the orchard by the church. I'd tied Monty's long flexi-lead to a fence and he was sat there perfectly happy minding his own business, when a large dog came galloping over to him from the far end of the field. I was fairly unconcerned as this dog seemed friendly enough but, in the blink of an eye and before I could do anything about it, things got out of hand when this apparently playful Golden Retriever appeared to go berserk and lock its jaws firmly around Monty's lower jawbone. Monty growled and struggled as I raced over to him and, aware I could also be bitten, did my best to grab the Retriever's jaws and force it to release its grip. As I did so, I was alarmed to see blood all around its mouth and realised it was oozing out of a nasty looking wound in Monty's lower lip.

Just as I finally managed to force the Retriever's mouth open and hold the snarling dogs apart, the dog's lady owner ran over to us from the other side of the field. Her first impression was of blood on her darling dog and Monty doing his utmost to take an almighty chunk out of it. She obviously thought Monty had bitten her dog, which was not the case as he hadn't actually had a chance to do so. I held onto both dogs which were still snarling and barking aggressively at each other, and just about managed to keep them apart. The lady was obviously quite upset and agitated at finding me doing my best to keep these seemingly ferocious dogs, both of which had blood all around their mouths, from tearing each other apart.

I was also upset and agitated and as she managed to take her dog off me, put it on its lead and pull it back, I told her as calmly and politely as I could that it was her dog which, for no reason whatsoever, had attacked Monty and bitten right through his lower lip. She more or less tried to tell me that, as Monty was tied up, it was my fault her dog had been a problem. I couldn't be bothered to argue with her, as I just wanted to get Monty cleaned up and attend to his wound. In any case it wasn't easy to converse sensibly with both dogs still barking and snarling furiously at each other. I just said that if she couldn't control or trust her dog, which she obviously couldn't or Monty wouldn't have been attacked, then she should keep it on a lead. Still a bit shaken up by this bad experience, I then took him over to the churchyard tap, washed him down and cleaned off all the blood.

After this altercation, every time we walked out in the village, I always scoured the horizon to see if this particular dog was on the loose and, if so, prepared to take avoidance action. Whenever I saw it lurking in the distance, I'd always turn around and either hurry back the other way or wait until I was certain it was on a lead. If it was, we'd approach and pass each other very carefully with both dogs making a heck of a row and straining on their leads to get at each other, which was really embarrassing. No doubt this other dog was normally as good as gold, as was Monty, but now they'd both made a canine enemy for life and would never flinch in their efforts to take a bite out of one another.

Over a period of a few years, we were caught out a couple of times with this particular dog. One morning, Monty and I were just about to turn into the churchyard when, without warning, this snarling, monster Golden Retriever dog came careering out from behind the low wall by the churchyard. It all happened so fast and I couldn't prevent Monty from springing forward on his flexi-lead and locking his strong jaws firmly around the top of the Retriever's head. Instantly realising this was the same dog who'd previously given him such a painful kiss, this time he was taking no chances and swiftly decided the best form of defence was a pre-emptive attack. The two dogs were suddenly writhing around in front of me and the more they struggled, the more firmly Monty held his grip.

This time a man was with the dog and we quickly found ourselves struggling to force our pets apart. Eventually we did so, and the man put his dog on a lead. I must admit I was pretty shaken up by this second incident and, what with both dogs making such a commotion, it was again difficult to have a normal conversation. I could only apologise and mutter something to the effect that it wouldn't have happened if he'd kept his dog on a lead. As we solemnly parted company, I was aware that this time it was the Golden Retriever who would need a wound cleaning up, not Monty.

A few months later, I was walking along the muddy path by the churchyard when I saw our Retriever *friend* hurtling towards us with his man owner frantically running behind him, obviously in a bit of a panic at seeing the distance between his dog and Monty rapidly closing. Monty instantly spotted his enemy bearing down upon him and, being a very tough and brave terrier, he stood firm and barked as aggressively as he could, fully prepared to defend himself to the death.

Quick as a flash, I scooped him up and placed him on top of the four foot high stone wall which surrounded the graveyard. I got covered in mud for my efforts, but was still thankful I'd got him out of range in the nick of time. The snarling Retriever had quickly borne down on us barking loudly, and eager to get his revenge on Monty for previously biting him. It started leaping up the wall trying to get to Monty, who was barking back in the most ferocious manner. I held his collar tightly to stop him jumping off the wall and starting an even greater mêlée, but at the same time the Retriever was jumping up at me, depositing mud and gooey saliva all over my clothes. He even tried to take a bite out of my arm, but luckily I was protected by my thick winter coat and he didn't break my skin.

His owner approached as fast as he could and struggled to get his dog on a lead and pull him away. He was just as shaken up as I was and, again, I would have liked to have a sensible conversation with him, but with both dogs causing such a row it was impossible to do so. They were both straining on their respective leads and barking at each other so loudly and aggressively that it was little wonder they didn't wake the dead in the graveyard. I muttered something along the lines that he must be aware I often walked along that path at that time of the morning and, judging by our past experiences, we both knew our respective dogs had a problem with each other which wasn't likely to go away. Also that if he kept his dog on a lead, such incidents could be avoided. Or words to that effect!

Needless to say, after this third fracas, I was even more nervous when walking in the village in case this Retriever was on the loose. If we did see him, and he wasn't on a lead, I'd immediately turnabout and walk as fast as I could in the opposite direction. If he was on a lead, however, I'd make a point of keeping Monty on a tight lead and, as casually as I could, carry on walking past them. By doing so, I hoped to calm him down and demonstrate there was nothing to be alarmed about and the Retriever's owner would do the same. Nevertheless, both dogs would always pull aggressively on their leads and bark ferociously at each other in an attempt to continue their feud and tear each other apart. Consequently, we just had to accept the two dogs were enemies for life, and whenever we were walking in the same vicinity we always had to look out for each other and be prepared to take avoidance action.

The problem became worse insomuch that, whenever Monty sees *any* male Golden Retriever, he will get agitated, snarl and bark in a pugnacious manner. Of course this is very embarrassing and makes him look as though he's a nasty little dog, when usually he's so gentle.

For example, once when Emm and I were visiting Thirsk in Yorkshire, we were walking in the centre of this perfectly peaceful market town when, all of a sudden, my arm suddenly and involuntary extended as Monty yanked on his lead, bared his teeth and barked his most ferocious bark.

At first we wondered what on earth was going on as, much to our horror, everyone stopped and stared at us, utterly perplexed as to why our little Border Terrier was behaving in such a manner. We then realised that, on the other side of the road, walking happily along with a kindly looking mature couple, was an elderly dignified male Golden Retriever. If he'd not been on a lead, for no other reason than it was the same breed as his antagonist from the village, Monty would have immediately ran across the road and attacked this gentle and bewildered looking dog, who just stared back wondering what he'd done to deserve such hostility.

Leaving Monty with Emm, I crossed over the road and explained to the dog's owners that Monty was once bitten by a similar dog and now treats all Golden Retrievers the same. I gave the placid dog a stroke and made a fuss of him to try and impress upon Monty that he was no threat to us or anyone else, which he obviously wasn't. However, Monty has a very long memory and, it seems, will never forget that particular male Golden Retriever from Chiselborough. As far as he's concerned, all male dogs of that breed are tarred with the same brush, and unfortunately he will act aggressively towards all of them. Consequently, we always have to be very careful when we are out walking, especially when we let him off the lead. We have to constantly scour the horizon to ensure there are no Golden Retrievers about, and if we do see one have to get Monty back on his lead and walk off in the opposite direction as fast as our legs will carry us.

Anyhow, we arrived safely back at the campsite from Cadgwith, and as it was still warm and sunny decided to sit outside with a cup of tea and rest our aching feet. We noticed that, since we'd left the site that morning, a caravan had arrived and parked on the adjacent pitch, just like it had every right to do. However, Monty didn't seem to understand that his territory didn't extend to the whole of the campsite, and when he heard a noise from the caravan he began to bark. We managed to quieten him down and a bit later, after Emm had gone inside to prepare the dinner, a man came out of the caravan with a tiny Shih Tzu dog, which began to bark (actually it was more like a squeak) when it saw Monty. Luckily Monty appreciated that a Shih Tzu posed no threat and calmed down as soon as I told him to be quiet, and the man and I struck up a conversation.

I initially got the impression he was a seasoned caravanner, and not a novice like me. However, that illusion was slightly shattered when he asked me if I knew whether he could use his microwave oven on the electric hook-up. I initially thought it would draw too much current and asked him what the power rating of his microwave oven was, which he confirmed as 500 watts. I looked at the hook-up point and noted that the maximum current rating was 5 amps. Obviously, the mains voltage was 240 volts, or thereabouts, so a quick mental calculation, based on what I remembered from college, should have told how much current his microwave would draw. If this was less than 5 amps it was safe to use, but if more than that I would have to advise him not to use it.

The trouble was, I hadn't given electrical theory very much thought since I'd been at college many years before. Now, did I have to multiply the watts by the volts to give the current rating? No, surely not, that would be 500 multiplied by 240, which would be…?

Well, my mental arithmetic was never that good and I wasn't too sure how many amps that would work out to be. But I knew it would be a heck of a lot and, if that was right, the electric hook-up could have probably powered a small town. So I had to think again.

I wanted to make sure I got this right, especially as I remembered a story a friend once told me. He and his wife had had a static caravan on a site on the south coast near the New Forest. It was a much more modern caravan than the old one we once had at Durdle Door and it was connected to mains drainage, water supply and electricity. Rather than each caravan being metered separately, the cost of electricity was originally included in the annual ground rent. After all, with electricity only being needed for lighting, the refrigerator, a television, a toaster and maybe an electric kettle and the odd use of a hair-dryer, the cost should never have been that much, all the cooking being done by Calor gas, as was the hot water and room heater.

Apparently, someone else on the site, I think it was one of their immediate neighbours, ripped out all the Calor gas appliances and replaced them with electrical ones. And I'm talking here of an electric cooker, electric shower and electric heaters, all of which consume lots of current.

Now, just like our campsite here in Cornwall, this static caravan site also had a maximum capacity of 5 amps, and when all the newly fitted appliances were turned on the amateur electrician was initially mystified by a strange burning smell. Unsurprisingly, all the wiring in the static caravan started to overheat before bursting into flames, causing a fair bit of damage to their almost new holiday retreat!

Consequently, the use of this *free* electricity cost this caravan owner infinitely more than he could have ever hoped to save on Calor gas costs, and it must have been hugely embarrassing when he owned up to the campsite owners what he'd done. After all, he was virtually attempting to steal electricity from them. No insurance policy would have paid out to repair the damage and goodness knows what it cost to replace the entire wiring, repair any fire damage and re-install the Calor gas cooker, Calor Gas shower and Calor Gas heaters. As a consequence, *all* the caravans on the site then had their electricity supply individually metered.

Bearing this in mind, I paused for a bit, took a deep breath and tried to cast my mind back to those boring electro-technology lectures at technical college when I was an apprentice. After all, I didn't want to make a mistake and advise my new friend that it was safe to microwave his dinner, and then end up getting sued for the cost of replacing a fire damaged caravan. I had to think hard and then, somewhere from deep in the back of my mind, I remembered that the actual current drawn by the microwave would be around 500 watts *divided* by 240 volts. Accordingly, a simple mental arithmetic calculation told me that that was near enough 2 amps. So, feeling rather smug, I was confident enough to tell my new friend that it would indeed be safe to use, provided he didn't also have an electric oven, electric shower, electric heaters and suchlike plugged in at the same time.

He seemed very grateful for my technical expertise and proceeded to tell me his life story, which I must admit I didn't really want to hear. I can't remember all the details, but apparently he and his wife had tragically lost two dogs in the space of a week, which must have been absolutely heartbreaking. I think they lost one dog (I can't remember the breed, but I got the feeling they were small dogs) through illness and it had to be put down. All dog owners have to go through this at some time, and I know from experience how upsetting it can be. Anyhow, later that same week, this poor man and his wife then tragically lost their other dog when it was viciously savaged by an out of control German Shepherd that sunk its teeth into their dog's neck and shook it to death!

I didn't really know what to say to him in the circumstances, but my heart went out to him and his wife. They were obviously extremely upset by all this and vowed never to get another dog. However, their son had immediately bought them the little Shih Tzu and, even though this breed of dog has an unfortunate name (it apparently means *Lion King i*n Chinese), judging by the way this man was making a fuss of it, I was sure it would help him and his wife come to terms with their tragic losses.

Emm then called to say that our meal was ready and I bade my new friend goodnight as I went inside. As we'd eaten our main meal in the pub at lunchtime, we had some soup and bread, which was ample. Unfortunately, it was brown bread which I don't really like. Well, I don't mind it too much, but it doesn't like me and always gives me wind, so I knew I'd suffer later on. Anyhow, while we were eating, I couldn't help myself glancing out of the window and looking for any telltale signs of smoke coming from the caravan next door. Luckily, all seemed to be well and I was relieved that I appeared to have remembered my basic electrical theory correctly.

I decided to get cleaned up and go for a shower, wearing the minimum amount of clothes this time and definitely no socks. As soon as I got over to the washroom, the brown bread seemed to kick in and I needed to sit down on the toilet. Luckily I had the place to myself, so managed to give the wobbly toilet pan a miss and checked out the adjacent WC. It was clean enough, firmly bolted to the floor and, therefore, appeared safe to use. However, the concrete floor was quite damp where it had been mopped over and it was quite cold in there.

I didn't want to linger too long so tried to do what I had to do as quickly as I could. However, sitting there in the cold unattractive toilet, I momentarily wished I was back at home again in my clean warm bathroom where I could take my time and relax with a good book. However, there was nothing to be gained by dwelling on it, so I got on with the business in hand. This particular campsite was all right, but with the cold corrugated iron roofed toilet and shower block, plus the grass pitches, it certainly wasn't the best. Tomorrow, we would be at another campsite in St Ives and I very much hoped the facilities there would be superior to these.

Having finished what I had to do, I got into the shower, stripped off and felt much better under the flow of hot water. As I lathered the shampoo into my hair, I hoped that no one else would come in and reduce the flow by turning on another shower. Thankfully, no one did, so I completed my ablutions without incident, dried myself off, got dressed and went back to the motorhome where we spent a bit of time planning the route to St Ives.

We thought we'd take a fairly leisurely drive and stop off at Marazion, round about lunchtime, to see St Michael's Mount, which seemed reasonably straightforward. We then listened to some music on the radio and went to bed. Once again, we were really tired and I should have easily nodded off, just like Emm and Monty. However, just as I feared, I suffered with wind, which prevented me falling asleep straight away and caused me to have a rather unsettled night.

11

WATER TORTURE

I did eventually get to sleep and we both woke up feeling raring to go, in my case in more ways than one! We were keen to get to St Ives, and after a quick breakfast Emm packed up everything inside, whilst I did all the outside jobs. After turning off the gas, disconnecting the electric hook-up, coiling up the cable (again a messy job due to the dew and muddy worm casts) and remembering to raise the steps, I was ready to set off. But much to my annoyance, Emm insisted on checking everything once more. It was just as well she did, as we were about to drive off without our rubber mat again and the fridge was still set to the '240V' position, not the '12V' position. So many things to remember! Surely, we hoped, everything would eventually become second nature to us both.

Even though we'd used the site facilities for showering and most of our washing up, we'd inevitably used some of our water and I thought that we ought to empty our waste water tank and fill up with fresh water before we left the site. The waste disposal facility and fresh water tap were just around the corner by the toilet block and we had to drive past them on our way out. So, no sooner had we started off and turned the corner, I pulled up by the tap and stepped down from the motorhome. We'd bought a plastic bowl especially to collect the dirty water and I got it out of the side locker, put it under the motorhome's waste water emptying point underneath the steps, bent down and opened the drainage valve.

A stream of murky, smelly grey water gushed out all over my hand and the bowl quickly filled up. I crouched down to turn the valve off before the bowl overflowed, then slid it out from underneath the vehicle and emptied it into the special drain. Unfortunately, the bowl was filled to its brim and, as I carefully picked it up, the inevitable happened and some of the foul smelling water slopped down the front of my light coloured trousers. I thought it was just as well they were not my smartest pair and hoped nobody would notice the smelly wet stain down my crotch.

However, Emm's eagle eyes spotted it straight away and from the tone of her voice anyone would have thought I'd done it deliberately. I ignored her not-so-helpful comments and extracted another half a bowl full of waste water, which this time I managed to empty without any more embarrassing spillages. I then made a mental note to make up a piece of old washing machine hose which could be screwed onto the waste valve and hopefully drain the waste water straight into the disposal point in future.

Having emptied the waste, I then needed to top up with fresh water which I thought would be a straightforward job that wouldn't take long. We had a special hose which we'd bought especially for the purpose, and all I had to do was push its so-called universal tap connector onto the tap; remove the motorhome's water filler cap; put the other end of the hose in the water filler inlet; turn on the tap; wait until water flowed through the hose and started to pour out of the top of the filler inlet; turn the tap off; coil up the hose; put it back in its storage compartment; replace the filler cap, and drive off with a full tank of fresh water.

Nothing could be simpler, or so I naively thought as I uncoiled the hose. I pushed the connector firmly over the tap, walked around to the other side of the motorhome and placed the other end of the hose into the water filler inlet. As I then went back to the tap Emm asked if she could do anything to help, but I politely declined her offer saying that everything was under control and that I'd only be a few minutes.

How wrong I was! The moment I turned on the tap, the connector immediately shot off and a powerful jet of icy cold water sprayed all over my shoes, the bottoms of my trouser legs and my socks. I must have looked extremely comical as I jumped out of the way, cursing to myself under my breath. There was far too much water pressure and I'd obviously turned the tap on too far. I turned it off as fast as I could and confidently replaced the connector over the tap once more. Being forewarned regarding the high water pressure, I turned the tap on again, more gently this time, but the hose connector still shot off and more water gushed onto the ground, just missing my feet as I leapt out of the way once more!

I forced the connector back over the tap yet again, and in order to achieve the best seal possible pulled it up as tightly as I could. I gradually turned the tap on again to allow little more than a trickle of water to flow out. Then, pleased that the connector stayed put and water started to flow slowly through the hose, I went round to the other side of the motorhome to position myself next to the water filler inlet and wait for the tank to be filled. Of course, from where I was then standing, I could no longer see the tap. But even though I knew it would take a little longer for the tank to fill with the reduced flow of water, I was reasonably confident all would be well this time.

I waited and watched and watched and waited, but proceedings seemed to take forever. So, finally running out of patience, I lifted the hose out of the water filler inlet, and surprise, surprise, nothing was coming out. Not a single drop!

I cursed again, more audibly this time, put the hose back into the water filler inlet and stomped back round to the tap, where I couldn't believe what I saw. The hopeless hose connector had detached itself from the tap yet again and water was pouring straight out onto the ground to create a growing puddle of fresh clean water. Feeling stupid, frustrated and guilty that I'd been wasting such a valuable commodity, I thought I now needed to ask Emm to come down from her elevated position in the passenger seat and help. She'd been sitting there engrossed in a book, apparently oblivious to my difficulties and, when she looked up, she thought I was ready to go. When I enlightened her and asked if she'd give me a hand she reminded me that, when she'd offered to help earlier, I told her I had everything under control.

Consequently I had to eat a bit of humble pie, as it were, and tried to explain why it was taking so long. She sighed as she reluctantly closed her book, and then stepped down onto the wet grass to help. I asked her to firmly hold the connector onto the tap and make sure it didn't come off again. She then crouched over the tap with her legs spread wide apart to keep her feet out of the puddle, and held the connector onto the tap as tightly as possible with both hands. In fact, the way she squeezed her small hands around that tap looked as though she imagined she was throttling someone!

Feeling an imaginary tightness in my throat, I once more went around to the opposite side of the vehicle to ensure that the other end of the hose didn't fall out of the water filler inlet. I then shouted out to her to turn the tap on, which she assured me she did.

However, still nothing seemed to happen. So, assuming she'd not heard, I shouted a bit louder and repeated my request. Emm told me not to shout and, in no uncertain terms, told me that she *had* turned the tap on. So I had no choice but to wait for the tank to fill. Again, it seemed to take forever, so a touch too sarcastically, I yelled back for her to double check that the tap hadn't mysteriously turned itself off and that water was actually flowing out of it. She bellowed back to the effect that of course it was turned on. But still nothing seemed to be happening at my end.

I could see water in the hose and tried to be patient as I waited a bit longer. Then, thinking we should turn the tap on a bit more to increase the flow, I called out to Emm to ask her to *please* do so. Mystified that still nothing much appeared to be happening, I carefully took the hose out of the water filler inlet and couldn't believe what I saw. Or, for that matter, didn't see. Not one single drop of water was coming out of the hose!

I put the hose up to my eye and peered down it in a comical sort of way, fully expecting the water to suddenly gush out and give my face a good soaking, just like a scene from an old silent comedy film. But nothing happened, which was probably just as well. I thought that for some unknown reason Emm must have turned the tap off, as I just couldn't think of any other explanation. Surely she wasn't having a laugh at my expense?

I shouted out to her again, a bit louder this time, and told her that nothing was coming out of the hose and that, if she wanted to move on to St Ives, she'd better stop messing about and turn the bloody tap on properly. Or words to that effect! She informed me, in an even louder voice, that the tap most definitely *was* turned on and remarked whether I thought she was stupid or something!

I put the hose back into the water filler inlet, not so much to fill the tank but so it didn't fall out and drag on the ground in the mud, and then went back round to the tap. Actually, more like stormed round to see for myself precisely what Emm had been doing – or rather not doing – which could have caused the water to disappear into thin air along a few metres of translucent plastic pipe!

I'd half expected to find that she'd abandoned the tap and was back in the motorhome with arms crossed, not best pleased that I'd raised my voice. But no, she was still valiantly bending over the tap, legs spread even further apart, as the puddle under her had now reached the proportions of a small garden pond!

It was so incomprehensible until, on closer inspection, I deduced that the tap was lower than the motorhome's water filler inlet. Consequently the water would only flow so far along the hose until it reached the point where it was the same level as the tap. Then, rather than defy the laws of physics by continuing on its short but impossible uphill journey into the motorhome's water tank, it would make its way through the inevitable gap around the hose connector and pour out onto the ground.

I was really surprised with the design of the universal tap connector which was supplied with the hose. It was just a flexible, funnel shaped piece of rubbery plastic, which was meant to be pushed over the tap and supposedly kept in place by nothing more than friction. However, as soon as the tap was turned on, it was never going to stay in place, and if physically held in position, as we tried to do, the water was always going to take the least line of resistance by forcing itself through the imperfect seal between the tap and the connector before spilling out onto the ground.

It was a stupid design, and I thought we surely couldn't be the first motorhomers to experience this problem. I remembered I'd had similar problems at home before we set off, but then I was trying fill up from the utility room mixer tap. Although the connector didn't form a perfect seal, at least the mixer was physically higher than the motorhome's filler inlet and I did get water to flow into the tank.

Just at that point a man nonchalantly strolled up to the tap to fill his rather elaborate caravan water tank. This was a large (5 gallon?) cylindrical plastic tank which was fitted with a detachable handle and, when full and too heavy to carry, could be rolled effortlessly along the ground back to the caravan in a similar manner to a lawn roller. He appeared not to have witnessed our shenanigans, and rather than have him watch our difficulties Emm offered to let him fill his tank before us. But the poor deluded fool told us he was in no hurry, and insisted on waiting for us to finish topping up.

Judging from his reaction when we exchanged greetings, he seemed to think we knew what we were doing and that he wouldn't have to wait very long. I asked Emm, in a nice tone of voice this time, if she would please go round to the other side of the motorhome and make sure the hose didn't come out of the water filler inlet, whilst I held the worse-than-useless, so-called universal tap connector in place. Luckily, with my bigger hands, I managed to grip it much more firmly and achieve a much better seal.

As I turned on the tap, I immediately appreciated the problems Emm had encountered. Once water was flowing, there was no way the connector could ever stay in position, nor was there the slightest possibility that the seal could be made anywhere near good enough. And even though I had my large hands squeezed tightly around the connector to ensure the best seal possible, some water still poured out over my hands, up my sleeves and onto my feet. However, at last we somehow managed to get enough water to flow along the whole length of the hose and deposit itself inside the motorhome's water tank, where it was meant to go.

Whilst all this was going on, Emm and I stayed outwardly calm, and the caravanner had to wait no more than five minutes whilst we "expertly" filled our tank, disconnected the hose, coiled it up, stowed it away and replaced the filler cap ready to set off. He seemed genuinely impressed with our teamwork and, totally unaware that before he came along we'd gone through twenty-five minutes or so of extreme exasperation, must have thought that filling a motorhome water tank was a darn sight easier than topping up a cumbersome caravan water tank, then having to roll it back to his caravan on the end of a handle like a heavy lawn roller.

All this running water made us both need to rush to the adjacent toilet block, and once we'd attended to our calls of nature we were ready to hit the road at long last. As we finally drove away, I thought we urgently needed a hose connector incorporating a hose clip or suchlike, to enable it to be tightly clamped around a tap to form a perfect watertight fit. We certainly didn't wish to act out this water torture pantomime again, and I made a mental note to investigate what types were available and buy some at the earliest opportunity.

12

GOONHILLY, MARAZION & SHOPPING

After our fun and games filling up with water, we turned the heater on full blast in an attempt to dry the wet patches on our trousers and drove out of the campsite, along the narrow lane and across Goonhilly Down past the satellite earth station. The gigantic BT communication dishes, of which there were about sixty in number, loomed in to view through the early morning mist and looked eerily out of place in this remote part of Cornwall.

We'd been to the Goonhilly Visitor Centre on one of our previous family holidays with the girls and had all been impressed with the high-tech control centre and colossal satellite dishes, most of which were named after Arthurian characters.

The world's very first parabolic satellite communications antenna, known as *Arthur*, was built there in the early 1960s, and in 1962 was used to receive the first live transatlantic television broadcast from the USA via the Telstar satellite. I remember being somewhat underwhelmed by the fuzzy black and white pictures of this historic event, which was planned to be of President Kennedy giving a press conference to the world. Unfortunately he was late starting and a baseball match, which meant nothing to anyone on this side of the Atlantic, was transmitted to fill in time before JFK eventually arrived to speak his words about the peace and understanding that would inevitably come from speedy communications.

The technology rapidly improved, and more satellites were

launched to beam live television broadcasts via Arthur from all around the world to ordinary people's front rooms. The Cassius Clay/Muhammad Ali fights and the 1964 Tokyo Olympic Games were classic examples. In 1969 another giant leap in technology took place when Arthur received live pictures of the Apollo 11 moon landings, which I recall watching in the early hours of the morning. Today, we take instantaneous global communication for granted but back in the 1960s those early transmissions created quite a stir.

Arthur's stainless steel reflector is almost thirty metres in diameter and weighs well over 1000 tons. It must be extremely finely balanced, as it can rotate horizontally through 360 degrees in only three minutes and vertically at 30 degrees per minute, and along with all the other antennas it made a spectacular sight in this back of beyond part of Cornwall.[14]

Seeing these massive antennae, I imagined a scene from some future James Bond movie being filmed there. I could picture our hero somehow clinging onto the edge of a gigantic antenna in a brutal fight scene with a particularly nasty villain. Suddenly, the dish starts to move vertically upwards and simultaneously rotates horizontally at maximum speed. Whilst viciously fighting to the death, Bond and 'Mr Nasty' somehow manage to cling on as they are carried high above the ground on the rotating antenna. Then, as they reach the highest point, at over thirty metres off the ground, 'Mr Nasty' is left clinging by his fingertips to a flimsy piece of metal. He's utterly exhausted, looking up at Bond and pleading for mercy through his eyes. Bond looks at him with utter contempt, pauses for a moment, then ruthlessly stamps on his adversary's fingers, causing him to bounce all the way down the antenna dish and fall to his deserved death!

Or maybe they both slip and end up, still fighting, sliding down the inside of the huge dish at a furious speed. As they plummet towards the ground, Bond's beautiful semi-naked girl accomplice appears from nowhere as she drives past in a lorry loaded with hay, onto which our

---

14 The largest antenna, diameter 32 metres, known as *Merlin* was completed in time to transmit the 1985 Live Aid concert.

hero expertly and safely falls. However, the villain is not so lucky and is smashed to smithereens on the hard concrete. Bond suavely straightens his tie, makes some corny comment about the dish of the day being 'Mr Nasty's undoing, checks his weapon and rolls in the hay with the girl.

Too far-fetched? Yes, I suppose so, but if such a scene were to appear in a future Bond movie, remember it was my idea!

Later on, I read somewhere that BT planned to cut costs and dramatically scale down satellite operations at Goonhilly. All the dishes except Arthur, which had been made a Grade II listed building and therefore protected, would be dismantled. No doubt such plans would hit the BT workers very hard indeed, as there were bound to be redundancies with few similar job opportunities on the Lizard Peninsula. It appeared that the site could become a tourist attraction where I hope many of the redundant workers would be able to find alternative employment.[15]

Anyhow, leaving the Lizard behind us, we headed towards Helston to pick up the A394 towards Penzance. We were aiming to get as far as Marazion, where we knew it would be easy to park for an hour, stop for a bite to eat and see St Michael's Mount. We wouldn't actually have time to visit this famous Cornish landmark, which is managed by the National Trust, but at least would be able to see it in the distance whilst we ate our lunch.

This was another interesting place we'd been to with the girls and had particularly enjoyed. We'd walked across the causeway, which links the mainland with the island at low tide, and as the tide had come in during our visit had to return by boat. On that trip we bought a year's family membership of the National Trust which, with further visits that year to Kingston Lacey, Corfe Castle, The Vyne, Polesdon Lacey and Ham House, to name but a few, proved to be a bargain.

But somehow, St Michael's Mount was the most memorable, the

---

15 The site did become a Visitor Centre which closed at Easter 2010 until further notice. In January 2011, it was announced that the site was being sold to create a *Space Science Centre*. Hopefully, more technological jobs will be created.

most unique and the most spectacular. The fact that it's built on solid rock towering up out of the sea, and that for a short time each day it's possible to walk there, whilst a few hours later it's completely cut off from the mainland, makes it particularly magical. During its long and astonishing history, the Mount has been a church, a priory, a fortress and a private house and, almost unbelievably, still remains home to a modern family.

During the English civil war the Mount was under the ownership of Sir Francis Basset, who was loyal to the King and became Commander of the Mount. After he died in 1645 he was succeeded by his brother, Sir Arthur Basset, who just a year later was forced to surrender the Mount to Cromwell's Parliamentary troops. Parliament then nominated Colonel John St Aubyn to be Captain of the Mount, and a year after Cromwell's death in 1658 he bought it from the Basset family to use as his private home. It's not clear how much he paid, but having been defeated royalists I imagine the Bassets were probably forced to sell for a sum significantly below the true market value.

Since that time generations of St Aubyns have lived at and looked after their unique home. However by 1954, finding it more and more expensive to keep up the island, the family gifted it to the National Trust but still retained a nine hundred and ninety nine year lease, thus enabling them and their successors to carry on living in the castle with a licence to operate the visitor business. This has proved to be a very successful arrangement, with the National Trust ensuring the preservation of the Mount, whilst the family continue to live and have a role on the island. Since then millions of people from all over the world have had the opportunity to experience and share this mystical place, whereas before it became under the custodianship of the National Trust I doubt whether many ordinary people ever had the chance to go there.

Anyhow it wasn't long before we were turning off the main road at the roundabout and heading towards Marazion. As I drove slowly towards the town, we both looked across at the imposing castle towering up out of the sea on our right hand side. The tide was out and we momentarily considered walking across the causeway and briefly stepping onto the island. However, dogs were forbidden and in any case there just wasn't the time to do it justice. No matter, we put St Michael's Mount on our wish list of places to revisit and promised to come back soon when we'd allow much more time.

We must have been daydreaming as, before we knew it, I'd virtually driven into Marazion town centre where, not wanting to get stuck in any narrow streets, we started to panic a bit. However, our fears were unfounded and it was quite easy to turn around and drive back along the sea front, where we found an ideal parking place on the side of the road smack bang opposite the castle.

We'd never been to the town of Marazion before so we decided to walk along and have a quick look-see. Monty enjoyed running around on the sands whilst we made our way along the beach towards the town, and we were both impressed with what we found. I imagine that, just like us, many people have gone to St Michael's Mount, but then totally ignored Marazion itself, which was a shame. It proved to be well worth a short visit and we found it to be a bit like stepping back in time to the 1950s, with little traffic, picturesque houses and a good variety of quality shops and eating places.

We browsed around for a while and, as usual, Emm was keen to have a leisurely look in all the shops. At first I didn't mind too much, as they were mostly interesting and different and not at all like some of the usual dismal town centre or tourist shops. Refreshingly, we found an excellent variety of individual craft and gift shops all selling quality local products and art, with not a cheap and tacky souvenir in sight. However, even though the sun was shining, I did eventually start to get fed up waiting outside with Monty whilst Emm went to browse inside each and every one for what seemed like an inordinate amount of time.

She would eventually come out and tell me about something she was tempted to buy, not necessarily for herself but for a birthday or Christmas present for someone else. Then, whilst she held on to Monty, I would be sent inside to look at whatever it was that had caught her eye so I could offer my opinion. I can't remember now what it was we were specifically looking at but, as I said, everything was of a good quality and the prices were also reasonable. Therefore, I really did start to think it wouldn't be a bad idea to buy a few presents, especially if it meant we didn't have to spend so much time trekking around crowded stores near Christmas time, which is not my idea of fun at all!

But, no, she kept dithering and never did make a decision, so in the end we bought nothing, which in some ways really annoyed me. I thought of all the weekends we'd inevitably end up having to go shopping with all the other hordes of last minute shoppers in December, when some of it could have been avoided if we bought some gifts here and now in a far more leisurely fashion.

Like most men, I have to say I don't like wandering round shops at any time of the year. But, without sounding too Scrooge-like, Christmas shopping is the very worst and shopping at that time of the year, when hordes of people descend on the stores in a mad frenzy to spend their money, is my idea of purgatory.

Being mostly in the shade in winter, our nearest big shopping centre in Taunton is invariably cold. Furthermore, the shops and buildings create a perfect wind tunnel and the Arctic winds, which often whistle along the River Tone, swirl icily along the streets before blowing down my neck, round my torso and out through my trouser legs. I'll be freezing cold and will have to wear a thick winter coat, scarf and gloves to keep warm. Then, when we go inside the crowded stores, the heating will be turned up to maximum, I suppose to keep all the scantily dressed shop assistants warm, and it's like stepping into an oven full of perspiring, overheated humanity!

It's absolutely unbearable on Saturdays before Christmas, when all the extra body heat inside the store will push the temperature up way beyond normal comfort levels, and it's no wonder I get irritable! Emm will somehow manage to steam-roll her way through the crowds and, whilst being pushed from pillar to post and struggling to keep up, I will do my utmost to stay outwardly patient and calm, but all the time get more and more impatient and hot under the collar.

Buying Christmas presents then becomes much more of an ordeal than any sort of season of good will pleasurable activity. Even though we always go armed with a well prepared list, we still seem to get sidetracked and rarely end up sticking to it. After just a short time in the shops, the crowds and the heat will befuddle our brains so much that we give up and have to go back the following weekend, then the next and the next, before we finally get something for everyone. So that's why I thought it would be a good idea to buy a few more interesting and unusual gifts now – anything to avoid some of the late Christmas shopping ordeals.

The general perception is that most women love shopping for clothes and are all perfectly happy to wander round all the big stores for hours on end trying this on and that on, before finally making up their minds what they do want. Sometimes, they will see just what they're looking for in the very first shop they go in, but won't buy it in case they see it cheaper elsewhere or see something they like better. They will then leave it for now and think about it and five hours later, when they're exhausted and just before the shops close, will rush back to buy it – only to find it's sold out!

In my experience, it's usually me who gets blamed for not insisting we bought whatever it was when we first saw it! Then, rather than go home empty handed, Emm will end up in a total panic racing around to buy something – *anything* – before it's too late. Then, nine times out of ten, when she gets her purchase home she will decide she doesn't like it after all and will inevitably drag me all the way back into town the following weekend to get her money back and choose something else!

If I were the owner of a store, I would only give refunds if the goods were proven to be faulty and not because someone had just changed their mind. After all, they'd had hours to decide whether to buy it or not in the first place, and if they couldn't stick by their decision why should the store owner be held responsible? Judging by the queues at the returns desks in the big chain stores, I'm convinced that loads of women buy a dress or something on a Saturday afternoon, wear it in the evening and then take it back the following week to get a refund on the basis *that they changed their mind* or *were not entirely satisfied with it,* whatever that means?

A friend of ours, who used to work in a very well-known and long established store, which can be found in most high streets, once told me she was working on the returns desk when a little old lady brought back some men's underwear. There were no receipts and the garments were not in the original packaging, let alone an original store bag. The only means of identifying that they were bought in a branch of this particular store were the labels.

This lady's husband had apparently sadly died and she'd been going through his drawers (no pun intended) sorting out his clothes. She then had the nerve to take a collection of assorted underpants and vests back to the store and expect a refund. Irrespective of the fact that they were all a few years old and had obviously been worn and washed on numerous occasions, our friend was told by her supervisor to follow company policy, not to make a fuss and reimburse her. I thought it was no wonder the store was in financial difficulty a few years ago. Business has perked up since then, but they still have enormous long queues at their returns desk.

Like most women, Emm just loves going shopping for clothes and will go to the shops at every opportunity, which I don't mind at all. The only problem is that she hardly ever wants to go by herself and always insists I go with her to hold her bags and give her my opinion. After trudging round the store for what seems like an eternity, she will want to try something on and I will have to stand outside the changing room with all the other bored looking men, holding her coat and bag whilst she takes forever trying on a selection of different outfits.

She will emerge at varying intervals wearing a different garment and ask me what I think. But it never really matters what I think. If I tell her I like it, she won't be so sure. And if I don't like it, and am stupid enough to say so, she will ask what's wrong with it? I never have the right answer and always seem to plant doubt in her mind, so she won't buy it. In the end, we will waste the whole day and she'll either go home empty handed or buy something she later decides she's *not entirely satisfied with*. So I'll be dragged round again the following weekend to get a refund and do it all over again.

On the other hand, like most men, if I want to buy a pair of socks or a shirt, for example, I will go straight into the store, head straight to the socks or shirt department, pick out something in my size and the colour I want, pay for it and go home again. Then I can get on with doing something more interesting and useful, like cleaning the toilet or rodding the drains. In fact, I'd prefer to do anything really rather than wander aimlessly around overcrowded, overheated stores for hours on end.

Fair enough, as Emm will often remind me, in my haste I have been known to buy the odd thing that's not been quite right. The classic example was when I went to a branch of the same well known store our friend used to work in and bought several pairs of their underpants. I marched into the store, went straight to the men's underwear display and, quick as a flash, made my choice. I looked for the shortest queue, paid and, mission accomplished, was on my way home again to enjoy the rest of the day.

However, when I later put a pair on, they somehow didn't feel quite right. Sure enough, they were the right size, but instead of the briefs I normally wear they were the more old fashioned and larger *Y-front* type. However, no one was ever likely to see them – more's the pity – and rather than go all the way back and change them I kept them and wear them in the winter to provide additional warmth in my nether region. Anyhow, I'd already taken them out of their wrapping and tried a pair on, so would never have had the nerve to take them back and ask for an exchange or a refund.

The funny thing is that both our daughters have grown up to be just like me and not like shopping at all. They hardly ever go to the shops and buy virtually everything on-line in the comfort of their own homes. In that respect, they've both been a huge disappointment to Emm as she couldn't wait for them to grow up and accompany her on her weekend shopping expeditions (and come to that, nor could I).

The girls both recall frequent trips around the big stores in

Portsmouth and Southampton when they were children, and would get so tired and fed up being dragged along with us. I remember having to look after Emm's bags, whilst pushing Rowena's push chair and holding on to Joscelin's hand. Of course, the girls had a low boredom threshold and it was a job to keep them happy. They would get very niggly and the only light relief was when I tried to amuse them with my Harry Worth impressions, which never failed to make them laugh.

For those of you who may not remember, Harry Worth was a bumbling bespectacled comedy actor, who was very popular with his BBC television show in the 1960s. At the beginning of each programme, he would be seen walking down a high street – I don't know why, he just did. He would stop by the corner of a large shop window, which just happened to be very reflective and mirror like. He would then stand in the shop doorway with the centre of his body as close as he could get it up against the edge of the large window. The right side of his body would be hidden from view behind the window, but with his left side visible and being reflected in the mirror like surface, he would almost look like his normal symmetrical self. He would then balance himself on his right foot – the one that was hidden from view – and raise his left arm and leg in the air as high as he could. The reflected image in the window would appear to show him simultaneously raising both arms in the air and defying gravity by lifting both legs off the ground at the same time.

Childish I know, but when I repeated the same trick using the full length mirrors in the department stores it never failed to amuse the girls. I may have got a few double-takes and funny looks from anyone else who happened to see me, and Emm may have told me to stop messing about but, as I apparently raised both arms in the air and magically lifted both feet off the ground, the girls always laughed and I was never bothered about what anyone else might think! Not so long ago, much to the amusement of an adult Joscelin and Lily, my three-year-old granddaughter, who were both with Emm and me at the time, I did the same thing in a large store in Bournemouth. I just felt I had to keep the old tradition going and, at my age, couldn't care less what anyone else thought!

Anyhow, I'm not too sure how we got from picturesque Marazion to me bemoaning about shopping trips and my Harry Worth impressions. So, returning to Marazion, although we didn't buy any presents or anything for ourselves, we couldn't resist the smell of pasties coming from a traditional Cornish pasty shop. It was lunchtime, we were hungry and the smell of the freshly baked pasties wafting over the road was just too much to bear. I wouldn't have been surprised if they'd installed a big fan especially to blow the baking smells out into the street to lure passers-by inside the shop. It certainly worked with us and we couldn't resist the temptation to follow our noses and make our way inside.

The problem was that there was so much choice. I never imagined that a simple pasty could have so many different fillings. As well as the traditional steak, potato and swede there were numerous other speciality types, all of which came in medium or large size, including cheese and ham, spicy chicken, lamb and mint, beef and stilton, pork and apple, to name but a few. There was even one described as *breakfast*, which I assumed was the full English breakfast baked in pastry, which I didn't really fancy as I like my sausage, egg and bacon the traditional way served up on a hot plate. Vegetarians were also very well catered for with varieties such as cheese, potato and onion, vegetable, cheese and mushroom or broccoli and sweet corn.

The list seemed endless, and even though they weren't exactly cheap the smell was addictive and we had to have our fix. In the end I decided on a medium traditional and Emm, after her usual deliberation, finally chose a cheese, potato and onion, and as we intended to go straight back to the motorhome and eat them with a cup of tea we asked for them to be heated up.

They certainly lived up to expectations and were far, far superior to the so called Cornish pasties we sometimes buy in the supermarkets. The only problem with coming to Cornwall was that we tended to exist on a diet of pasties and fish and chips, but we didn't care – we were on holiday!

13

4 STAR ST IVES & MODERN ART

Once we'd polished off our pasties, we set off again on the short but uneventful journey up to the north coast, where we'd booked into the 4 star *Ayr Holiday Park* in St Ives for the next two nights. According to their brochure, the site enjoyed *'beautiful coast views'* and had a *'superbly equipped shower and toilet block'* which, after the rather disappointing washrooms at the other campsite, I was keen to try out. We'd been particularly looking forward to staying there as we had fond memories of St Ives and, as an added bonus, the site was within easy walking distance of the town centre and beaches.

Emm used her improved navigation skills to the full and, to my surprise, directed us straight to the holiday park with no deviation whatsoever. The sun was burning brightly in the vivid blue sky, which was only interrupted by a few puffs of wispy white clouds, and we both felt the omens were good with respect to our short stay in St Ives. After our stress free journey we certainly felt better and far more relaxed then forty-eight hours previously when we arrived at The Lizard in the rain. I pulled up outside reception where a very pleasant young lady booked us in and showed us our designated pitch on a plan of the site. As it wasn't too far away, we left the motorhome where it was, put Monty on his lead and ambled across to carry out a reconnaissance.

We were both pleased that we'd been allocated a gravel hard standing rather than wet grass to park on this time. But, even so, it wasn't immediately obvious as to how we'd actually approach the pitch, which was on a sort of step in a hill – rather like a large strip lynchet – with magnificent views over St Ives Bay. We worked out that I'd have to drive round the one-way system on the tarmac road, turn left onto a narrow area of grass and drive past several parked motorhomes, caravans and cars. Then, as the pitch was situated at right angles to this grassy approach, in order to correctly position the motorhome facing forward onto the gravel, I'd finally have to turn left very sharply through ninety degrees.

However, it was never going to be that simple. The gravel pitch was a fairly small area, and as there had been a fair amount of rain over the weekend the surrounding grass had been churned up by the previous occupant, leaving deep muddy ruts close to one side of the gravel. That wasn't my only concern, as it clearly wasn't going to be easy for me to position the vehicle facing forward on the gravel as we'd been asked. The pitch itself wasn't that long, not much longer than the motorhome in fact, and the ground directly in front of it dropped down a metre or so to a lower level. Therefore I was acutely aware I couldn't afford to misjudge the distance and drive too far forward. If I did, and my front wheels strayed over this sheer drop, I would find myself in a very embarrassing and costly situation needing a specialist recovery vehicle to pull a damaged motorhome back up the slope!

Notwithstanding this nerve racking precipice at the front of the pitch, at the rear was a metre high grassy bank which I knew I'd have to be extra careful not to hit when turning onto the gravel or when reversing out again! Trying to park on this particular pitch was going to be a daunting manoeuvre and we thought about asking for a different one. However, it was obvious the campsite was very popular and we couldn't see a single vacant space anywhere else, so we just had to get on with it.

Not feeling all that confident, but not wishing to worry Emm too much (after all, she worries enough for both of us at the best of times), I tried to mentally work out the best way to approach this parking place from hell. I reckoned that, once I'd turned off the tarmac onto the wet grass, I'd have to move slowly forward keeping reasonably close to the bank on my right hand side – but not so close that the rear of the motorhome would hit the bank as I turned. Then, precisely at the right moment, I'd have to put full lock on the steering wheel, swing the motorhome sharply round to the left onto the gravel, straighten up and stop before we toppled down the bank at the front. Having carefully analysed what needed to be done, I was still apprehensive about actually doing it. Psyching myself up, I thought it must be possible for a fully skilled motorhome driver: it was just that I only had four days' experience under my belt and was very much a motorhome novice!

Emm stayed by the pitch with Monty ready to marshal me into position and, knowing I could delay the inevitable no longer, I cast my eyes over the pitch and its approach yet again before thoughtfully walking back to the motorhome. After taking a couple of deep breaths, I nervously pulled away and drove slowly around the edge of the caravan and motorhome camping area before turning off the road onto the narrow grass strip towards our pitch.

Being acutely aware the grass was damp and slippery, I drove even more slowly and hoped the tyres would retain their grip and not sink into the soft ground. All started off well, and when I approached our pitch I concentrated hard on keeping the driver's side of the motorhome as close to the grassy bank as possible, but not so close that the back of the vehicle would swing into it as I turned. I would like to say that all went to plan and I managed to perfectly position the motorhome without further ado. Unfortunately, however, that wasn't the case and there was much more *ado!*

I ended up being a bit too close to the bank and, as I sharply turned the steering wheel to the left, the rear corner of the motorhome was just about to gouge into it. Just in the nick of time Emm frantically signalled me to stop, and I then had to straighten up, reverse a bit and try again. I then positioned the motorhome a little too far away from the bank and it proved to be impossible to turn through anything like ninety degrees before I would have driven over the dreaded precipice at the front of the pitch.

So I had to try again, which was similarly unsuccessful, and ended up shunting the vehicle backwards and forwards *ad infinitum*. Each time, Emm frantically ran from the back of the motorhome to the front, then from the front to the back again, whilst banging on the bodywork as a signal for me to stop before I hit the bank or went over the precipice. It all got extremely hectic, and with every attempt I made to correctly align the motorhome on our pitch, the small gravel area appeared to get smaller and smaller and the vehicle larger and larger!

At one point, I did reverse back just a little too far and, to our horror, actually struck the grass bank. Fortunately the bank was muddy and soft enough to have a little bit of give in it and, apart from my pride and a dirty mark on the flimsy motorhome panel, no real damage was done.

Notwithstanding that mishap, I continued to shunt back and forth for an inordinate number of times, and even though we hoped we were as inconspicuous as possible we both became aware of numerous pairs of eyes watching our every move. Even so, nobody offered any help or advice and we must have provided the best free entertainment anyone had seen for a long time, easily surpassing the usual first time campers' antics when struggling with enormous frame tents or awnings. Eventually, I managed to park more or less parallel on our pitch, but with only the nearside wheels on the gravel and the driver's side wheels on the grass.

At that point, I gave up as a bad job and accepted the fact that there was just no way I'd ever be able to position the motorhome slap bang in the middle of this minute pitch where it was meant to be. The surrounding grass had got even more churned up, and if I'd carried on shunting backwards and forwards I was sure the wheels would have ended up getting completely stuck in thick gooey mud.

We both agreed it was the best I could do and, almost expecting a round of applause from all the people who'd been watching us, we brought our farcical performance to an end. Being within walking distance of the town, if the worst came to the worst, we wouldn't necessarily have to move again until it was time to travel on to our next campsite a couple of days later, by which time, we hoped, the mud would have dried out.

I then realised that most of the other motorhomes had been driven up onto ramps and that ours was nowhere near level. There was a pronounced slope towards its front which, as we didn't have any ramps, we could do nothing about. Not that we were too bothered; it just meant that we'd have to be extra careful whilst cooking on the hob and put up with rolling towards each other in bed. Even if we'd had some with us, after all our efforts trying to position the motorhome, I wouldn't have used them. If I'd tried to drive up onto ramps, the offside one would have surely sunk into the soft mud, and with our track record it wasn't beyond the realms of imagination that one or both of the front wheels could have slipped off the ramp and slewed over the precipice, with catastrophic consequences. We'd already provided enough entertainment for our attentive audience, which was seated all around us in their caravans and motorhomes, and the consequences of such an unintentional and spectacular encore didn't bear thinking about!

Doing my best to act nonchalantly, I finally climbed down from the cab, turned on the gas bottle and connected the electric hook up. Then, as I retracted the steps and placed the rubber doormat outside the rear door, I thought it was a good job it opened out onto the gravel, rather than the other side of the motorhome where we would have been forever dragging thick mud into the motorhome.

Having put the kettle on, I left Emm to make a brew whilst I climbed up a few wooden steps which were set into the dreaded grass bank at our rear, and went over to inspect the toilets and shower block. The outside looked nothing like the usual campsite facilities I'd been used to. In fact, I didn't immediately realise that the swish chalet-style building with its shiny varnished wooden panelling housed the showers, wash basins and toilets. It looked far too impressive. Then, when I opened the door to the Gents, I could hardly believe what I saw.

The amenities were unlike anything I'd ever seen at any campsite in the UK or France and were poles apart from the cold concrete floors, basic basins, tottering toilets and shivering showers we'd *enjoyed* at our previous site. These washrooms were more akin to what I would have expected to find in a 5 star hotel, let alone a 4 star campsite. The wall tiles were far more upmarket than the ones I'd put on our own bathroom and shower room walls at home. Likewise, the taps and fittings were of a much higher standard and price bracket than our own; the sea blue moulded inset washbasins were top of the range, with gleaming circular mirrors above; the floor was covered in beautifully clean ceramic tiles; there were free electric hairdryers and shiny full length mirrors! Nothing would have looked out of place in a top hotel. Everything was that opulent.

Similarly, all the toilets and urinals sparkled, with no trace of anything unpleasant: no toilet paper was strewn all over the floors; no cubicle had a broken or missing lock; readers of graffiti would have been disappointed, and no giant spiders or cobwebs were to be seen. In fact, I wouldn't have had too much of a problem cooking and eating a meal in there if I had to. There was even piped music to keep everyone entertained whilst they went about their business, and the whole place was centrally heated. It was just as comfortable as home and I couldn't anticipate any constipation here!

I went back to the motorhome and, whilst we drank our tea, raved about the toilets to Emm. I don't think she really believed me when I told her they were inside the smart chalet type building or how good they were. I'm sure she thought I was joking, but when she came back from her first visit after tea she was just as impressed and relieved as me.

Anyhow, we'd read about the beautiful coastal views from the campsite and were certainly not disappointed. The panoramic vista from our front window looked right across St Ives Bay and was truly breathtaking. We couldn't wait to get out and explore, so after a quick snack we set off to walk into the town where we planned to spend the remainder of the afternoon. We strolled out of the caravan park and up into a field where some tents were pitched, and joined a small track which led us through a wild bushy area towards the coast path, which would take us right into St Ives itself.

Although in a hurry to get there, I just had to stop and explore a rocky promontory which jutted out into the sea. I climbed up as high as I could and took in the views from all angles. To my left was a huge solitary rock, which resembled a squatting fat man looking out to sea, and to my right was a splendid view of St Ives at the far end of a sandy bay. There was hardly a cloud in the sky, the sea was sparkling in the bright sunshine and the grass behind us and to our left was a vivid green. Having completely forgotten about our misery in the monsoon just a few days before, the magnificent scenery and marvellous weather made me wonder why so many people rush to go abroad when there are such places as St Ives here in the UK.

Emm, however, started to get a bit impatient with me scrambling around on the rocks and, obviously wanting to get to St Ives before the shops shut, had already started to stride on ahead with Monty. So I had a last look around and hurried on to catch her up. Passing a well-kept bowling green, which must have been in one of the most picturesque locations possible to play bowls, we joined a road which led us down towards Porthmeor Beach and the town beyond. To our right there was a large cemetery, which judging by some of the gravestones was pretty old, and just beyond that was the very modern looking Tate Art Gallery. It would have been interesting to have gone inside, but we didn't have time to do it justice and, in any case, Monty was with us so we would have had to take it in turns. Also, we noticed that it would have cost £5.85 each, but that if we came back in a couple of years' time, when we were both over sixty, we would be eligible for free entry. So that's what we decided to do.

We were soon wandering around the labyrinth of narrow cobbled streets and alley ways in St Ives, Emm looking in all the shop windows and me looking at all the varied architecture. Most of the buildings appeared to be hundreds of years old and the old part of town looked more like a costume drama film set than a modern living community.

The houses were largely painted in different pastel colours, and although not many had much of a garden, their green fingered owners had proudly crammed glorious floral displays into tubs and hanging baskets. Being laid out centuries before motor cars were even thought about, the narrow streets were virtually traffic free, and the lack of vehicles added to the picturesque and olde-worlde atmosphere of the place.

We remarked that, for such a popular holiday resort, there was a distinct lack of amusement arcades, tacky souvenir shops selling cheap imported pottery or kiss-me-quick hats and suchlike. Not that we were looking for such establishments – far from it in fact.

What there was, however, was an abundance of art galleries. Every other shop seemed to be full of original paintings or reproductions by local artists, especially seascapes and local scenes. They came in all sizes to suit all budgets and we were sorely tempted to buy one – or two, or even three. However, we just couldn't make up our minds which we liked best; they were all that good. So in the end, we ended up with nothing, which we later regretted.

Since the coming of the railways at the end of the 19th century, artists have been drawn to St Ives where many settled to make a living selling their work to the ever increasing number of tourists. Being surrounded by sea on three sides, the sun's rays reflect off the mass of water to give a brilliantly bright, unpolluted light to paint by, and whether looking out to sea or towards the town, the scenery is superb with virtually every view a potential work of art. The sparkling turquoise sea, the bright yellow sands and the pastel buildings all provide the perfect contrast which has inspired St Ives' artists for generations and, judging by what we saw in all the art galleries, I could well appreciate their work.

As well as painters, St Ives has also attracted some notable sculptors, the most famous being the late Barbara Hepworth. Even though I'm not a fan of modernist sculpture, whilst in St Ives it would have been interesting to visit her museum and sculpture garden and see for ourselves what all the fuss was about. Personally speaking, although I acknowledge the infinite patience and skill required by the Renaissance sculptors, for example, in transforming a huge block of marble into a perfectly proportioned human figure or animal, I remain unconvinced regarding the artistic merit and skilfulness of the modernist sculptors in shaping a block of stone into some obscure and holey abstract form.

I can just imagine those sculptors centuries ago, as they very carefully and very precisely tapped away with a mallet and chisel to metamorphose a gigantic block of expensive marble into an instantly recognisable mythological or historical figure. After months of painstaking dedication, the masterpiece is virtually finished with only a few more taps of the mallet required to finish the last prominent feature – say its nose. Being so near to completing his prestigious project, I imagine the sculptor being very excited, and after all that time rather tired. Unfortunately in his excitement, and because he's over tired, he very slightly over hits the final mallet stroke and with a deafening thud the almost perfectly shaped snout crashes to the studio floor!

I imagine that utter disbelief and tears of frustration would follow whilst our sculptor realises that all those hours, weeks and months (even years) of toil have been totally wasted. Not to mention his tarnished reputation! His only options would be to start all over again, or else change the name of the statue to something like '*The Man With No Nose*' and pretend that that was what he meant to produce all along. During his lifetime, such work probably wouldn't receive much critical acclaim, but after his death it could well be hailed as a masterpiece.

After all, in 1504 Michael Angelo clearly made a bit of a boob with his famous four metre high marble statue of *David* of *David and Goliath* fame. Fair enough, there's no doubt the statue may look like a very muscular human being, but even a relative philistine like me can see that his head is about twice as big as it should be. Nowadays his creation may well be critically acclaimed, with millions of people flocking to Florence from all over the world to marvel at it. But at the time, I understand Michael Angelo's artistic rivals consistently ridiculed him for his *'David with the Big Head'*, and he probably wished he'd spent another couple of months chiselling the head down to more realistic proportions!

However, I don't think the modernist sculptors would have much of an issue with out of proportion body parts or chipping too much off the block. After all, they don't seem to sculpt lifelike figures any more. That would take far too much time and require far too much skill. As far as I can see, in today's modernist world they just knock a hole or two in a block of stone and they've created a *'masterpiece'*. Well, according to those select few modernists, they may have, but I'm afraid lesser mortals like me just don't get it.

Perhaps we're just not clever enough? Or maybe it's a bit like the fairy story about the Emperor's new coat, with some art connoisseurs not wanting to admit they don't get it either. Fair enough, an oval block of stone with a nice smooth oval shaped hole in it can look rather nice in a garden surrounded by plants with sunlight shining through the hole. But where's the real skill in that? I mean if the sculptor makes a mistake when cutting out his hole and chips away a bit more than he bargained for, he (or she) only has to make the hole a bit bigger and smooth it out a bit. Don't they?

After all, what difference will it make? And who's going to notice? Yes that's right – nobody! It's not like the Renaissance sculpture with the missing nose or oversized head, is it? No I'm sorry, I don't wish to belittle anybody's work, but I just don't get the modernist stuff. Mind you, if they can receive critical acclaim and sell such *art* for vast sums of money, what do I know? So, good luck to them – but don't expect me to pander to their work.

That goes for abstract paintings as well. Surreal pictures of dark aggressive shapes sprouting weird body parts, with piercing eyes staring out at me, just assault my eyeballs. And I can't help thinking that the products of naked artists rolling on a paint covered floor, or randomly flicking it at a wall, remind me of what my daughters used to bring home from playschool.

I'm sorry, but I like the pictures hanging on my wall to look like something I can relate to, like a nice landscape or seascape which reminds me of pleasant holidays or days out. Mind you, my pictures don't necessarily have to be absolutely precise and resemble photographs. After all, it's dead easy these days to get an exact likeness and capture any scene with a modern digital camera. And I do like quirky cartoons that make me laugh and fully appreciate the skill in that.

Likewise, I very much admire the Impressionists' stuff, especially Monet, whose work, which I've seen in London and Paris, almost blew my mind. The way he painstakingly dabbed huge numbers of tiny blobs onto large canvases to build up his pictures is amazing. Close up, these randomly placed dabs of varying colours don't look much. But stand back, and they magically transform themselves into extraordinary and recognisable images of his world famous water lilies or scenic views. That's my idea of great artistic skill and what I call *real* art. His later work is particularly inspiring, especially as he was going blind by then.

I know it's all in the eye of the beholder and maybe it's a failing on my part, but modern art does little for me. That's why it was rather gratifying to see that virtually all the paintings in the St Ives galleries and art shops were my kind of art. There was hardly an abstract offering to be seen which proved to me that, if they wanted to make a living, the St Ives artists realised they had to paint pictures that mirrored my own artistic taste and appealed to the majority of people. And not what a minority of modernists thought was special.

I remember when I first worked in London in 1983 and visited a modern art exhibition on the South Bank. The main exhibit, which was in all the papers at the time, was six thousand used car tyres arranged into the shape of a life sized *Polaris* submarine. It was outside the Festival Hall building, and I first caught a glimpse of it when walking to the office on the Monday morning. At the time, rather than commuting each day from where we were living on the south coast, I was staying in a cheap hotel during the week and once I'd finished work had plenty of time on my hands.

I must admit I was fairly intrigued by this *tyred* submarine, so after work the next day I took myself down to the South Bank to get a closer look. Although I appreciated it must have taken a fair amount of time and skill to cleverly arrange all the old tyres into the shape of a full sized submarine, I couldn't really reconcile it to myself as *art* – well not my kind of art anyway.

After all, it couldn't be placed on the mantelpiece or realistically put in anyone's garden like a statue, so I couldn't see any artistic significance. I wasn't the only one though, as a few days later someone felt strongly enough to set fire to it and, for his pains, burnt himself to death in the process. Apparently, the artist created the tyre submarine as a protest statement against nuclear weapons, and if that was the case I suppose he succeeded in his endeavours. He certainly got plenty of publicity, as did the person who set fire to it!

Anyhow, the main exhibition closed at six o'clock, so I didn't have much time to explore all the other modern art on offer, and if there'd been an entrance fee I doubt whether I'd have bothered. However, I think it was funded by the old Greater London Council, which seemed to have money to burn in those days, and it cost nothing to go in. So having nothing to lose (except a bit of my time and I had plenty of that to kill) I ventured inside the weird and wonderful world of modern art, where I spent a very strange forty-five minutes or so.

There was a pile of house bricks, stacked up just like they would be on any building site; ladders, which led up from the floor through holes in the ceiling to the next floor; old car roofs shaped into abstract *tables*, with all sorts of strange, multi-coloured miscellanea dangling from the inside of the roofs on pieces of wire or string; plus all sorts of other incomprehensible and surreal objects knocked together out of scrap metal and other odd bits of rubbish. I was amazed that anyone could take this seriously and even more than amazed that the Greater London Council, or whoever it was, could finance and encourage so many seemingly long haired layabouts to create all this crap.

However, my views were not shared by everyone and I overheard other people praising the wacky exhibits. Nevertheless, it seemed to me that the *artists* must have been under the influence of illegal *recreational substances* when creating all this colourful junk, as were the people who thought it was highly expressive. Or maybe, just maybe, these modern artists were cleverer than I thought and were just poking fun at all the punters who praised their work as wonderfully creative art!

Anyhow, how I got from scenic St Ives to my opinions of modern art I'm not too sure so I'd better return to St Ives before I upset too many people. We carried on exploring the narrow lanes, the shops, the harbour and the beaches, and when we climbed to the old chapel on top of St Ives Island – which is not an island at all but surrounded by sea on three sides – to take in the view, we truly appreciated the unique unpolluted light which had drawn all those artists to St Ives in the first place.

Unfortunately there wasn't time to visit Barbara Hepworth's sculpture garden, so feeling hot, tired and hungry, we retraced our steps back along Porthmeor beach and, deciding to take the road back to the campsite rather than the coast path, dragged our aching legs up a very steep hill alongside the cemetery. The sight of an unoccupied seat near the top spurred us on, and when we reached it we gratefully plonked ourselves down for five minutes rest.

The cemetery was much larger and more impressive than it appeared to be when we passed it earlier in the day. For a start, it was built on the side of the hill where it rose up as far as I could see. All the gravestones were of a dark grey stone, which I assumed to be granite, with a fair proportion being very large and obviously erected in memory of some pretty important and wealthy people. I was curious and would like to have spent some time looking around to see who'd been interned there, how old they were and when they departed this earth.

Unfortunately there wasn't time to do so, and in any case Emm would have thought I was a bit morbid. However, I'm pretty sure there would have been lots of sailors who perished in shipwrecks a hundred years or so ago and that many of them would have been very young.

Also, I imagined there would have been a fair number of very young children, babies even, who would have perished due to long forgotten illnesses that just a few generations ago would have been incurable. It also struck me that if the ground was as hard and rocky as it certainly was on the nearby cliff top, it must have been pretty back breaking work for anyone to actually dig the graves.

I was still thinking about all the poor souls in the graveyard when we arrived back at the campsite. Being uphill all the way, it had been a fair old slog and we needed to rest awhile before cooking our meal. The sun was still shining brightly, so we decided to take full advantage and sit outside to unwind with a cool drink and admire the magnificent view. Whilst relaxing in our chairs, we noticed that the hot sun had started to dry out the muddy wheel ruts in the grass, which reassured us somewhat about having to back off our pitch when the time came to do so. All seemed right with the world, and after the disappointing start to our holiday we both felt that we'd taken to this motorhome life style after all.

After resting up and eating our meal, I went over to the washing up area to wash up (well, why else would I go there?) and got talking to a man at the next sink (funny, how it's always the men who wash up when camping and caravanning!). It transpired that he came from Kingswood, near Bristol, which was not too far away from us in Somerset and, coincidently, also where our youngest daughter now lived. Consequently, we immediately built up a rapport and carried on chatting like long lost friends.

It turned out he was also touring in a motorhome, and I thought I'd impress him by telling him we were motorhomers as well. However, he already knew that. He'd instantly recognised me as the motorhome novice who'd entertained him and his wife whilst we made a right old hash of parking earlier in the day! It appeared that, whilst eating their late lunch, they'd really enjoyed the show we'd put on, and had had a good laugh at our expense! However, he told me this in a light-hearted way so we both had a chuckle about it, and he went on to tell me what I'd done wrong and what I needed to do next time. He'd owned several motorhomes so, compared to me, he was an absolute expert and his advice was well worth listening to. We carried on making small talk whilst we finished our washing up, after which I excused myself and went back to the motorhome.

Emm and I then walked up to the designated dog walking area so Monty could do his business, and as we made our way slowly past the other caravans and motorhomes we noticed a Border Terrier, just like Monty, tied up outside a caravan. When we came back twenty minutes or so later, the dog was inside the caravan constantly barking and whimpering, and as the car had gone it was obvious the owners had driven off somewhere and left the dog behind. There was no problem with the heat, as it had rapidly cooled off as the evening wore on, but the poor dog obviously wasn't happy being left on its own and was making quite a racket. Luckily its owners weren't away too long, but we were quite concerned about the dog at the time and it spoilt our evening a bit.

Anyhow, what with our journey and being out in the fresh sea air for most of the day, we were both dead tired. And after an early night, we slept almost as soundly as all the poor souls in the cemetery!

14

THE MERMAID OF ZENNOR

When we woke up and opened the curtains across the front window, the sight that greeted us was out of this world. Indeed, if we'd been staying in a hotel we would have been paying a hefty premium for the superb sea view we enjoyed from our relatively modest motorhome that morning.

With the brilliant early morning sunshine, the deep blue sparkling sea and the magnificent scenery, we really felt as though we could have been in some Mediterranean hot spot rather than Cornwall. Everything was spectacularly different from the weekend when we felt lethargic and thoroughly fed up with the dark grey skies, strong winds and heavy rain. It then felt as though we were enduring some sort of character building exercise, rather than a relaxing holiday, and we were on the brink of packing up and trying to get a refund on the motorhome on the basis that *we weren't entirely satisfied with it*. However, having enjoyed warm sunshine and blue skies for the last couple of days, we were really enjoying ourselves, felt good about motorhome life and were raring to go. But raring to go where we wondered?

We were booked into this superb campsite for another night and, after all the problems we'd experienced parking on our compact gravel hard standing, we didn't really relish the idea of driving off and then having to park up again later in the day with everyone staring at us. However, we were both keen to drive along the scenic B3306 coast road to Land's End, so a decision had to be made. Over breakfast, we chewed it over, and finally agreed that, rather than stay put and spend the day in St Ives, we would set off early and do the trip to Land's End. We'd driven along this route many years before and both knew it would be well worth repeating, especially in the motorhome where we'd be sitting higher up than in a car and would therefore get a much better view of the scenery over the top of the hedgerows.

Having cleared away the breakfast things and taken advantage of the fabulous 4 star facilities, we both set off to take Monty for his morning walk just beyond the top field where the tents were pitched. The poor little Border Terrier, which we'd been so worried about the night before, was tied up outside its caravan keeping guard and, as we walked past, seemed to go completely bonkers. Instead of regarding Monty as one of its long lost cousins and being happy to exchange a friendly sniff, it started to bark like a banshee and strained on its lead in a frantic effort to get to a bewildered Monty, seemingly to tear him apart.

We quickly reduced Monty's flexi-lead to its shortest length and walked past as fast as we could. Even so, as we hurried on, the barking continued and we felt rather conspicuous as the commotion drew numerous pairs of eyes from behind caravan and motorhome windows in our direction. The owners of the barking Border, however, seemed content to ignore all the noise and just carried on casually eating their breakfast, or whatever it was they were doing from within the confines of their caravan.

In our experience, Border Terriers usually recognise their own breed and are very passive towards each other, if not a little aloof. However, any sympathy we may have had the previous evening for that particular Border when it was distressed at being left on its own, sort of vanished. Even so, we knew it wasn't the dog's fault but its owners who took no notice of him. Border Terriers are extremely affectionate dogs and crave human contact, and he obviously didn't like being tied up on his own outside whilst his owners completely ignored him. Nor would he have liked being left alone in the caravan

Tree Ferns at Trebah Gardens after the rain finally stopped.

The remains of the Victorian Serpentine Factory we stumbled across at Poltesco on the way to Cadgwith.

I

Overlooking Cadgwith Harbour - The Cadgwith Cove Inn beckons.

The worse-than-useless universal tap connector in action which caused so many problems when filling up with fresh water.

Gripping the connector tightly made little difference.

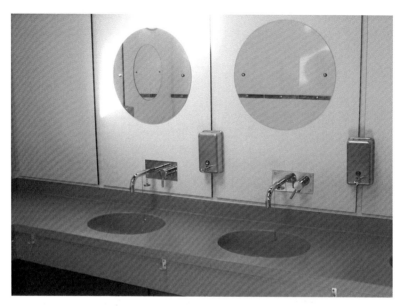

The Imaculate washrooms at Ayr Holiday Park, St Ives, were more akin to a 5 star hotel than a campsite.

Remembering my mother's washdays using a copper, just like this one in the Wayside Museum, I imagined my glasses were steaming up!

The legendary Mermaid carving in the 600-year-old church pew at Zennor.

IV

The wreck of German ship RMS Mülheim, which tragically ran aground in bizarre circumstances off Land's End on 22nd March 2003.

Rowena Cade's marvellous open-air Minack Theatre on the cliff tops near Porthcurno.

The precarious foot bridge over the lockgate at Charleston.
Note the different water levels either side.

Divers at Charleston Shipwreck Museum, including a replica of John Lethbridge's
early 18th century 'barrel' diving machine.

The Beatles in CLOUD CUCKOO LAND, Mevagissey.

The Shell House at Polperro.

Jean & Gren's damaged seat by Polperro Harbour.

I still wonder who Jean & Gren were & what happened to their seat.

the previous evening, when his owners disappeared down the pub or wherever it was they went.

When we returned after our short walk, the poor dog was still tied up outside his caravan looking and sounding sorry for himself, and even though we gave him a much wider berth this time he still barked loudly at us. We both felt really sorry for him by now and wished his owners would give him the attention he obviously needed. However, with him straining on his lead and barking aggressively, I certainly didn't fancy approaching him to give him a stroke. Consequently, there wasn't a lot we could do about it and just had to carry on and get ready to go out for the day.

Once we got Monty inside, the distressed dog thankfully settled down and we prepared to get ready to drive off. Luckily, the muddy patches alongside our gravel hard standing had pretty much dried out, so I didn't think there would be too much of a problem, either when reversing off our pitch or when we had to park up again later in the day. That is, provided I took great care and didn't repeat all the mistakes I made the previous day.

Emm got out to direct operations and, turning the steering wheel sharply to the left, I eased the motorhome slowly back towards the grassy bank at the rear. Just as I got really close, Emm banged the body work as hard as she could with her hand, which made me think I'd misjudged the distance and actually hit the accursed obstruction. Fearing the worst, I was much relieved when Emm told me I could go back another foot or so. Thankful that I hadn't damaged the fragile bodywork, I ever so slowly eased back a bit, then a bit more and then a bit more, all the time watching Emm's wavering arm in the wing mirror until the bodywork reverberated with her thud of finality, as she banged to signal me to stop. I then put full opposite lock on the steering wheel, selected first gear and eased forward.

However, immediately behind the adjacent caravan to my right, there was a parked car which prevented me from moving any further forward. Therefore, being carefully guided by Emm's arm waving signals and banging, I then had to shunt backwards and forwards a few times before I could finally proceed along the grass strip behind a few more parked cars and caravans towards the safety of the tarmac roadway, where I stopped to let Emm hop in.

Even though the grass had dried out considerably since we'd arrived at the campsite, I was aware my tyres had churned up the ruts even more. I dreaded having to park up again when we returned, and hoped the sun would shine all day to further dry out the soft ground. But for now, I was relieved to have manoeuvred off our hellish hard standing, and as we made our way out of the campsite towards the coast road I was determined to enjoy the day and put all thoughts of parking up again out of my mind.

The B3306 is a very scenic route indeed, and as we drove slowly along we enjoyed magnificent sea glimpses over the walls and hedges in the bright sunshine. However, it was quite hilly in places and rather narrow, so I certainly couldn't afford to lose my concentration. After a mile or so, we found ourselves held up by a long procession of bicycles stretching out in front of us. It looked like a race of some kind and all the cyclists were dressed in multi-coloured skin tight Lycra cycling suits and aerodynamic helmets. They were all peddling like mad down a fairly steep hill and there was no way I could overtake. This wasn't too much of a problem, as we were in no particular hurry and slowing down to a cycling pace allowed me to appreciate the scenery that much more. I almost wished I was on a bike as well, as it would have been easy to stop as and when I wanted and admire the views, which wasn't quite so easy or practical to do in the motorhome.

After following the bicycles for a fair old way, we came to a long straight stretch in the road where they all pulled over to the left hand side and formed a single regimented line which stretched out for a hundred yards or so. Still peddling furiously, all the cyclists at the rear veered from side to side as they turned their heads to look behind them and wave me on. There was nothing coming the other way so, after checking my rear view mirrors, I eased out to the other side of the road to overtake. As we carefully passed them, Emm counted around fifty male cyclists all crouched over drop handlebars with their colourful, skin tight Lycra covered bottoms, of varying shapes and sizes, stuck high up in the air and wobbling from side to side in unison with each other. All in all, a rather spectacular sight!

Unfortunately, we all had a bit of a scare as, before I'd passed all the wobbly bottomed riders, a van headed right towards us. Luckily, its driver quickly appraised the situation and slowed down to a virtual halt, which just about allowed me to safely pass the leading cyclists before moving over to the left hand side of the road again. It was certainly not a moment to lose concentration lest we ended up with a scene reminiscent of some old silent comedy film, with fifty colourful cyclists and their expensive machines scattering and tumbling all over the road like skittles, which would have been nowhere near as funny in real life. Just a little further down the road, we saw some large vans parked by the side of the road, which obviously belonged to the cycling group, and some people who looked like they were marshalling the race. From the writing on the side of the vans, it was apparent that they were from Germany and I hoped they were enjoying their peaceful invasion of southern England.

Being on the exposed north Cornish coast, the landscape was very wild and desolate. Huge granite boulders were strewn around and there was hardly anything of significance growing there, certainly no tall trees. On a fine balmy day such as this, it seemed a bit surreal but still a pleasant place in which to drive, walk or cycle. Even though both we and the German contingent had chosen a good day to come this way, I couldn't help thinking it would be a bleak and inhospitable road to travel along during one of the frequent gales that blew in off an angry Atlantic Ocean.

About four miles out of St Ives, we reached the tiny village of Zennor on our right hand side and decided to turn off and explore for a while. There aren't that many words in the English language that begin with the last letter of the alphabet and, for that reason, words and names beginning with '*Z*' seem to have a rather special ring to them. Or should it be *zing*? Whereas the letter '*S*' is very common, '*Z*' seems to be reserved for rather special names and places, so I was ever so slightly disappointed to find out later that *Zennor* was named after a *Saint Senara* whose name starts with the most common letter in the alphabet. More of her later.

Anyhow, here we were in Zennor and I parked up facing a stone wall in one of the few remaining spaces in the small free car park. I was well aware I would have to back out again later, but didn't think that would be too much of a problem, as there was loads of space between us and the row of cars behind. Besides, I'd already had plenty of practice reversing the motorhome on this trip and Emm was on hand to direct proceedings. We locked up and decided to wander up the road a short distance to visit the 13th century church. Postcards we'd seen in St Ives depicted a rather intriguing centuries old carving of the *Mermaid of Zennor*, which was intricately carved in the end of a wooden bench in this very church. Consequently, we just had to take this opportunity to go and see this antiquity for ourselves.

Just before the church, I saw a footpath on the left hand side leading to a part of the coast path we'd never been to and I was itching to explore. However, I was outvoted by one vote to one, with Emm having the casting vote! To be fair though, it was a fair old walk to the sea and we would have needed virtually the whole day to do justice to this part of the cliff top walk. So, reluctantly I again had to concede and made a mental note to add this walk to our ever increasing list of places to go in the future.

Having gone into the church whilst Emm looked after Monty, I found it to be quite dark inside and it took me a while to find the famous bench. At first it didn't strike me as all that special and the mermaid was hard to make out. But when I considered it was around six hundred years old and thought of all the long dead people whose backsides had polished the dark and shiny seat throughout the centuries, it was pretty awe inspiring. In the dim light inside the ancient church, I could almost feel the presence of generations of ghostly worshippers who would have sat on that very seat virtually every Sunday of their comparatively short times on Earth.

Even though their lives would have been extremely hard, they would have all given thanks and been grateful for their lot. Every Sunday they would have knelt in prayer, listened to sanctimonious sermons and sang hymns of praise. They would have gathered there for happy family occasions, like marriages and christenings (in that order), as well as sad occasions like funerals, and I wondered what sort of lives they led and how different their existence would have been compared to ours.

As I said, I initially found the mermaid carving to be a bit disappointing as it wasn't easy to make out in the dark wood. However, once I'd removed my photo-chromatic spectacles, which had darkened in the bright sunshine outside, I could clearly make her out holding a round mirror in one hand and combing her long hair with the other. She'd obviously been knocked about a bit over the last six centuries, but that was to be expected and, if you ask me, anyone that old was perfectly entitled to have knocked about a bit. It amazed me she was still in the church where anyone could come and see her for free, rather than in a museum somewhere locked away from prospective vandals and thieves.

When I was a young boy in the 1950s, I was always told at my Church of England primary school that churches were never locked because they were the house of God, and that no one would ever steal from Him. There may have been some truth in that back then but, sadly, not today. Many old churches are kept locked to keep out undesirables who unfortunately wouldn't hesitate to steal or vandalise centuries old artefacts. Lowlife scumbags even steal the lead off church roofs and once it's replaced, often through the generosity of the parishioners, they often have the nerve to go back and steal it again. Yes indeed, our lives are so much different today, but it was refreshing to know that in that remote part of Cornwall, some old values still seemed to hold true.

Anyhow, I later found out the story behind the Mermaid of Zennor. Once upon a time there was a mermaid who lived in the nearby Pendour Cove, where she would listen to the Zennor church services. She became enchanted by a particular lone male voice which always sang the closing hymn. So enchanted by this alluring voice, she just had to see for herself who it belonged to. Of course, being a mermaid and having no legs, it would have been quite difficult for her to get from the cove to the church. Not only that, she realised the villagers would be somewhat disturbed to see a non-human figure joining in with their worship, so she certainly wouldn't have wanted to be recognised as a mermaid.

Nevertheless, she just had to see for herself who owned the beautiful singing voice and hatched a cunning plan. No one knows where she got it from, but legend has it that she put on a very long dress to hide her tail and then walked awkwardly to the church. (Well walking for her would have been just a bit awkward, what with having a fish's tail instead of legs). Anyhow, when she reached the church, she sat incognito in the back of the pews and saw for herself the masculine singer with the amazing voice. Having already become bewitched by his singing, now that she clapped eyes on him at long last, she became even more captivated and fell head over heels, or rather *head over tail,* in love with him.

She continued to come to every church service to see the object of her heart's desire, ogle his virile young body and marvel at his incredible singing voice. His name was Matthew Trewhella and, as well as being a pretty good singer, he was extremely good looking. The mermaid must have been quite a looker as well because, on one of her subsequent visits, their eyes met and Matthew instantly fell in love with the mysterious stranger.

However, the mermaid had a bit of a problem insomuch that, although she'd been able to leave the sea for the time it took to put on her dress, walk awkwardly to the church, listen to the singing and then get back to her home under the water, there was a limit as to how long she could remain on land and she knew that if she lingered too long she would dehydrate and die. On the day when Matthew's eyes met hers, knowing that she'd already stayed too long in the church, she started to leave and hurry back to the ocean. Matthew, however, plucked up enough courage to rush after her and ask her to stay. She insisted she had to go, and he begged her to tell him her name and where she lived.

Reluctantly, she owned up and admitted she was a mermaid who lived in the sea and had to get back there straight away, or else she would die. Presumably, this must have been a bit of a shock to the lusty young man but, being so love-struck, he told her he didn't care one jot about what she was or where she lived, and that he would follow her to the end of the earth (or even to the depths of the ocean) if only they could be together. Then, being a big strapping lad, he picked her up in his muscular arms and effortlessly carried her all the way back to the cove, where she swam back into the sea. He then followed her beneath the waves and was never seen again in the village.

That was not the end of the story, however, as some years later, a ship dropped anchor in the cove just off Zennor and the captain heard a beautiful female voice calling to him. To his utter amazement, he saw a mermaid swimming alongside his ship, who politely asked him to pull the anchor up again. She explained that it was resting on her door and preventing her from getting inside her house at the bottom of the sea, where she lived with Matthew, her husband, and their children. Another story tells that little *merboys* and *mergirls* were sometimes seen swimming in the sea just off Zennor and, even to this day, it's said that at sunset on a summer evening at Pendour Cove, Matthew can still be heard singing faintly in the summer breeze.

However, the Zennor mermaid legend is a bit confusing and it's quite difficult to know what to believe. As I previously mentioned, Zennor gets its name from St Senara who is the present day patron saint of the village. The church is still named after her and, of course, has always been the home for the centuries old bench seat with the magnificent mermaid carving. We know the mermaid, depicted in the carving, and Matthew Trewhella fell in love with each other, that he went to join her under the sea and they had a couple of *merbabies*, if not more.

At this point, however, the plot thickens somewhat and the story becomes a bit more hazy. St Senara was originally a certain Princess

Asenora of Brittany, who married a King Goello. Not much seems to be known about her for certain, but apparently she had a wicked stepmother who, jealous of her beauty and virtuous nature, falsely accused her of being unfaithful. The king must have been a bit thick and, believing the stepmother's evil lies to be the gospel truth, cruelly condemned poor innocent Asenora to death by burning, as was the law in those days. Anyhow, just before they could light the fire, they found out she was pregnant which her accusers took as further evidence of her certain guilt. Not thinking for a moment that the child could be his, the king nevertheless felt just a wee bit merciful and spared his wife the death by burning sentence. He then had her nailed inside a barrel and thrown into the sea instead!

From then on, the story gets just a little unbelievable. It's not clear as to how long she was cruelly imprisoned inside the barrel, how big it was, whether it sank to the bottom of the sea or floated on top. All we do seem to know, however, is that she was fed by an angel and gave birth to her child in the barrel, which was eventually washed up on the coast of Ireland where she raised her son. She named him Budoc (which meant the drowned one) who, as he grew up, wasn't particularly keen on the Irish.

Some years later, the evil stepmother, who'd caused all this turmoil, confessed on her death bed that she'd lied about Senora's supposed infidelity and King Goello finally accepted his wife had been faithful and that the child was his. Full of remorse (well, if he wasn't, he should have been), he somehow sent her a message begging her to return to Brittany with their child so they could all be one big happy family. Strangely enough Senora agreed and on their way back from Ireland, they stopped off in Cornwall where they founded the parishes of Zennor and Budoc (near Falmouth).

However, that's not the end of the story, as at some point Senora was supposed to have been a mermaid who then converted to Christianity. All incredible stuff and there the trail seems to go cold and much is open to speculation. Maybe she changed into a mermaid inside the barrel after it was cast into the sea. After all, how else could she have survived and given birth in such dire conditions? Was the angel who fed her, presumably on a diet of fresh fish, responsible for her metamorphosis into a mermaid and then converting her to Christianity? Did Senora and her son ever return to Brittany to reunite with her untrustworthy dim wit of a husband, King Goella? Or was she the same mermaid who fell in love with Matthew Trewhella and lived happily ever after? It all sounds a bit fishy to me and the truth seems to have been lost in the mists of time.

Anyhow, returning to present day reality, I went back outside to look after Monty whilst Emm went to see the mermaid for herself. However, she soon came back and told me she couldn't find her. I then tethered Monty to a drainpipe and accompanied her back inside to point out the ancient carving to her. However, she wasn't nearly as impressed as I had been and thought the medieval mermaid was no more than an old piece of worm eaten wood.

Some people have no imagination!

15

THE WAYSIDE MUSEUM

Having both seen the mermaid, we made our way back to the nearby Wayside Museum, which due to the prominent waterwheel by its entrance we couldn't fail to notice when we'd turned into the village. Well-behaved dogs on leads were welcome and it only cost £3 each to go in, so we decided to spend a couple of hours looking round.

At the campsite, we'd picked up a leaflet which stated that, '*The Wayside is a tranquil, some say magical, place where you can spend an enjoyable hour or two, although many visitors stay much longer.*' And that proved to be no exaggeration. Apparently, there were over 5,000 artefacts, dating from around 3000 BC to the 1950s, which all reflected the lives of the Cornish people who lived and worked in this remote and harsh area. We both found the museum to be full of interest and could easily have spent more time there than the two hours or so we did stay.

There was an extensive collection of prehistoric and Bronze Age tools, arrowheads and suchlike which, although interesting in their way, for me were rather inanimate and dull. Emm definitely doesn't enjoy peering at ancient artefacts in glass cabinets, so we didn't spend too much time looking at them. Like most people, we find more recent history to be much more fascinating, especially the 1950s when we were growing up. In any case, there are far more everyday objects from recent decades, which people can easily relate to, still around today. That's why nostalgia has become a thing of the future with museums having sprung up all over the country to fuel this interest and cash in on the past, with hardly a glass cabinet in sight.

When I was a young boy, however, I was pretty enthusiastic about prehistoric Britain right up to Roman times and always said I wanted to be an archaeologist when I grew up. I'm not really sure what happened to that ambition, but it may have had something to do with an aversion to getting my hands and nails dirty and hating being outside in the cold and wet. So, as I got older, I suppose it gradually dawned on me that being on my hands and knees for hours on end in a cold windswept part of, say, northern England in the pouring rain, carefully scraping away at the mud with a tiny fork trying to unearth some barely recognisable arrow head, or part of a Roman chamber pot, was never going to suit me after all!

Consequently, my interest in early history diminished whilst my interest in more recent social and economic history increased. Until they visit somewhere like the Wayside Museum, many people don't appreciate how much has changed in recent times to make everyday tasks so much easier than they were for our parents and grandparents, let alone people living in the 1800s, 1700s and before. Life was so much harder, especially for folks living in such out of the way places like Zennor. With no labour saving devices, very limited opportunities and certainly no holidays, just keeping a roof over their head and feeding their families was all that concerned most people. That is, unless they were the aristocracy or the super-rich landowners. They had plenty of labour saving devices, known as servants, who were paid a pittance and could be hired and fired at will. However, even though life must have been especially hard, everyone appeared to be reasonably happy with their lot and went to church every Sunday to give thanks.

A couple of hours at the Wayside Museum certainly showed us how ordinary people lived and worked in days gone by and, more interestingly, how things gradually improved for everyone. There was an extensive display of tin mining equipment which, although this industry brought wealth to the area, brought home just how hard and dangerous it was. It would have been back-breaking work and in this day and age, it seems incomprehensible that men and young boys were happy to hack their way through solid rock, then tunnel out horizontally for vast distances under the sea using nothing more than a pickaxe and temperamental explosives.

Labouring in wet, cold and pitch black conditions, with just a candle fixed with a blob of clay onto their helmet to provide the only illumination, the risks would have been enormous with high incidences of tunnels collapsing and flooding. How they managed such dangerous work is beyond our understanding these days and, just like early coal mining and working in Victorian factories, there was hardly any consideration given to the workers' health and safety. Life was cheap and, as far as the bosses were concerned, if someone was killed or injured and no longer able to work, it was just too bad. There was always someone else to take their place. Later on came the Factory Acts, but health and safety as we know it today would have been incomprehensible to those tin miners back then.

Not like today, when health and safety seems to have gone mad. Some Councils, for example, refuse to display flowers in hanging baskets lest they fall on someone's head; the consequences of conkers dropping from trees and striking unsuspecting members of the public are considered such high risk that perfectly healthy horse chestnut trees are cut down; likewise, unless children wear protective glasses, schools deny them the pleasure of playing the traditional playground game of conkers. It all sounds bonkers to me, as it does to most people of my generation.

My particular health and safety pet hate is the *Danger of Death* signs that adorn every single pole carrying electricity cables. What it cost to have millions of these labels produced and then for workmen to go round screwing them to all the poles is anyone's guess. But to me it hardly seems necessary and whether they have actually prevented one single fatality is very debatable.

In my day, we played conkers for hours on end and I don't recall one single accident. We never doubted that the hanging baskets had been firmly screwed to the wall, and even though we loved climbing trees, we all knew that if we were stupid enough to climb an electricity pole we could get electrocuted. So we didn't do it! It seems to me that the people who actually make these decisions are over cautious basket cases and it's the tax payers and council tax payers who are being screwed.

Looking back at our childhood in the 1950s and early 1960s, we had far more freedom than children today. We learnt to take risks, got loads of exercise and were free to explore far and wide into the countryside. Today's youngsters just don't have that freedom. It's not only that parents fear their children will have an accident, be molested or murdered – and the media has a lot to do with that fear – but also the health and safety brigade have gone well over the top. Also, there is the attitude that every single accident has to be somebody's fault and therefore some individual or organisation has to be found to be culpable and made to pay.

In days gone by tin miners, coal miners, factory and farm workers faced very real dangers every single day of their working lives with hardly any monetary reward. As far as the mine owners, factory owners and landowners were concerned, labour was cheap as well as expendable, and if anyone was brave or stupid enough to complain they could instantly lose their job and be evicted from their tied cottage! So they just couldn't afford to question their working conditions or ask for a pay rise. In the main they were so very humble and grateful to actually have a job at all, no matter how dangerous, and were content to be able to earn a regular wage, no matter how small. Of course, in those days workers deserved far, far more protection than they could have ever hoped to get, and what they would have thought of the modern day compensation culture is totally beyond me.

Nobody could argue that health and safety is not a good thing these days. But maybe, just maybe, it's gone a little too far the other way. Over the last century or so vast improvements have, quite rightly, been made so that everyone can go about their work and daily lives in maximum safety. But how can working in a flooded mineshaft with a high risk of a life threatening accident occurring, for example, be anywhere near comparable to the remote possibility of a hanging basket full of summer flowers crashing down onto an unsuspecting member of the public and causing a serious injury?

Anyhow, I'd better get off my soapbox and return to the museum. Tin mining was only one of the themes depicted. In all, there were twelve themed areas to look at, including displays of blacksmith's, wheelwright's and carpenter's tools, all set out in living workshops. There were also displays of shops and other buildings including a cobblers, a mill with original machinery, the old school and waterwheels from the Cornish mining industry, all of which were well set out with plenty of easy to read information. Even Emm, who usually rushes round museums so she can get to the gift shop as soon as possible, was impressed and took her time soaking up the atmosphere of how ordinary people lived and worked in this remote area.

As I mentioned before, it was the extensive displays from the 1950s which especially took my interest, and looking around the old school room took me back to my Church of England infants and primary schools in Fleet, Hampshire. The small individual wooden desks with their inkwells, carved initials of former pupils and lift-up lids, were very similar to ones I sat at in the 1950s learning joined-up writing with a nibbed pen and ink. I wondered what became of all the Cornish children who once sat at these desks and what sort of lives they led when they left school at the age of fourteen or even younger. No doubt most of the boys worked in the nearby tin mines or went to sea, and the girls got married and had loads of children.

I also wondered what happened to most of my old school compatriots who, like me, had higher aspirations than the girls and boys who sat at the desks in the museum. I smiled to myself as I remembered fixing pen nibs to the front of paper aeroplanes and flying them around unsupervised classrooms. Having the slight weight of the pen nib added a bit of aerodynamic stabilisation and, if thrown hard enough, they would zoom across the room and stick, dart-like, in the blackboard or an upturned desk lid. Although we'd never heard of the words *health and safety*, we knew we could be caned if unlucky enough to be caught by a teacher. We were even luckier that no nibbed paper aeroplanes ever flew into anyone's eye!

The ancient cast iron coke-fired boiler in the museum school room was just like the ones which provided the only heating in my old classrooms. During the cold winters they were constantly fed with coke from tall galvanised iron containers which, in turn, had to be kept topped up with coke from the store at the far end of the playground. Sometimes too much coke would be put on and the fire would roar away, the black cast iron would glow red hot and everyone would swelter in the excessive heat.

I remembered the day a friend did something to annoy a teacher – I think it was to punish him for his consistently bad handwriting – and he was told to stand in the corner facing the wall by the stove. He didn't have to wear a dunce's cap, but no doubt if we'd been a generation earlier he almost certainly would have been humiliated in that way as well. Anyhow, he stood by the hot boiler for almost the whole lesson and certainly wouldn't have been very comfortable in the heat. Later in the day, he got his own back by putting an elastic band on the top of the hot boiler. The rubber began to sizzle and melt giving off the most obnoxious fumes which, as soon as I saw the fireplace in the museum classroom, I imagined I could still smell. I'm not sure now whether the teacher ever found out who was responsible but seem to recall that, much to our delight, all the doors and windows had to be opened to dispel the fumes and, best of all, the lesson had to be abandoned early.

I can't imagine how exposed solid fuel boilers in classrooms full of young children would fit in with today's health and safety regulations. I'm sure there was a fire guard around them, but in any case we all knew they were hot and we'd get burnt if we got too close. I can't recall any accidents, but in those days everyone had a real coal or coke fire at home and from an early age I think we were all aware of the dangers.

Another display, which especially took my eye, was of pre-electricity clothes washing equipment and early washing machines, and when I saw the old gas boiler I couldn't help thinking of my mother's washdays. She would have to get a similar cylindrical contraption, which we always called a *copper*, out of the shed, lift it over the back door step and drag it next to our old ceramic kitchen sink. It seemed to weigh a ton and, being more than a metre high and about half as much in diameter, not that easy to manhandle.

Built into the underneath of the copper was a large rusty looking gas ring, which she'd have to connect to a gas tap in the corner of our kitchen via a perished rubber hose. She would then pour five or six bucketfuls of water into the tub before turning on the gas tap and lighting the gas ring with a match.

This was never easy as my mother had to get on her hands and knees to reach the burner and invariably the match would go out. So she would have to strike another, and possibly another. Meanwhile the space beneath the boiler would fill up with gas and when it did eventually light there was often a minor explosion. Thinking back, having a gas tap in the kitchen at floor level where inquisitive toddlers could easily turn it on, as well as a great big temperamental gas ring to light, was genuinely dodgy and a *real* health and safety issue.

However, people in those days were a far more hardy lot than we are today and didn't worry too much about the hazards of lighting the gas. Perhaps that was because once it was lit and the ten gallons or so of water eventually reached boiling point, adding the washing soap and dropping a full load of dirty washing into this boiling, frothing mass required maximum concentration lest one's arms got scalded.

Whilst the clothes, sheets and pillow cases were left to boil for twenty minutes or so, the whole house would fill with steam as well as the combined smell of Fairy soap, human sweat and coal gas. During the boiling process the contents of the copper had to be agitated with a washing dolly, consisting of a large wooden handle with either an inverted copper dish shaped device or three wooden prongs attached to one end, which was pushed into the frothing, cauldron of boiling water to move the dirty washing around and agitate it in much the same way as a modern washing machine does.

My mother never had a proper dolly and made do with an old broom handle to do the job. She also never owned any wooden washing tongs which were specifically designed to lift the scalding washing out of the cauldron. So she improvised and, after turning off the gas, would use the broom handle to lift the heavy, dripping, steamy washing out of the boiling water into the sink where she rinsed it under the cold tap. The washing would then have to be carried outside and squeezed out through our old mangle, of which there were many fine examples in the museum.

I remember we had a very heavy, cast-iron contraption which was kept in the shed, but dragged out onto the lawn on wash day. It had a pair of adjustable wooden rollers which, when a large handle was turned, were driven through a cast iron gearing mechanism so they would rotate. The wringing wet and heavy clothes would be passed through the rollers and most of the excess water would be squeezed out, or *mangled*. The clothes would be mangled several times, with the rollers being adjusted closer together by turning a large screw on the top, thereby causing more and more water to be squeezed out. When I was a bit older I would have to help and woe betide me if I ever dropped any of the freshly washed sheets, or whatever, onto the wet muddy grass!

We did eventually get rid of the ancient cast iron mangle and replaced it with a brand new *ACME Wringer*. This was a much lighter portable contraption which could be clamped onto a table top, and was made of white painted steel with lightweight rubber rollers. It also had a much simpler adjusting mechanism, which was just twisted one way to bring the rollers closer together and the other way to move them further apart. I must have been a bit of a masochist (or just plain stupid), as I sometimes used to see how far I could pass my small fingers through the rollers before I could bear the pain no longer; the secret being to make sure the rollers were spaced as far apart as possible.

After we got the *ACME*, I don't think we called it *mangling* anymore and referred to *wringing out* the wet washing instead. Even so, whether *wringing out* or *mangling*, it still then had to be pegged out on the washing line to dry in the wind and the sun. Ours stretched the complete length of our large back garden and in sunny weather it was never a problem to get everything dry. However, in the winter or when it was wet all the clothes would be brought inside and hung up on a variety of wooden clothes horses and put in front of the coke boiler or the coal fire to dry. This was fine for the clothes, but not that pleasant for us as, in those pre-central heating days, the wet clothes shielded us from our only source of heat and we would have to put on extra woolly jumpers to keep warm.

After hanging everything out to dry, the dirty water had cooled down a bit and then had to be emptied out of the copper. There was no easy way to do this and my mother would scoop it out into the sink with a saucepan (probably the same one she used to boil the potatoes and cabbage!). Finally, when the copper itself had cooled down enough to touch, it would be manhandled back to the shed where it would stay until the following washday, which was always Mondays.

As I stood by some of these laundry exhibits in the museum and remembered my mother slaving away in the heat and the steamy atmosphere, the old familiar washday smell seemed to fill my nostrils again. And for a moment I imagined my glasses were steaming up.

Apart from stirring up these childhood memories, seeing the museum's extensive collection of washing implements made me realise just how much washday has changed in such a relatively short space of time. Whereas not so long ago my mother, Emm's mother and millions of women like them endured hours of physical hard work doing the weekly wash, these days virtually all that needs to be done is put a bundle of dirty clothes into a combined washing/drying machine and press a button. Then, after putting one's feet up for an hour or two, just empty the clean, fresh smelling and dry washing out of the machine and put it away, with hardly a puff of steam in sight. Also, of course, now that washing is so much easier, our clothes are washed much more often than they were back in the 1950s and 60s. We also change our socks and underwear every day, and not just once a week!

Sometimes, Emm has a little moan about having to wash my smelly squash gear. I do try to play at least two matches a week and appreciate that my sweat soaked socks, shirts and shorts can hum a bit, especially if they're left languishing in the laundry basket for a few days prior to getting washed. If she had to stand over a boiling copper all day I could understand it being a major problem. But, even so, I'd be pushing my luck if I dared to point out that she only has to chuck it in the machine and press a button, and should think herself lucky she doesn't have to cope with washdays like our mothers had to!

Anyhow, after we'd seen all the exhibits, we took a short walk in the sunshine around the garden which was packed full of interest, both in the planting and additional artefacts on show. We thoroughly enjoyed the Wayside Museum, which was excellent value for money and would highly recommend a visit to anyone passing that way. The fact that Monty was allowed in with us was a great help, as we could take our time and not worry about leaving him in the motorhome or, alternatively, take it in turns to look around.[16]

When we got back to the car park eager to move on to Land's End, we found a flashy, red sports car parked right behind our motorhome and, until it was moved, we could go nowhere. I was dumfounded, as well as annoyed, that anyone could be so arrogant enough to park in such an irresponsible and selfish manner, especially as there were plenty of legal parking spaces on the side of the road. There was no sign of its driver and I wondered whether I could muster up a few hefty helpers from the museum and literally manhandle the small car out the way.

I was still pondering what to do when a young man, a *Hooray Henry* type, and a rather over made-up young lady, who was tottering along in a pair of high heels, appeared from the direction of the church and I asked if they knew who owned the car that was blocking us in. Henry or whatever his name was – *Dick Head* would have been

---

16 I noticed that, almost two years later, the museum's website now states that *only guide dogs are allowed* and assume that some irresponsible dog owners allowed their dogs to misbehave in some way.

appropriate – looked at me down the end of his snooty nose and admitted it was his. Then, in a very condescending voice, he asked if I would like it moved.

At times like these many people, me included, don't always say what they really mean. I wanted to use a few choice words like *pompous, inconsiderate* and *idiot*, for example. But those were nothing like the words that actually came out of my mouth, as I heard myself politely say that we'd only just got back and it was no problem.

Without another word, he swaggered over to his expensive sports car, started the engine and disturbed the peace for miles around with his excessively loud exhaust as he roared, rather than moved, out of the way. We were no longer blocked in, but I still needed to be extra careful not to hit our *friend's* phallic symbol of a car which he'd now parked to one side of the motorhome, ready to move into our space when we left. Luckily I'd had enough practice by now and with Emm's help managed to expertly back up and move out of the car park like I'd been driving the motorhome for years.

Muttering under my breath, we were then on our way again. But I wondered what would have happened if we'd got back to the motorhome thirty minutes or so earlier and *Hooray Henry* and *Henrietta* were nowhere to be found?

16

WRECKED OFF LAND'S END

As we slowly carried on towards Land's End the scenery became more and more barren and, as we virtually had the road to ourselves, we could admire the bleak but beautiful scenery with occasional distant sea glimpses. We were lucky it was such a fine sunny day with only the slightest hint of a breeze, which we knew wasn't often the case in this part of the world. The small number of stunted bushes, struggling to grow in the harsh rocky landscape, all leaned markedly in the direction of the strong prevailing winds which blew in off the Atlantic and made it impossible for any significant vegetation to thrive.

Suddenly a tall cylindrical brick chimney loomed up out of the treeless terrain ahead, and as we approached I slowed to a snail's pace to get a better look. It was joined to an imposing wall, which was virtually all that was left of one of a pair of derelict, three storey stone buildings. However, the adjacent building had fared rather better and all four walls were still proudly standing, albeit the roof had long since collapsed. I later discovered they were engine houses belonging to the old Carn Galver Tin Mine, which closed down well over a hundred years ago. Both buildings were an imposing monument to the area's proud mining heritage and I was tempted to stop and have a closer look. However, as we'd spent far more time in Zennor than originally planned and wanted to get to Land's End, I only pulled over very briefly and, without getting out of the motorhome, just took a quick photograph.

I realised we were well and truly in the heart of the old Cornish tin mining country when, a bit further down the road, we saw signposts to both the Levant Mine and Beam Engine (National Trust) and the Geevor Tin Mine. We could just about see them in the distance by the coast and, having found out so much about this dangerous occupation at the Wayside Museum, I would have loved to visit these modern day tourist attractions to discover more. However, once again, I had to accept we couldn't do everything and concede that these visits would have to wait until another time. We both really wanted to push on, and it didn't take us much longer to complete our scenic drive and find ourselves in the large car park at Land's End where we'd been several times before.

We first went there together in August 1971, having driven all the way down to Cornwall in our old Fiat 850 for a week's camping holiday. Although we did enjoy some fine weather, the wet and windy days outnumbered the sunny ones and the day we went to Land's End was particularly foul. However, unable to think of anything else to do and because we were so close to the end of the land, we just had to go there. On arrival, we paid what we thought was an over inflated price for parking the car, then braced ourselves against the incessant rain and howling wind as we set off to explore England's most westerly point.

Although we knew it was scenic, we couldn't see much of it through the dark, low clouds and driving, horizontal rain. The wind forced us to bend double and lean over in a similar manner to the diminutive shrubs we passed on the way, and our eyes were permanently screwed up to protect them from the huge raindrops, which almost felt as though they were machine gun bullets smacking into our faces. Fair enough, even with our hands cupped over our eyes to fend off the blinding rain, the scene below us with the powerful waves battering the rocks was indeed spectacular. But it wasn't a place to hang around for too long, and certainly not when the weather was as foul as it was that day.

Back then there wasn't all that much for visitors to do anywhere in Cornwall during the frequent inclement weather, and Land's End was no exception. After getting a thorough soaking looking out to sea we would have gone to the *First and Last House Gift Shop*, bought a postcard to send home and then seen the famous privately owned signpost (more of that later). And that was about it really, apart from a small suspension bridge across a small ravine, which we remembered walking over. However, over the years the tourist industry has really taken off, and as well as being drawn to Cornwall for the beautiful scenery today's visitors have many more attractions and places of interest to keep them amused. Consequently, even on the frequent wet days there's always something to do.

We remembered going back to Land's End again, this time with the girls, on a reasonably fine day sometime in the early 1990s when we were staying in a caravan at Kennack Sands. Peter de Savary, a businessman and successful entrepreneur, had acquired Land's End and ploughed a great deal of money into developing it for tourism. As well as improving the hotel complex he'd built a couple of new buildings, one to house the new exhibitions he introduced and the other, an arched building at the entrance to the site, to house all the various administration offices.

Mindful of the environment, he called upon the expertise of Dr. David Bellamy to advise on the conservation of the area, in particular on how to regain and preserve the greenery and wildlife. As a result, some footpaths were tarmacked to encourage visitors not to wander all over the cliffs, thereby reducing erosion and allowing the majority of the cliff tops to return to their natural state. De Savary obviously had to finance this somehow, so he introduced shops, restaurants and various attractions, both indoors and out, which encouraged visitors to come for the whole day and spend their money.

He was very interested in the history of the area and particularly the legends of King Arthur and the Lost Land of Lyonesse which, according to legend, is a sort of Atlantis that lies beneath the sea off Land's End and is said by some to be the lost Camelot of King Arthur. De Savary chose this to be the theme for his main tourist attraction, known as *The Lost Labyrinth*, which we took the girls to see and very good it was too. The legend is dramatically depicted in a multi-sensory theatre show, which also includes true smuggling and shipwreck stories associated with Land's End.

As I'd once worked on Sea King helicopters, the part of the show that particularly made an impression on me replicated the dramatic rescue of scores of yachtsmen during the fateful Fastnet race of August 1979. Over three hundred yachts were taking part in the race when freak storms blew up in the Irish Sea. Rescuers from both sides of the water, including a Dutch warship, French trawlers and helicopters from RNAS *Culdrose* came to their rescue in the largest peacetime rescue operation in horrendous conditions.

Many sailors were successfully rescued, but the fearful storm took its toll with twenty-five yachts sunk or disabled and fifteen lives tragically lost. As we stood in the packed auditorium, the deafening sound effects of the violent storms were very realistic and culminated with a Royal Navy Sea King search and rescue helicopter apparently hovering noisily overhead to dramatically winch survivors up from the raging sea.

Many people were not endeared to this development of Land's End, but I think it's been tastefully done. After all, thousands of people would visit and find, as we once did, that there wasn't that much to do when they got there. That is, apart from having a photograph taken by a signpost, buying a cheap souvenir in the gift shop or exploring the coast path, which isn't much fun for families in the usual Cornish weather and, in any case, not possible for the less able bodied. Now, whole families can go to Land's End for a complete and enjoyable day out, which makes the car parking fee worthwhile.

Fair enough, the attractions still have to be paid for, but they cost no more than similar ones and, what with the retail outlets for local businesses and craftsmen, the development has created much needed jobs. In any case, if people solely want to walk the coast path they only have to pay for car parking, which I'm sure is cheaper now than before the site was expanded. They are then free to wander through the tourist traps and beyond to join the coast path where the development is soon out of sight, which was just what we intended to do.

In 1996, De Savary sold the site to a company called *Heritage Attractions Ltd*, which also owns other controversial UK attractions, such as *The Needles Park* on The Isle of Wight, *Snowdon Mountain Railway, Lightwater Valley Theme Park* and, appropriately, *John o' Groats* which, for good or bad, have all been similarly further developed for tourism.

Anyhow, today the weather was unbelievably warm and totally different from our wet and windy visit in the early 1970s, so we were looking forward to seeing Land's End at its very best. After parking up, we quickly made our way through the modern attractions and headed towards the much photographed Land's End signpost, where we watched various people having their picture taken.

The signpost is not real, but part of a family photography business dating back to the 1950s. It shows that the distance to New York is 3147 miles; to John o' Groats 874 miles; to The Isles of Scilly 28 miles, and to the nearby Longships Lighthouse just 1½ miles. There is also a blank "arm" on the signpost, into which the photographer can slide an assortment of letters and numbers to make up his customers' home town and distance from Land's End, thus providing a unique photographic memento of their visit.

If the customer lives in the UK, then I guess the signpost will always point in the general direction of everyone's home town, or at least to the only road that leads there. However if someone from America, for example, wants to take home a souvenir photograph, I'm not sure if the signpost can be adjusted accordingly.

Many people don't realise the signpost is a commercial enterprise and think it's a real one that's been hijacked for profiteering. They feel exploited having to pay for a photograph standing by it (it cost £9.50 when we were there and I believe the price has gone up since then) and can't understand why the legal owners get agitated when they pose there to have pictures taken with their own cameras. Even so, I couldn't help feeling that far more people would invest in a legitimate souvenir photograph if it was a bit cheaper.

Anyhow, as we then made our way to the land's end, just like we'd done all those years before, I was disappointed to see that the suspension bridge was now blocked off at each end by a high wire fence and locked steel gates. This was a pity, as I'd enjoyed walking along the rickety bridge back in the early 1970s, but with today's health and safety regulations I wasn't surprised. (I seem to remember we walked over it when we came with the girls in the 1990s, but can't be sure.)

We carried on to the First and Last House, where Emm stood outside just long enough for me to take a photograph of her. Of course, there was no stopping her from then disappearing inside to inspect all the souvenirs. I was itching to get away from the tourist traps to explore the coast path, and when she emerged I managed to gently guide her away to the same spot on the cliff edge where we'd stood together in such contrasting weather conditions all those years ago.

Today the views were truly spectacular with the blue sparkling sea gently lapping, rather than roaring and crashing, against the granite rocks and cliff faces. There wasn't a cloud in the sky and only the gentlest southerly breeze. We felt exhilarated and comfortable in short sleeves with the balmy sunshine warming our faces and bare arms, and took our time marvelling at this amazing scene, which was a far, far cry from when we huddled together there in the early 1970s in gale force winds and driving rain.

Over to our right, towards Sennen Cove, we were shocked to see the rusting wreck of a huge ship resting at the bottom of the cliff. The wreckage looked fairly recent and a massive part of the vessel – I think it was the stern – was lying on the rocks with vast amounts of metal debris strewn all around it. We'd never seen anything like it before and learned from a nearby information board that it was the wreck of a German ship, the *RMS Mülheim*, which was driven onto the rocks on 22nd March 2003.[17] It was carrying over two thousand tons of scrap

---

17   Later on I found out that the cause of the shipwreck was rather bizarre. The ship ran aground in the early hours during which time there was "moderate visibility and fog patches". On investigation it transpired that the chief officer, who had been on watch at the time, caught his trousers in the lever of his chair when trying to get up, which caused him to fall and be rendered unconscious. By the time he regained consciousness, *RMS Mülheim* was already bearing down on the shoreline with disastrous consequences!

car plastic destined for a landfill site in Germany and hundreds of tons of it escaped into the sea to be found in fishing nets and washed up on local beaches. As plastic doesn't break down naturally, it will pollute the environment for an incomprehensible amount of time, which is a thoroughly depressing thought.

The information went on to say that plastic waste, raw sewage and chemicals are all types of marine pollution that threaten life around our coasts, and that a staggering *four hundred million gallons of sewage and toxic waste are discharged into UK coastal waters every single day!*

This was indeed dismal reading and we wondered how long mankind could go on polluting our beautiful planet in this manner. On such a calm and sunny day, the sight of the wreck was a powerful image and a harsh reminder of the power of the sea and man's abuse of our planet. Consequently, it was with heavy hearts that we carried on towards Sennen Cove.

When we looked back, the tourist complex was hidden from view and all we could see was a wild and desolate landscape with huge granite rocks strewn amongst low lying vegetation. As we got closer to the shipwreck, seeing the sheer size of the pulverised vessel with all its wreckage spewed out over the rocks below us, we realised the sea must have been extremely powerful when the RMS *Mülheim* met its sad end. In today's calm and peaceful conditions, it was difficult to imagine how the sea could have possibly been whipped up into such a frenzy to reduce the enormous metal vessel to what we witnessed below us. But we couldn't ignore the evidence of our own eyes, especially as we remembered how wild the sea was the first time we stood together near this spot. As we got closer still, it was even more surreal and difficult to comprehend the sheer magnitude of the wreckage at the bottom of the cliffs, and I wondered how long it would take the sea to completely destroy it. Unfortunately, I imagine it will remain there for many decades to come as a permanent reminder of the power of the sea in these waters, as well as a tourist attraction.

As we got nearer to Sennen, the views in that direction weren't bad either. Of course, I would have liked to have gone further, but we couldn't do everything so we turned around and made our way back to Land's End where Emm wanted to look in a couple of the tourist shops before finally calling it a day. After I prised her away and led her back to the car park, we saw a couple of large German coaches that were towing special trailers. They were surrounded by dozens of multi-coloured Lycra covered cyclists, whom we presumed were the same ones we'd overtaken earlier, all loading their expensive looking racing bicycles onto the trailers.

Back inside the motorhome, we watched them finish loading their bikes with military precision and then line up to climb aboard the coaches in a very orderly and precise fashion. This surprised me somewhat, as most of the stereotype German tourists we've met on European coach holidays have just pushed and shoved everyone else out of the way in their mad rush to be first on board the boat, the coach or get to the front of the queue for the toilets, for example. Maybe this was a military group, who had far more self-discipline than their civilian tourist countrymen and women!

Anyhow, they all looked pretty tired, which wasn't that surprising considering they'd been out in the hot sunshine pedalling up and down hilly roads in their Lycra cycling suits. No doubt they would all enjoy a few steins of cold lager later on.

17

THE MARVELLOUS
MINACK THEATRE

I wouldn't have minded a beer myself, but as I was driving I had to make do with a freshly brewed cup of tea, which went down really well. It was still only mid-afternoon, and after our cuppa we decided to drive the few miles to Porthcurno to visit the extraordinary Minack open air theatre, which we knew was open to the public during the daytime when performances weren't taking place.

It really is amazing how an outdoor theatre can thrive in such an out of the way part of Cornwall, but thrive it does and has done since before the Second World War. It's totally unique, having been literally carved out of granite rock in the cliff top high above the Atlantic Ocean, and almost looks like an ancient Roman amphitheatre. Incredibly, since the 1930s to the present day and pausing only because of the insane territorial ambitions of a certain Adolf Hitler and his evil cronies, sell out performances of all kinds of theatrical productions have taken place there in all weathers.

I'd never heard of the place until Emm mentioned it during our Cornish camping holiday in 1971. I'm not sure how she knew about it, but whilst camping in a nearby field we took the opportunity to go there and see a play called *The Net*. When we booked the tickets on the afternoon of the performance, the weather was warm, dry and sunny. However, when we went back in the evening it had already turned much cooler and, although we were wearing thick jumpers and anoraks, we soon realised we were never going to be warm enough to sit on a cliff top at that time of night and watch a play in the open air.

We sat on hard concrete seats and there was a cold sea breeze blowing in right off the Atlantic Ocean. It wasn't too bad when we first sat down for the seven thirty curtain up (there wasn't actually a curtain, but you know what I mean), but as the evening temperature plummeted we soon felt pretty darn cold. It was just about bearable for the first half hour, but after the sun went down and the evening wore on we felt more and more frozen.

To make matters worse, sitting on the cold concrete seats, our backsides started to get increasingly more uncomfortable and, as we shifted our weight from one cheek to the other, we painfully realised why virtually everyone else had brought thick cushions with them. Then, to add to our misery, squally showers soaked us during the second half and we reached a point where we just wanted the play to end so we could leave and get warm again.

Although I can't remember much about the play now it involved some sort of sea creatures, and the backdrop of the rough Atlantic Ocean was very dramatic with the characters seemingly appearing from the sea and then disappearing back into it. I do remember, however, that although we weren't as warm and comfortable as we would have liked, we felt sorry for the performers who must have been covered in goose pimples in their scanty costumes.

By the end of the play, the cold and wet had penetrated right through to our bones and we felt as though we could be suffering from hypothermia. We made a dash for our car, turned the heater full on and couldn't wait to get back to our small tent so we could cuddle up in our sleeping bags and do everything possible to warm each other up.

Today it couldn't have been more different. The sun's balmy rays beat down on us with the temperature somewhere near the mid-twenties and we were dressed in light summer clothes. Unfortunately though, in our eagerness to get there, we somehow took a wrong turning and ended up in the car park at the Portcurno Telegraph Museum (another place I would have loved to have visited) instead of the Minack Theatre. However, rather than find our way back along the minor roads to the correct car park, we decided to leave the motorhome where it was and walk the short distance to the theatre.

We made our way along a lovely sandy footpath, past a lifesavers' hut and across Porthcurno Beach which was quite stunning in the glorious sunshine. The sands were golden, the sky was blue and the turquoise sea was shimmering in the afternoon sun. Even though it was September, there were scores of people making the most of the late summer weather sunbathing and splashing about in the clear sea water. It was just like a scene from an upmarket Mediterranean resort and I again wondered why we go abroad when we live in such a beautiful country. I then did a reality check and admitted to myself that today's weather was the best we'd ever experienced in Cornwall. It was truly exceptional, and when I remembered how cold and miserable it was when we last came to Minack it was clear why so many people do forsake our own country to holiday abroad.

It was so hot that Emm couldn't resist removing her socks and shoes and heading off towards the sea for a paddle. I'm afraid I'm a bit of a wimp when it comes to exposing my feet to sea water and didn't join her. It's not the actual paddling I dislike, but having to put my socks and shoes back on wet, sand covered feet. No matter what I do, I can never get the stuff off and find it so uncomfortable walking around with abrasive sand stuck between my toes. Of course Emm eggs me on and sometimes, just to humour her, I succumb, but only if I know I'll be able to wash and dry my feet properly afterwards.

Whilst Emm was dipping her feet in the ocean, I had a sudden feeling that dogs were probably not allowed on the beach and didn't want to draw attention to Monty by taking him down to the water's edge. We hadn't seen a notice but I became aware there were no other dogs around, and as it was such a fine sandy beach thought it was almost certainly meant to be dog free until at least the end of September. There wasn't time to go back to the motorhome and drive around to the theatre car park, so I thought that now we'd got this far we might as well carry on and, if challenged, plead ignorance. After all, I always carried a good supply of plastic bags with me and if the need arose would obviously clear up any mess. Consequently, in order to keep as low a profile as possible, I kept Monty close to the bottom of the cliff edge and urged Emm to hurry up.

She kept goading me to take off my shoes and socks and join her in the water, which I must admit was tempting, but I just wanted to climb the cliff path and see the Minack Theatre without further delay. We were some distance away from each other and it was difficult to communicate without drawing unwanted attention to Monty and myself. Blissful in her ignorance about us probably being on a dog prohibited beach, she kept waving and hollering at me not to be so wimpish and to bring Monty and join her in the shallow warm water.

I couldn't very well shout back at the top of my voice that I didn't think dogs were allowed, and tried to use hand signals to tell her to get a move on. Of course, the more I waved and tried to hurry her up, the more she took her time and the more attention I drew to myself.

Finally, rather disgusted that I'd refused to paddle, she gave up on me and emerged from the sea. She then walked over to a rock, where she plonked herself down and did her best to brush as much sand off her feet as she could. This was no mean feat, as the sand seemed to be of the stickiest kind imaginable and countless grains of the stuff were firmly stuck between her toes. As she wiped off as much of the beach as possible and shook her feet around in the air in an effort to get them dry, I knew I was in her bad books and tried to remain as patient as possible. At last she put her socks and shoes back on and, not before time, we were ready to climb the path to the top of the cliff where the Minack Theatre awaited us.

I decided not to mention my suspicion that dogs were banned from the beach. After all, we were virtually there and I didn't want to worry her about it in case she insisted I carry Monty all the way back to the motorhome and drive round to the theatre car park. Time was getting on and I was impatient to get there without further ado.

The path was pretty steep and a bit scary in places and I was mindful about Emm's dislike of heights. However, as long as she didn't look down she was fine and Monty obviously enjoyed it as he bounded up the sharp incline and stone steps, pulling me behind him on his lead. As we paused to look at the truly magnificent scenery, I couldn't help wondering who'd actually built the steps that were set into the solid rock in places. Thinking I'd never know the answer, we completed our exhilarating climb and arrived at the very top of the cliff where we found ourselves in the car park right outside the theatre entrance.

It seemed very different from how we remembered it on our last visit thirty-five years previously. For a start, the modern looking exhibition centre looked relatively new and we were sure the tarmac car park, with marked out parking bays, was no more than a piece of waste ground way back then. We remarked to ourselves that a lot can happen in thirty five-years, which it obviously had, and we wondered where all the time had gone.

We were pleasantly surprised that dogs on leads were welcome in both the amphitheatre itself and the exhibition centre, aptly called *The Rowena Cade Exhibition Centre* after the extraordinary lady who created the unique theatre in the cliff face below us. This was an unexpected bonus, as we could both go in together and not have to limit our time taking turns.

We paid our entrance fee, but before we could go on in had to wait for about ten minutes until the matinee audience left. They were all smiling and talking excitedly and appeared as though they'd thoroughly enjoyed the performance of *Macbeth*. Sitting in the strong afternoon sunshine, they certainly would have been a lot warmer than we were whilst shivering in the cold watching *The Net*. When the doors eventually opened, we went inside, and by looking at the wealth of photographs, models and audio-visual displays we found out for ourselves how the remarkable Rowena Cade created her unique open air theatre on this isolated Cornish cliff top.

Miss Cade was born in 1893 and died in 1983, so it's quite possible we may have seen her at some point during the performance we saw in 1971. Her family originated from Derbyshire where her father owned a cotton mill. But in 1906 when her father retired, presumably having made a comparative fortune, the family settled in Cheltenham where they apparently lived a genteel life.

However, this was rudely interrupted by the First World War and Miss Cade left her mother and father to work in stables on an estate at Elsenham, some miles south of Cambridge. Whilst there, she lived in an old shepherd's caravan and was responsible for selecting and breaking horses which were then sent out to the front lines in France and Belgium, where almost all of them would have met a sickening and bloody end.

After the war, her father had died so her mother sold the house in Cheltenham and decided to settle in Cornwall, where she rented a house at Lamorna. Miss Cade returned to live with her mother and apparently fell in love with the nearby Minack headland, which she immediately decided to buy for the princely sum of £100. She must have been quite a wealthy lady as on this land, using granite from the nearby quarry, she promptly had a house built for herself and her mother. A short time later, she had it extended to accommodate her sister and family who returned from Australia where they'd been living for some years.

In those days, there was hardly any organised entertainment in that remote part of the country and people had to provide their own recreation. Right from when she was a child, Miss Cade had always been interested in the theatre and many local productions took place in her garden. Her special talent lay in costume design and the subsequent making of them for her family and friends. In 1929 a far more ambitious production of *A Midsummer Night's Dream* was staged in a meadow a mile or so away from her house, and Miss Cade took on the role of wardrobe mistress. She worked very hard behind the scenes to design and make many of the props and costumes and, even though another year's growth meant many of the children had difficulty squeezing into their original costumes, the play went down so well that it was repeated to great acclaim the following year.

Flushed with success, the group were keen to perform again and decided on another Shakespeare favourite, *The Tempest*. Someone then suggested that the rugged coastline in Miss Cade's garden would provide a far better backdrop for this play than the meadow. However, as there was nowhere in her garden suitable to seat an audience, she wasn't convinced. Consequently she looked for an alternative setting and came up with the most outrageous venue for a stage right on the edge of the cliffs overlooking the sea. She must have had great imagination and incredible vision to even consider that a stage and suitable seating could be created there, and many people must have thought she was mad.

Then aged thirty-eight, it took her and her two gardeners, Billy Rawlings and Thomas Angove, the whole winter of 1931–32 to literally carve some simple seating and a stage out of the solid rock. Having sat there in 1971 and experienced the intense cold, I fully appreciated how difficult it must have been to labour in such an exposed position, high up on the cliff face during the winter months, with a sheer drop into the Atlantic Ocean below them. Although the hardest physical work Miss Cade had done before was mucking out horses, she did far more than her fair share of the manual toil and proved herself to be far different from the usual well off and genteel ladies of that time. The three of them somehow transformed piles of boulders into granite blocks which they slowly inched into place entirely by hand. Terraces were created which they filled in with earth and small stones, all of which had to be shovelled down from the upper slopes. It must have been back breaking work, but in August 1932 the perfect stage was eventually set for *The Tempest*.

After collecting their tickets at a table in the garden, the expectant audience made their way in the moonlight down a gorse-lined track to the stage, which was illuminated by some car headlights and an assortment of battery powered lights. As they took their seats for the first performance in the new theatre, Miss Cade and her helpers must have experienced all sorts of emotions, ranging from excitement to nervousness and extreme trepidation. But, of course, any doubts were proved resoundingly wrong and the production of *The Tempest*, staged high up on the cliffs, was an outstanding success. The unique performance was even mentioned in *The Times* which, to my mind, considering Cornwall's relative isolation from London in those days, must have been quite remarkable. And that was the beginning of the marvellous Minack Theatre.

Miss Cade must have realised she'd started something very special indeed and, whether she knew it at the time or not, her *hobby* become her life's work from then on. She spent the next seven years or so making many more improvements and, at the same time, further plays were put on each summer, including lavish productions of *Twelfth Night, Anthony and Cleopatra,* and *The Count of Monte Cristo.*

With the outbreak of the Second World War, her endeavours were forced to an abrupt end when the army moved in to clear the site for coastal defensive purposes. A gun post was built and barbed wire entanglements placed all around. Even so, Miss Cade still managed to regularly crawl under the wire to cut the grass and it's a good job the Germans never invaded when she was the wrong side of the wire! After the war, much damage had been done to her *pride and joy,* but she remained unperturbed and resolved to carry on and bring the theatre back to life. She succeeded brilliantly.

First of all she recycled the gun post and transformed it into her new box office. Then she decided the theatre needed to be separated from her garden. So she, Billy Rawlings and Tom Angove built more walls, an access road, a car park and a flight of ninety steps up from the beach (the very ones we'd just walked up). Unable to afford the cost of any more granite, she then devised her own method of manufacturing imitation stone with sand and cement.

Remarkably, although she was now in her fifties and, judging from photographs, quite a frail looking woman, she still managed to manhandle (or, in these days of political correctness, should it be *womanhandle?*) bags of sand up from the beach. She would then mix it by hand with cement and water to make imitation stone seats which, before the cement set hard, she would skilfully decorate with intricate and very realistic Celtic patterns using the tip of an old screwdriver and a teaspoon.

Miss Cade must have been deceptively strong and one morning she single-handedly hauled a dozen fifteen foot beams, which she found on the shore, right up the cliff path to the theatre. This timber had been washed up from the wreck of a Spanish ship, and later in the day some Customs and Excise men met her on the beach and asked if she'd seen any timber. She replied that she had indeed taken some wood that morning and that they were more than welcome to climb the steps and inspect it. The men obviously thought the frail looking lady couldn't possibly have carried the timber they were looking for up all those steps and left her to it. Sometime later, when she and Tom Angove were incorporating the twelve beams into the new dressing room she was known to have remarked, I imagine with a twinkle in her eye, that she didn't tell them a lie. I suppose she didn't and imagine that the beams are still there to this day!

After the war, in terms of productions, things got off to a slow start with only one play performed in 1949 and another in 1951. Then, three plays were put on in 1952 (including *The Net*) and the following year, four plays (including *King Lear*). After that, things really took off and throughout the 1960s and into the 1970s ten or even twelve productions per season were regularly performed to enthralled, if not freezing cold, audiences. All this was a true labour of love for Miss Cade who never managed to cover all of her costs, so always had to make up the shortfall from her own pocket.

In the 1950s, she tentatively approached a London Drama School and the National Trust for financial help, but they both declined. However, the Cornwall branch of the National Council of Social Services, of all people, did agree to help, but unfortunately had to give up after three years of losses. No doubt disappointed, but still unperturbed, Miss Cade carried on working on a shoestring as always. Then, in 1976, when she was over well over eighty years young, she finally gave the theatre to a Charitable Trust which was especially set up for the purpose.

However, she still couldn't have been that all strapped for cash as a short time later she managed not only to buy another bungalow, which was used to provide the theatre with its own independent office, but also some more land to provide a larger car park. The Trustees put the theatre on a much more commercial footing and one of the best things they did was to build the exhibition centre, thus giving visitors the chance to fully understand how the theatre was created, as well being able to see it without necessarily having to watch a performance. This explained why the modern car park and the exhibition centre were not there when we first came in 1971.

Anyhow, we came out of the exhibition fascinated by the story of this remarkable woman and how the productions put on by local players way back in the 1930s led to the twenty week summer season in the Minack's seven hundred and fifty seat fully equipped outdoor auditorium.

I wondered why she was never honoured with a Damehood for her lifetime's work in creating the Minack. After all, it appears to me that these days too many people with questionable private lives, regarding drink, drugs and sordid sexual habits, have had the highest honour in the land bestowed upon them. I like to think that maybe Miss Cade was offered such an honour, but was so modest about her achievements that she chose to turn it down. But surely there can't be that many Dames who deserved to be honoured for services to the theatre more than she did?

With these thoughts going round in my head, we looked down on the actual stage and seating area which was even more spectacular than I remembered. If I'd been transported there blindfolded by some unknown force and then had the blindfold removed, I would have sworn I was in the Mediterranean sunshine somewhere looking down on a Roman amphitheatre. But no, I was in Cornwall, one of the wettest counties in England and it was superb. We looked right down onto seating terraces and the stage with its various balconies and dressing room, all precariously perched on the edge of the cliff, and marvelled once again as to how it all came about.

With the backdrop of the sparkling ocean, it looked far more impressive than I remembered from before when it was so overcast and getting darker as the evening wore on. Back then, even though we felt the full force of the cold wind blowing in off the Atlantic and swirling all around us, I don't think we fully appreciated that the sea was quite so near. But now, having climbed the steps up from the beach, we certainly realised how close the stage was to the ocean below. Pausing frequently to wonder at the awesome views and take some photographs, we slowly followed the steep steps down to the seating area where we were even more astounded at the originality and inventiveness of the place, which was the last thing anyone could have imagined being here in this wild location, hundreds of miles away from theatre-land in the West End of London.

We could see the intricate patterns which Miss Cade had made in the cement seats, and were astonished by their realism and sheer ingenuity. All the cement seats and walls had weathered and had, to all intents and purposes, transformed themselves into real granite, such was their craftsmanship. The other feature that impressed us was all the salt tolerant succulent plants which grew from virtually every crevice in the rocks and reminded us of the tropical gardens we'd visited in Monte Carlo on several occasions.

We wandered around for half an hour or more, just soaking up the atmosphere in the bright sunshine, and were sorry we wouldn't actually be able to see a play. It would have been too hot to leave Monty in the motorhome during a matinee although, with hindsight, we later thought he would have been fine if we'd gone to an evening performance, provided we really wrapped up warm of course! Anyhow, we promised ourselves we would definitely come back some other time to see a play and our list of places to visit in future had yet one more entry.

Regrettably it was soon time to leave and we made our way out through the obligatory gift shop. However, this was no tacky souvenir shop and even I was quite impressed. Apart from Minack Theatre T-shirts, sweatshirts, books, mugs, postcards and all the other usual things that one would expect, there seemed to be much emphasis on suitable clothing to wear during the performances.

On one hand there were shelves full of sun hats and sun block for people lucky enough to come to a matinee when the weather was kind. On a day like today, with the sun beating down and very little breeze, they would have been essential items for the audience. With hardly any shade in the theatre and with the sun being reflected back off the rocks, it would have been like sitting in a cauldron, and anyone not having the foresight to bring their own sun protection or sun hat with them would have been very wise to purchase some in the shop.

On the other hand, I noticed there were twice as many shelves crammed with cold and wet weather clothing. There were loads of warm woolly hats and thick fluffy fleeces, as well as various waterproofs, which all came in a multitude of shapes and sizes. It was just the sort of clothing we desperately needed when we came to see *The Net* and even though we were on a very tight budget back then, rather than risk hypothermia, we may well have forked out for a couple of sweatshirts.

The proportion of cold and wet weather clothing as opposed to warm weather gear on sale gave a pretty good indication of what sort of conditions to expect during the majority of performances at Minack's exposed open air theatre! However, that's not entirely fair as for all evening performances the theatre would be in the shade, and as the sun went down the temperature would rapidly fall with even the gentlest of sea breezes accentuating the cold.[18]

The other essential items I noticed in the shop were some rather fancy cushions, which came complete with their own back rest. I think they could be hired for a pound which, as I knew from personal experience, would be a pound well spent for any member of the audience who hadn't brought their own cushion with them. The

---

18 It amused me to later read a frequently asked question on the Minack's website, i.e. Is the theatre air conditioned or heated? The answer being, "The Minack is an open-air theatre and the temperature is dependent on the weather!"

alternative of having to sit on a rock hard cold seat for a couple of hours doesn't bear thinking about!

I was somewhat surprised that they didn't appear to have blankets for hire. I felt sure that, rather than suffer the plummeting temperatures during the latter part of any evening performance, most people who'd been caught unawares would gladly pay out a nominal sum to wrap themselves in a blanket. Therefore, in that instance, I felt the Trustees had possibly missed a money making opportunity. Or maybe they had thought of it, but hoped that freezing cold members of the audience would feel desperate enough to splash out far more money on an expensive fleece and woolly hat, etc.

As we climbed back up the steps, we passed through an impressive and fairly new looking sub-tropical garden. There was a huge rockery crammed full of salt tolerant succulents which thrived in the usual windy conditions, plus all sorts of other exotic plants. There was also a very extensive plant stall which sold all the varieties that grew there. After much deliberation, we bought a small Aeonium Schwarzkopf which when fully grown to around three feet has huge rosettes of dark red tinged leaves. We were pretty confident it would survive in a pot on our south facing patio in the summer but expected to have to bring it into the conservatory during the winter.[19]

The whole Minack organisation was certainly far more commercial than when we came in 1971, but definitely not in a cheap and tacky way. From its early beginnings right up to 1976, the theatre only managed to carry on because of the extraordinary efforts of, and frequent cash injections from, Rowena Cade. However, when the trust took over they must have quickly realised that more income urgently needed to be generated and that, if it were to survive, the theatre had to be run on a much more commercial basis. Consequently it was a master stroke to create the Exhibition Centre, where visitors could come in all weathers and learn about the fascinating history of the place. Also, making the distinctive theatre a tourist attraction in its own

---

19 It did brilliantly well, until we foolishly let it get caught by an early frost.

right, not only generates more income, but whets peoples' appetites to tempt them back another time to see an actual performance.

They also created a first class coffee shop,[20] which is like a conservatory high up on the cliffs with spectacular and breathtaking views down over the theatre and the sea. As well as serving cream teas, snacks and light meals, it also offers simple take-away meals for people coming to a performance and I imagine that their hot soup goes down a treat most evenings. All this enterprise generates much needed income, as does the gift shop with all the warm and waterproof clothing, cushions, sun hats and sun block which are sold there. Likewise, the plant sales must also bring in much welcome income.

Just for a moment, a cynical thought passed through my head as I wondered what if Rowena Cade had never built her theatre? Then I wondered what if some businessman today proposed to build such an attraction on the very same spot, or just up the coastline, say at Land's End? I couldn't help thinking that modern day public opinion would be outraged; that there would be huge opposition from all sorts of pressure groups; and that planning permission would be refused! Thank goodness Miss Cade did succeed in creating her wonderful masterpiece and long may her legacy continue to thrive and attract audiences from all over the world. I know we will definitely be going back in the very near future.

Anyhow, it had been a long and tiring day and we reluctantly started to make our way back to the beach. As we took our first tentative steps down the well-worn path, I imagined Rowena Cade all those years ago struggling to create the steps with her gardeners and then carrying bags of wet sand, as well as all those heavy wooden beams, all the way up this very path to her theatre.

When we got to the bottom, I didn't say anything about suspecting we were walking Monty along a dog free beach. I just hurried us along and luckily nobody said anything. It had been a wonderful afternoon,

---

20   The Visitor Centre was built in 1986 and the Coffee Shop completed in 1999.

and all too soon we were back to reality in our motorhome trying to decide what to eat for dinner.

We'd run out of meals and knew we'd have to get to a shop or supermarket to stock up, so knowing there was a Morrisons on the outskirts of Penzance we decided to call in there on the way back. Also, as we were both tired after our long day and didn't relish the thought of cooking, we decided to treat ourselves to a meal in the supermarket restaurant. So, having made a positive decision for once, we pulled up in the car park, fed Monty and left him to have a snooze in the motorhome whilst we made our way straight to the restaurant. However, much to our disappointment, the restaurant closed at seven o'clock and it was now ten past!

By now we were starving as well as tired and I said we could go to a pub for a meal, but couldn't think where to go. I then suggested buying an easy-to-cook supermarket ready meal which we could just pop in the oven when we got back. We looked at everything they had to offer, but not being in the best frame of mind couldn't agree on anything. Emm wanted to settle for oven-cook frozen fish and chips, but I wasn't keen on that idea. I told her I'd rather get freshly cooked fish and chips from a chippie, and that there must be one in Penzance.

Much to my annoyance, Emm vetoed that idea and, in desperation, I volunteered to cook spaghetti bolognaise. But she didn't want that either. So we spent ages looking at all the prepared meals again in the hope of finding something we'd both be happy with. I can't remember what we got in the end (I think it probably was frozen fish and chips), but by that time we were so hungry and tired that I, for one, no longer cared what we had to eat, so long as we had something.

Anyway, having finally agreed on our meal (whatever it was) we had to get the rest of our provisions to keep us going for the next couple of days. I hate going food shopping at the best of times and we took forever trying to find what we needed in the large unfamiliar supermarket. I have to admit that, as we'd had such a long busy day and were both tired and hungry, we started to get a bit ratty with each other – which was a shame as we'd both had a brilliant day up until then.

Finally, having sorted out the shopping and barely speaking to each other, we made our way back to St Ives, and when parking up I decided not to make another exhibition of myself by shunting the motorhome back and forth in a futile attempt to park facing forwards in the correct manner. This time I just drove in and parked sideways with all four wheels just about on the gravelled hard standing, which was good enough for me.

Having then connected the electricity and turned on the gas, Emm cooked our oven meal, which we hungrily devoured. She then washed up whilst I took Monty for a very short walk. We were both absolutely shattered, so had another early night. We'd certainly packed a lot into the day, having been to Zennor, Land's End and Minack, not to mention Morrisons, and, virtually before our heads hit our pillows, were both dead to the world.

18

COMMUTING &
MOVING ON

I woke up fairly early after a good night's sleep and, as Monty was wide awake and appeared to be a bit restless, decided to leave Emm in bed and take him for an early walk. As we headed out of the campsite and along the cliffs, I was pleased I'd made the effort to get out of bed and realised that first thing in the morning was one of the best times to go for a stroll. There was no one else around and I had plenty of time admire the scenery, think my own thoughts and contemplate.

I cast my mind back to the mid-1970s and early 1980s, when we lived near Lee-on-the-Solent and would see the sea virtually every day. Five days a week, at seven thirty in the morning, I'd leave home and cycle the short distance along the seafront to the old HMS *Daedalus* airbase where I worked as an Electronic Calibration Engineer. It only took me about ten minutes to travel from door to door and that short cycle ride was a great energiser and a perfect start to the working day. Also, apart from the odd puncture repair kit now and again, my journey to work cost virtually nothing and was certainly preferable to commuting to London by train, which I never, *ever* wanted to do.

I would look out across the Solent to the Isle of Wight and think how lucky I was to live so close to the sea and have such an easy, cheap and stress free journey to work each day. The only downside was that, more often than not, it would be windy along the seafront and if the wind happened to be against me in the morning it could be a fairly strenuous, albeit short, cycle ride. I would console myself with the foolish thought that the wind would then be behind me on the way home. However, Sod's law would invariably operate and, during the eight hours or so I was at work, the wind direction would turn around through one hundred and eighty degrees and I'd still have to peddle hard again and battle against the strong sea breeze on the ride home.

Even so, it was great exercise which helped keep me fit and I always knew I'd soon be home. When the girls came along, I'd also cycle home at lunchtime which was great as I could see them during the daytime. I used to think I was one of the luckiest fathers alive to be able to spend so much time with my young children, and I fully appreciated the quality of life we had then and never wanted to move.

However, my job was pretty poorly paid and calibrating and repairing the same old electronic test sets day in and day out became excruciatingly boring. Even though I had reasonable qualifications, I knew that if I'd insisted on staying in the area my promotion prospects were virtually zilch. In order to bring in extra money, I'd taken on a succession of gardening, painting, decorating or any other odd jobs which came my way. Even though I brought in a fair bit of extra cash, I knew moonlighting was no good in the long term and that I ultimately needed to be promoted. I also knew that promotion inevitably meant taking up a post in London, which I always insisted I'd never do.

Partly to become better qualified and partly to spend a day away from my boring job, I asked my line manager if I could be released for one day a week to go back to college and study for another technical qualification, which was something the MoD actively encouraged. His initial reaction was that I already had more qualifications than necessary for the job I was doing at the time and he wasn't at all encouraging. However, as tactfully as I could, I pointed out that I didn't want to stay in that particular job for the remaining thirty-odd years of my working life and needed to progress. Luckily he then understood where I was coming from and supported my application, which was accepted.

Every week for the next three years, I dutifully attended Portsmouth College of Technology (it's now a university) for one day and one evening and obtained my *Higher National Certificate in Electrical and Telecommunication Engineering*. That may sound rather grand now, but I was never that interested in the subjects and only passed the exams because I was pretty good at maths. I could work out the majority of questions using calculus, complex numbers and all the rest of the baffling mathematics, but never really had much of a clue what it was all about and learnt most of it parrot-fashion. I remembered working really hard to cram all the incomprehensible facts and mathematical formulae into my overburdened brain and, after baby Joscelin came along, revising at home for exams with cotton wool stuffed in my ears to stifle the sound of her crying.

Anyhow, it was quite satisfying when I passed and, now that I had more qualifications than my line manager, I thought my big chance had come when I was selected for the next promotion review. However, pride comes before a fall and I wondered if all my studying had been worthwhile when the interviewers, obviously impressed with my academic qualifications, concentrated on asking me far too many in-depth technical and theoretical questions. And I failed!

Another two years battling the boredom dragged slowly by before I was asked to grace the selection board with my presence again. This time I revised all the technical stuff until my brain was crammed full of complex theorems, formulae and circuits and, realising it was a *do or die* situation, was ready for them this time. Strangely enough though, they only asked a couple of very simple technical questions and mostly grilled me on my management potential. They asked what equipment I'd had been working on and, if I was in charge of our workshop, whether I would reorganise any of our working practices. At first, I wasn't too sure whether to make out that the workshop was as efficient as it could be, or tell them what I really thought.

After a moment's hesitation, I decided to tell the truth. Then proceeded to explain precisely what changes I would make to improve efficiency and, at the same time, raise staff morale by making the job much more varied and interesting for all concerned. I knew my opinions were in direct contrast to my rather dictatorial line manager and thought I'd probably blown it, especially as the interview came to an end after a comparatively short time. Consequently I was flabbergasted when I later received a letter telling me I'd been successful and that I would soon be offered a post on the higher grade!

On the following Friday afternoon the careers officer phoned to say I'd passed with flying colours and that he had the perfect job for me. He was full of congratulatory comments and was obviously trying to boost me up. However, this *dream job*, as he called it, was in London and I'd already told the promotion board that I wanted to stay in the local area and never wanted to be considered for a job in town. When I reminded him of this, he made it clear my promotion prospects were very dim indeed if I didn't accept. So, being on a high because my potential had been recognised at long last and I was on the brink of promotion, but feeling low because it looked like I would have to commute to London, I reluctantly told him I would give it serious consideration over the weekend and let him know my decision on the Monday morning.

After agonising over this life changing decision all weekend, when the crunch came to the crunch, I reluctantly accepted. I could have commuted daily from Lee-on-the-Solent for a couple of years and then gone back to another post on the south coast, but the thought of having to get up at five-thirty every morning and not getting home until seven each night appalled me. That and the fact that Emm's elderly parents were both suffering with their health at the time, made us decide to move, at the MoD's expense, to Farnham where they lived. Consequently, that reduced my commute time somewhat and allowed us to buy a larger house for our growing family.

Life became so much different then and, even though it turned out to be a very good career move, I always resented the time it took me to travel to work and back. To start with I became a weekender, travelling up to London on Monday mornings, staying in a cheap hotel during the week and going back to Lee-on-the-Solent on Friday afternoons, all paid for by the MoD.

I remembered my first day quite clearly. It was just before Easter 1983 during the fourth year of Margaret Thatcher's controversial premiership, and Emm dropped me off at Fareham station at some ungodly hour on the Monday morning. I was looking very smart in a new jacket, trousers, shirt and tie and was carrying a brand new briefcase in one hand and a small suitcase, containing just enough clothes for the week, in the other. The six-thirty train took me to Eastleigh, where I had to dreamily change platforms and wait ten minutes for the fast train to take me on to Waterloo, where I was spewed out of the carriage along with thousands of other weary eyed commuters.

The journey so far had taken over two hours and I hadn't even got to work yet. As I felt myself being jostled along with a throbbing mass of zombie-like humanity towards the station exit, as well as wondering how on earth all these people put up with commuting backwards and forwards like this every working day, I was feeling pretty apprehensive about my new job. For a moment I dearly wished I was back on my bike, cycling along the seafront to the Calibration Laboratory and to hell with the promotion. However, it was a bit late to change my mind now. I'd well and truly burnt my bridges so just had to get on with it.

At least I could stretch my legs a bit whilst I walked for twenty minutes or so across Waterloo Bridge and on to the office. I never had any intention of catching the Tube for two reasons. Firstly, I knew that after sitting on the stuffy crowded train for all that time, a walk would do me good and help wake me up. Secondly, I just hated the idea of going underground with thousands of other people pushing and shoving each other in a mad scramble to fight their way onto an overcrowded train.

So, mentally singing The Kinks' 'Waterloo Sunset' to myself, I walked down the steps and out of the station where I was greeted by the early morning sunshine. However, the sunshine and all romantic thoughts of 'Waterloo Sunset' promptly disappeared as I made my way through the underpass past the depressing sight (and smell) of all the down-and-outs living in cardboard boxes with their dogs.[21]

When I emerged into the sunlight again on Waterloo Bridge, I was stunned by the relative silence which greeted me. There was a considerable police presence and the bridge was cordoned off with yellow tape. Bearing in mind this was at the height of the IRA terror campaign, I asked one of the policemen what the problem was.

It turned out that it was indeed a bomb scare which greeted me on my first day in London. However, it wasn't the IRA who were responsible, but the Third Reich. A German World War Two unexploded bomb had been found right under Waterloo Bridge and the police were waiting for the bomb disposal unit. I didn't want to hang around there too long and asked whether I could walk along to the adjacent Hungerford footbridge and cross there. However, he told me that it was also closed, as was Blackfriars Bridge in the other direction. Consequently there was no alternative other than to go back to Waterloo, descend into the bowels of the earth and catch the Tube to Tottenham Court Road.

As I said, I don't like the Underground at the best of times, but on this particular day it was an absolute nightmare and heaving with sweaty humanity. Of course, I wasn't the only person reluctantly having to travel by Tube that morning. Every single person who usually walked across the bridge, caught a bus or jumped into a taxi had no alternative other than do exactly the same as me and go by on the Underground. Consequently the walk down to the platform, the wait for the train and the terrible overcrowding was almost unbearable. In

---

21 From 1983 until 1998 the pedestrian underpasses under the Bullring roundabout outside Waterloo Station was home to many homeless people who slept rough in cardboard boxes. During my time in London the numbers seemed to increase all the time *(at one time, there were around 200 such people)* and it was truly depressing to start the day by walking past these unfortunate people. They were eventually evicted and re-housed but many couldn't cope with normal life living in flats. It was known as *Cardboard City* and was a sad symbol of Mrs. Thatcher's Britain.

the light of terrible disasters which happened later in the 1980s where huge crowds of people were gathered, such as the King's Cross fire and the Hillsborough Football Stadium catastrophe, I've always felt that the crush I experienced that day could have easily resulted in a similar tragedy...

Luckily it didn't, but by the time I finally emerged back into the daylight I was bathed in sweat and totally disorientated. I had no idea how to get to the office from Tottenham Court Road which I knew was the nearest Underground station, and more than ever sorely wished I was back in Lee-on-the-Solent monotonously calibrating the same boring test sets after cycling along the seafront.

Anyhow, I eventually found my way, met my new colleagues and gave my excuses for being late on my very first day. They understood and, despite the terrible start, I seemed to settle into my new job relatively quickly, but never again used the Tube for the journey from Waterloo to the office. Nor did I encounter another of Hitler's bombs for that matter.

Of course, this lifestyle was completed different from what I'd been used to and a far cry from my pleasant ten minute commute along the seafront. Weekending didn't suit me or the family very well at all and, even though I was paid good expenses and was never out of pocket, I quickly realised that money wasn't everything. After a couple of months enjoying the bright lights of London in the evenings, the novelty wore off and I longed to be able to go home each night to Emm and the girls.

I looked forward to the weekends when I could get home again but, bizarrely, Emm and I often ended up squabbling over some stupid triviality or other and I then looked forward to going back to London. Finally, after six months of living an unsatisfactory life out of a suitcase in cheap hotels and just going home for the weekends, we finally moved house to Farnham and I became a fully paid up daily London commuter.

Even though the journey was shorter than from the south coast, it still took me an hour and a half to travel from door to door. It would take ten minutes to cycle to the station, followed by a fifty minute train ride, plus the twenty minute walk, along with thousands of other robotic commuters, across Waterloo Bridge to the office. Or in other words, a total of three hours a day spent travelling to and from my place of work, which was a major culture shock compared to my previous travelling time.

Although I'd been promoted, I was certainly no better off financially either. It all looked good on paper, as I was paid what sounded like a generous London Weighting Allowance. However, it nowhere near covered the cost of my British Rail season ticket, so my travelling costs had gone up from virtually zero to around a £1,000 a year, which was much more money then, than it is now. Also, we had to have a larger mortgage and interest rates, which were already in double figures, seemed to increase virtually every, finally peaking at over fifteen percent! All in all, after my so called *promotion*, taking into account the additional time it took me to get to work and back, which I always considered to be part of my working day, my hourly rate of pay went down – not up!

However, in spite of all this, I then had another quick promotion and a series of far more interesting jobs. I also had to travel around a fair bit by car, which meant I didn't have to commute to the office every day and was paid very good expenses. However, the downside was that I saw the family much less as I often had to stay away overnight. Then, after ten years commuting to the capital and travelling around the country, which was enough for anyone, I wangled a transfer to Yeovilton in Somerset, which was great for my career and another promotion soon followed. However, for a number of reasons, Emm never truly settled there.

For some reason, all these old memories went through my head on my solitary stroll along the cliff top and I knew we'd have to live by the sea once again when we retired.[22] I'd always enjoyed walking in the beautiful Somerset countryside, but in my book a coastal walk,

---

22   We did when we retired to Highcliffe in Dorset.

especially along a cliff top, usually outscores a walk without sea views. Whether the sun is beating down or it's grey, overcast and stormy, a coastal view is always different and full of interest.

That morning the sea certainly looked different from the previous day, when it was a deep blue colour sparkling in the bright sunshine. The waves were now pounding, rather than just lapping onto the rocks below, and it was much windier and more overcast. However, it was still relatively peaceful and calming in its own way, as well as dry.

I must admit that, on days when I didn't have to go to work, I've usually been too tired or just too lazy to get out of bed as early as I did that morning, especially in the winter when it's dark. I resolved to make more effort in future and make the most of the days, especially when I retired in a few years' time.

I took a long last look towards St Ives then, somewhat reluctantly, made my way back as quickly as I could to the motorhome. We were moving on from St Ives that morning and hadn't yet decided where we'd head for, let alone booked into any campsites for the remainder of our holiday. Over breakfast we tried to agree where to go, what to do and where to stay for the next few nights, but, as I've touched on before, combined decision making has never been our strong point. Our usual indecisiveness was made worse as the sky was more overcast than it had been for the last few days and it looked as though it could rain. In the end, however, we both agreed to head towards St Austell which was in the direction of Somerset, and if the weather turned nasty and was anything like we'd endured at the beginning of our trip, it wouldn't be too far to carry on home.

Of course, we hoped the weather would remain kind. After the rain we'd experienced at the beginning of our trip, it had turned out to be far better than we could have ever hoped for but, if it did pour with rain again, we'd have the option to pack up and go home. Mind you, that was the worst case scenario and we hoped it would stay dry so we could enjoy the rest of our week's holiday. By heading towards St Austell, we thought we could possibly go to Mevagissey and Charlestown, where neither of us had been before, or travel further on towards Looe, where we'd spent several good holidays in the past and would like to visit again. In the end, we made a decision to make a decision later in the day depending on how long it took to get to St Austell and on how the weather was shaping up. Even though we hadn't booked a campsite, it wasn't the height of the season and I persuaded Emm that it would be OK to take pot luck when we got to wherever we ended up.

So, having more or less settled on the direction we'd head in, we soon finished packing up and were ready to go. I slowly drove off our pitch which, having parked sideways on this time, was a far easier manoeuvre than it was the previous morning. Then, having set off round the one-way system, I decided to take the opportunity to fill up with fresh water and empty our grey water tank before we left.

I parked up by the motorhome service area near the toilet block and emptied the grey water without incident and, after all the lessons we'd learned a few days previously, didn't think it would take too long to carry out the supposedly simple task of filling the fresh water tank. However, just like before, the tap was lower than the motorhome's water filler inlet and the stupidly designed universal hose connector didn't make anything like a perfect seal on the tap. Consequently, most of the water gushed out onto my feet and sprayed all over my trousers, with hardly a drop finding its way into the tank where it was meant to go. Once again I had to grip the connector onto the tap as tightly as I possibly could and eventually this supposedly straightforward, but frustrating, task was finalised.

I again made a mental note to buy a selection of more suitable hose connectors before our next motorhome trip and, hopefully, avoid this exasperation in future. Once I got that sorted out, I knew it would make filling the tank much easier with far less precious water wasted. Also, I'd stand half a chance of keeping my feet dry, as well as not getting water sprayed all over my trousers and ending up looking as though I'd wet myself!

Having finally got the water sorted out, I drove slowly out of the campsite and headed towards the A3074, past Carbis Bay and on to the A30. Once we'd joined the main road the sun came out, the motorhome warmed up and I soon dried out. Also, we gave up all thoughts of going home. There wasn't much traffic about so we made good progress and it didn't seem that long before we found ourselves turning off on the A390 towards Truro. After constantly discussing and changing our minds about where to head for, we both more or less agreed to find a campsite somewhere in the St Austell area and leave Looe for another time.

I asked Emm to look in our campsite books to see if she could find a suitable place to stay for the night near Mevagissey. However, as she tends to feel sick when taking her eyes off the road, she finds it difficult to read a book or map whilst going along. I must admit I find this a little frustrating at times, but after years of experience just accept that, if I'm driving and we need to consult a map, we will have to stop. And that's just what we did at the next lay-by. I needed to stretch my legs anyway and we took the opportunity to brew a quick cup of tea and study our campsite books.

There seemed to be loads of campsites thereabouts, so I was sure there would be plenty of vacancies and that we'd have no trouble if we just turned up at one later in the afternoon. However, Emm insisted we shouldn't leave it to chance and that we book a pitch for the night in advance.

We didn't want anywhere too expensive and didn't particularly want to pay over the odds for facilities we wouldn't use. All we really needed was a level pitch, with electric hook-up, clean toilets and showers, and we quickly picked a site that fitted the bill. I turned on my mobile phone, dialled the number and effortlessly made the booking. Unlike the other sites we'd stayed at, they were happy for us to pay when we arrived and didn't want us to pay in advance with a card over the phone. So, now we'd made a firm booking and no longer had to worry about where we'd be staying that night, we could relax and enjoy the rest of the day, which we did – until later.

For now, we both agreed to go to Charlestown and, if we had time, look at the Shipwreck and Heritage Centre. We had a leaflet for this interesting looking attraction, but there was no indication as to whether dogs were allowed inside or not. If they weren't, we'd have the same old problem of having to visit separately whilst the other one of us stayed outside and looked after Monty, which was not particularly ideal if time was short. However, a quick phone call confirmed that well-behaved dogs were allowed inside, and before we had a chance to change our minds I started the engine and set off towards Charlestown on the outskirts of St Austell.

19

MUSEUM & FILMING IN CHARLESTOWN

We soon arrived in Charlestown and, keeping our eyes peeled for somewhere to park, we spotted a car park sign at the end of the road. Without hesitation, I drove on in to find just one vacant space which was far too small to take our motorhome, and it seemed that we might have to think again about where we could go for the afternoon. Remembering that we'd passed loads of parked cars on the side of the wide approach road to the village, more in hope than expectation, I drove back to see if there was a vacant space we could squeeze into.

Surprisingly, right at the end of the road between the start of the double yellow lines and the last parked car in the row, there was just enough room for our motorhome. Not quite believing our luck, I quickly parked up before someone beat me to it.

Not wanting to get a parking ticket or, worse, get clamped or towed away, we meticulously checked to see how long we could park there. The road was lined with large trees which were in full leaf, and we half expected to see a restriction sign obscured by foliage high up on a lamp post. Much to our delight, however, our pessimism proved to be unfounded and we could legally park there free of charge for the rest of the afternoon. So, thankful for our good luck in bagging the last free parking space in Charlestown, we set off down the hill towards the harbour.

The Shipwreck and Heritage Centre looked impressive, and when we saw a lifeboat and a diving bell on the outside of the building, we were drawn to the entrance where there was a life size dummy of a pirate with a peg leg and a hook instead of a right hand. I remarked that it must cost an arm and a leg to go inside, but my feeble joke was lost on Emm and, in any case, the cost was very reasonable. Double checking that Monty would be allowed to go with us, we decided to have a quick look around the harbour before coming back and going on in.

We walked up a hill and around the back of the museum where we found ourselves looking down on a very impressive, but empty dock. A photograph on the front of the tourist leaflet we'd picked up showed three magnificent tall sailing ships berthed alongside. It was disappointing not to see them, and as we carried on looking around I couldn't help wondering where they were.

Even though we'd never been there before, it looked vaguely familiar and I thought I must have dreamed about it or even lived there in a previous life. The harbour, the cottages and all the buildings belonged to a bygone age, with little to indicate that we were visiting in the early part of the 21st century. There were several old derricks, which I assumed would have been used for loading and unloading ships' cargo in days gone by and below us, adjacent to the dock, a complex of old buildings, which looked like old warehouses. To our left, was a row of very pretty and well-kept whitewashed cottages which looked to be of Georgian origin. Only a couple of cars parked nearby and some television aerials gave away the fact that we'd not been transported back to the 19th century or beyond.

Soaking up the atmosphere as we continued on down towards the sea, I noticed a narrow and precarious looking metal footbridge leading across to the other side of the harbour. Looking more closely, I realised it was perched on top of a large rust coloured steel gate, which completely blocked the entrance to the dock we'd just been looking at. The dock was, in effect, an inner harbour and there was a smaller outer harbour on the other side of the steel gate. The water level in the dock was a good six feet or so above the level on the seaward side, with the gate preventing the water from flowing out of the dock and back into the sea.

At high tide, the water level would be the same on both sides and the gate could be opened to allow ships to enter or leave the dock. Then, as the tide started to ebb away, the gate would be closed to prevent the huge volume of water from flowing back out to sea. Consequently, there would always be sufficient draught for a large ship to float in the dock. It would have been interesting to have seen this in operation, but high tide was hours away and unfortunately no ships were going to be able to get in or out of the dock during our short visit.

The footbridge itself didn't look as though it would pass today's stringent health and safety regulations. It was well worn, and when wet would have been especially slippery. Also, there were only four thin strands of wire on either side to hold on to and prevent anyone falling off. There was very deep water to potentially fall into on the dock side, and at low tide on the seaward side a very big drop into much shallower water and thick, oozing mud. Although unlikely that anyone could actually fall through the wires, it was clear that anyone suffering from the slightest fear of heights would be nervous about crossing this rickety looking footbridge.

I suspected that, rather than make this short but somewhat daunting crossing, Emm would insist on walking all the way back to the museum and round the other side of the harbour. For as long as I've known her, she's expressed both a fear of heights and of being near deep water. So I knew she wouldn't relish the thought of traversing this particular bridge, which in some ways was akin to walking the plank.

Her fear goes way back to when she was a young child on a family boating holiday on the Norfolk Broads. Apparently, when negotiating a lock, her father fell overboard and ended up floundering in very deep water. As he was a non-swimmer, he must have been in considerable danger and it was very scary for all concerned. He was as blind as a bat without his thick glasses, which fell off during this frightening escapade and ended up at the bottom of the lock. Thankfully, much to everyone's relief, someone had the presence of mind to throw him a lifebuoy and haul him back onto dry land. But, once he'd recovered from this terrifying ordeal, he had to continue the rest of the holiday in a virtually blind state without his specs.

Emm obviously didn't want to cross this unsteady looking bridge, nor did she want me to, and as soon as I stepped onto it with Monty she shouted at me to come back. However, I can never resist such a challenge and told her I'd be perfectly all right. She replied, as she has done on numerous occasions when I wanted to do something similar, that that was exactly what her dad said all those years ago when he fell in the lock!

However, I don't think she was really bothered about the remote possibility of me falling in the water. As far as she was concerned it would have been my own stupid fault, and she would have just walked on as though she didn't know me. No, she wasn't perturbed about me at all. She was just overly worried that I'd either let Monty slip over the edge into the deep water on the dock side, or end up with him dangling by his neck on the end of his lead over the mud on the seaward side.

I said I was just going for a quick look around the other side of the harbour, and if she didn't want to go over the footbridge I would meet her by the museum entrance. Then, making sure Monty was on a tight lead, I effortless led him across. I looked back to see Emm hesitate for a moment, then take a couple of deep breaths. She waited until no one else was on the footbridge, tightly gripped the wire handrails with both hands, kept her eyes straight ahead without once looking down, and quickly walked the twelve paces or so to the other side. I must admit that, knowing she was genuinely nervous about walking across the deep water on this unsteady looking bridge, I was a bit surprised and rather proud of her.

We then strolled around the impressive outer harbour wall which swept around from the western side to provide protection from the full force of the prevailing winds. On the eastern side, there was a narrow entrance to allow ships into the relative sanctuary of the outer harbour. However, to then be able to pass through the gate at the even narrower entrance to the inner harbour required a very sharp ninety degree turn to starboard. Of course this could only be achieved at high tide, and must have required immense coordination and seamanship in getting the large ships in and out of the dock during that time frame. Marvelling at the skill of the sailors, and regretful that we wouldn't be witnessing any ships entering the harbours, we walked back up the road to the Shipwreck and Heritage Centre where we paid our entrance money and went inside.

There was so much to see and we soon realised there was never going to be enough time to do it all justice. However, we did our best as we meandered our way through the comprehensive and informative exhibits. We learned that around two hundred years ago, what is now Charlestown was just a small fishing village, known as West Polmear, which had no harbour and just nine inhabitants. However, at the end of the 18th century when the china clay pits started to become a huge concern, a local businessman, Charles Rashleigh, saw a growing need for a sheltered harbour where this precious commodity could be safely and efficiently loaded onto ships.

Both china clay and china stone were essential elements for the manufacture of porcelain and these were found in abundance in nearby St Austell, thus providing much needed employment for many of the out of work tin miners after that industry started to decline. Somehow or another, Rashleigh managed to fund the building of the harbour, firstly by constructing the outer wall which would shelter the ships, and secondly by blasting out huge amounts of rock to construct the deep inner harbour we'd been looking at. He also built the complex of warehouses, where the clay would have been dried and stored before being transported by sea to the English pottery manufacturing areas and beyond.

To protect the village from anyone who might deem to attack, he also installed a gun battery on the end of the harbour wall, which was found to be the perfect place for the Huer, or look-out man, to spot shoals of fish and guide the fishing boats to them as they put out to sea. Having just walked out to where the battery would have been, I wondered what became of the cannon and whether it was ever fired in anger.

Anyhow, West Polmear became known as *Charles's town* in honour of Charles Rashleigh and that naturally evolved into *Charlestown*. It was the only outlet for the many tons of clay and china stone dug out from the local St Austell workings, and the harbour soon became very prosperous indeed. In 1876, for example, over thirty-four thousand tons of clay and china stone were shipped out to foreign and domestic ports. It must have been very tricky at times, as any ships taking their cargoes to the Staffordshire potteries had to sail around the notorious Lizard Peninsula and Land's End, where over the centuries numerous ships were reduced to wrecks, just like the RMS *Mülheim* which we'd seen the previous day at Land's End.

As well as china clay, the local copper mining industry also contributed greatly to the area's prosperity, and a smelting house for the production of copper was built in Charlestown. In the space of just four months during 1813, almost four thousand tons of copper were shipped out of the harbour in forty-nine separate ships, so it was obviously a very big concern indeed.

As the village prospered more cottages were built, as was a hotel, a chapel and, later, a church. Today, even though the china clay industry has declined and copper mining is no more, Charlestown is still a working port and home to a unique working fleet of three tall, square rigged, sailing ships called the *Kaskelot*, the *Earl of Pembroke* and the *Phoenix*, which are owned and operated by the Charlestown based Square Sail Shipyard Ltd.

As already mentioned, we were disappointed that none of these magnificent ships were in the harbour that day. However, we found out they are used for film work, as is the harbour and the village itself, and as we read about the considerable filming that had taken place and looked at the many photographs on display I realised why Charlestown had seemed so familiar to me. Of course, I'd seen glimpses of the harbour and the sailing ships many times on television and in feature films. In fact the whole place was virtually a great big film set, where numerous period films and television programmes have been made.

For example, some harbour scenes and a Charlestown based tall ship, *Søren Larson*,[23] were used in the old BBC series *The Onedin Line* which, when it was originally shown during the 1970s, I never watched all that much. It went out during the summer months on Sunday evenings when Emm and I were courting and then first married, so I must have had other things on my mind. However, since then I've enjoyed the odd episode on video and, now I knew about its Charlestown connection, made a mental note to obtain the DVDs to catch up on the saga of Captain James Onedin's struggle to make a go of his small Liverpool based shipping line.

I also learned that some scenes from the superb *Poldark* television series were filmed there. This was a programme we always watched, albeit in black and white, and I would very much like to see again in colour, not only to try and spot the scenes filmed in Charlestown, but also because of its association with the Cornish tin mining industry, smuggling, parliamentary corruption and the wild scenery. The series, based on Winston Graham's books, was full of intrigue and romance and when it went out in the mid to late 1970s, again on Sunday evenings, I don't think we ever missed an episode.

Along with a large majority of the heterosexual male population, one of the main reasons I never missed an episode was the delectable Demelza, played by a young Angharad Rees. I could never understand why Ross Poldark was so upset at losing his original love, the rather aloof and anaemic looking Elizabeth, when he had the far feistier and much sexier Demelza to bed!

Apart from the gentry, who were mostly the villains, the Cornish accent was very much in evidence and I think that made Poldark a much better programme than *The Onedin Line,* which was supposed to be based in Liverpool. For me, one of the downsides of that series was that none of the cast made any attempt to speak with a regional

---

23 The Søren Larson was subsequently sold and now operates in Australia and the South Pacific.

accent. Consequently it lost some of its authenticity and the story line could have just as easily been based in Cornwall or Devon, where much of it was actually filmed, or Hampshire or Bristol, or anywhere else for that matter.

The more recent *Hornblower* programmes, which ran from 1998 to 2003, were very good indeed and the stars of the show were very much the sailing ships, at least one of which I now realised was based in Charlestown (the Square Sail Company also built sets for this series). Not surprisingly, the filming was more technically advanced than *The Onedin Line* and it would be interesting to watch them again to marvel at the sea battles, many of which were filmed off the nearby Cornish coast, and try to identify any scenes of Charlestown itself. Film work with these ships must be very interesting indeed and they are regularly re-rigged, adapted and made up in some way to replicate almost any period ship that might be required. Just like actors and actresses really.

I later found out that in the film *Where Eagles Dare*, the harbour doubled as a wartime German submarine base which was supposed to be in occupied Alderney, and the Pier House Hotel, which we'd earlier walked past, was used as the pub in the film. Some other films I've seen which, unbeknown to me at the time, have a Charlestown connection include several *Treasure Island* films, *A Respectable Trade*, *Rebecca*, *Moll Flanders*, *Longitude*, *Mansfield Park* and *Frenchman's Creek*. There have been many others, some of which I've seen, some I've not, and I made another mental note to obtain a selection on DVD and watch them again with renewed interest.

It was very hot in the museum and it was a relief to find ourselves walking down a tunnel which led us to a viewing gallery, where we were pleased to be able to cool down for a while in the fresh air whilst looking down at the dock. The tunnel was originally built to transport trucks full of clay from the old drying kilns above us, to where it would be poured down chutes directly into the holds of ships in the dock below.

Although disappointed that the dock was devoid of ships, having seen all the photographs in the museum and by recalling the

Charleston connected films and TV programmes, it was easy to imagine the scene below us as it would have been in the 19th century, with hordes of weather beaten Cornishmen frantically loading and unloading tall sailing ships with their various cargoes. And for a moment I could almost hear them busily going about their business.

Having contemplated and cooled down a bit, we then went back up the tunnel where we found ourselves standing in a full scale partial replica of the village as it supposedly would have been in Rashleigh's time. We could peer into cottage windows to see how families lived all those years ago and, for example, saw a display depicting a sailor sitting at the dinner table drinking out of a tin mug. His wife was cleaning a large cooking pot whilst he was just about to enjoy his meal comprising of a huge Cornish pasty. Perhaps he'd been toiling all day loading dried clay into ships' holds?

There was a blacksmith's forge, where the smithy was skilfully bashing out whatever needed to be bashed out of a red hot piece of metal. In those days, when the horse and cart was the only form of land transportation, he would have been a very important and busy man. Another major tradesman would have been the cooper, who was depicted making a large barrel, such as would have been used for storing and transporting fish, brandy or clay, for example, as well as many other commodities.

Another scene depicted the great man himself, Charles Rashleigh, sitting at his desk in a more up-market house with a feather quill in his hand. It was supposed to be just a year before his death in 1823 and he was talking in a broad Cornish brogue to his daughter, Martha. He was saying something about his financial worries, which were apparently due to his mistrust of certain rogue servants. I don't recall this being explained all that well in the museum and am, therefore, not sure what financial concerns he was supposedly alluding to. However, after all he did for Charlestown's prosperity, it would be very sad if he was cheated out of his vast fortune in some way.

Seeing a tableau of a working man sitting on an outside toilet reading the paper made me laugh out loud. It reminded me of a similar scene at the Milestones Museum in Basingstoke, with its huge indoor display of old shops and streets showing the way of life in and around North Hampshire from Victorian times to the 1930s. I took my elderly mother and stepfather there some years ago and we were looking around some early 20th century workers' cottages, which my mother would have been very familiar with. We peered through a window and saw a tableau of a working class family sitting at a table eating a meal, and then went through to the back yard, where there was a typical coal shed and outside toilet.

The door to the toilet was closed, but my mother couldn't resist opening it. As she did so, it revealed a bundle of torn up newspaper on a nail and a man sitting down on what may have been an old earth closet with his trousers round his ankles. He was also reading a paper and looked to be deeply engrossed in the business to hand. In fact he looked so realistic that my dear old mum very nearly jumped out of her skin and, deeply embarrassed, slammed the door shut and shouted out 'SORRY!'

Anyhow, back to the Shipwreck and Heritage Centre. At the end of the street there was a very interesting collection of old gas equipment and domestic appliances, including cookers, fires, refrigerators and old gas meters. Until then, I wasn't aware that the very first domestic gas lights were installed in a house owned by a William Murdock in Redruth, way back in 1792. I wondered how he'd ever conceived the idea of producing coal gas in the first place, then how he stored it and piped it to his gas lamps. It must have been extremely dangerous and I wondered if he ever had any accidents.

I remembered visiting my mother's grandmother many times when I was a boy back in the 1950s and 60s. She'd lived in her small house in Fleet since before the First World War and it had remained virtually unchanged since then. She'd lost her husband during the senseless carnage of that terrible conflict, where the conscripted army were mere cannon fodder for incompetent generals. Like thousands of women widowed as a result of that war, she had a hard life and had to bring up three children all on her own. Her house hadn't been modernised in any way since then and would easily have slotted into a similar museum depicting early 20th century life.

For example, there was no bathroom and, once a week or probably less often than that, she bathed in a tin bath which usually hung on a nail in the scullery. An old, smoky black range was permanently kept alight with coke, wood or anything else that would burn and provided her only source of heating, cooking and boiling water. On bath nights she would laboriously heat up countless saucepans of water before taking a bath in front of the range, and I remember a large blackened teapot full of piping hot, but well stewed and unpalatable tea was always simmering on top of the range ready to be offered to any visitors.

Today, when I see some of the house hunting programmes on television with naive couples drooling over solid fuel kitchen ranges, I always think of Gran, as we called her, and just can't comprehend why anyone in this day and age would want to heat their homes and cook using temperamental, labour intensive solid fuel ranges rather than clean and convenient electricity or gas.

Anyhow, Gran also had no flush toilet and if we needed to go after drinking her tea, we would have to go outside to a dilapidated shed in the garden and pee through a hole in a well-worn wooden seat into a foul smelling bucket. At some point the bucket would need to be emptied somewhere at the top of the garden where, during the summer months, there was always a bumper crop of tomatoes which I never fancied eating.

Her only form of entertainment was a huge wooden wireless, which was powered by a large lead-acid battery that had to be carried to the electrical shop in town every so often to be exchanged for a fully recharged one. She never had a mains electricity supply and her only forms of lighting were candlelight or gas, which is why thoughts of Gran were triggered off whilst reading about the history of gas appliances in the museum.

Thinking back to the early 1960s when I was a lad, Gran's gas lights would have been over fifty years old at that time and I wondered how safe they would have been. Although I can't actually remember going there at night when the gas lamps would have been turned on, I seem to recall the house always having a whiff of gas about it and don't suppose for one moment they were ever subjected to routine checks.

I must admit that I've never liked gas all that much and prefer electricity for cooking. This dislike goes back to a nasty experience that my mother had when I was about ten or eleven years old. Our gas supply was on a meter which had to be fed with two shilling pieces (ten pence in today's money) and one day, when my mother was cooking something in the oven as well as on one of the rings, the gas ran out. She put a few more coins in the meter to restore the supply and then relit the gas ring. However, somehow or another, the gas supply to the oven never got reignited. Maybe she forgot, or maybe she tried to light it and unbeknown to her it went out, but once the coins had been fed into the meter, the oven started to fill up with gas.

After a while, she smelled gas and bent down to open the oven door. As she did so, the gas that had built up inside the oven during the short time the supply had been restored, was immediately ignited by the flame on the gas ring and, without warning, violently exploded. A huge ball of flame shot out of the oven into my mother's face, and she was very lucky to escape with little more than singed hair and eyebrows, a few minor facial burns and more than a little shock. Of course it could have been far worse and she was incredibly lucky, but I've always been very respectful of gas after that nasty experience!

Also, somebody I used to have dealings with occasionally through work seemed to suddenly change and become very withdrawn. I didn't know very much about his personal life, but one of his colleagues told me that his newly married son and daughter-in-law had been asphyxiated by carbon monoxide poisoning from a faulty gas heater. I liked gas even less after hearing that, and as I looked at the antiquated collection of old gas appliances I wondered what the safety records were like in the early years of domestic gas supplies.

Reflecting on these sad thoughts, I realised that Emm had already moved on to the next exhibits and I tried to catch her up without missing too much. I found her looking at a fascinating underwater tableau depicting a varied collection of diving equipment. Numerous divers were displayed rummaging through wrecks, looking for treasure and salvaging lost cargoes. I thought it was very realistic until I realised that the array of diving suits and associated equipment were all from different eras, and ranged from a primitive wooden diving barrel to the latest high pressure diving suits in which a diver could descend to depths of up to four hundred feet. As I looked more closely, I certainly didn't envy the brave men and women who risked their lives working on the seabed.

From watching films and newsreels, most of us are reasonably familiar with various types of diving equipment. We've all seen the typical frogman suits, the brass diving helmet and great big lead boot type, as well as the much more sophisticated deep sea suits with robotic arms as used on the North Sea oil rigs, examples of which were all on display. Looking at these exhibits, with the possible exception of the frogman suit, it seemed to me that, no matter how modern or sophisticated, they would all be extremely claustrophobic and the divers would be completely and utterly reliant on other people for their safety and very life.

I personally wouldn't mind doing a bit of snorkelling in clear warm waters to look at fish just below the surface, and after a bit of training and under expert supervision I could possibly be persuaded to go a bit deeper with a pair of flippers and an oxygen cylinder on my back. However, there's no way I could ever voluntarily allow someone to lock me inside any sort of deep sea diving suit and lower me into the sea. Knowing I'd be completely dependent on someone else to supply me with oxygen, pull me back to the surface and then release me from the diving suit, would totally freak me out and the very thought of it almost makes me break out in a cold sweat!

So, what really caught my attention was a replica of the very first underwater diving machine. I was completely surprised to discover that it was invented as long ago as 1715 by a certain John Lethbridge, who came from Newton Abbott in Devon. Apparently he was a wool merchant and also a bit of an amateur inventor, but had no obvious connection with the sea. However, being aware there were numerous shipwrecks which contained untold treasures under the oceans, he developed an interest in exploring the sea bed solely as a money making venture.

He probably needed much more money than he made in the wool trade to support his ultra large family of seventeen children, so he forged ahead with his strange and unique diving machine invention which he hoped would make him rich. It simply consisted of a leather coated oak barrel, which he'd modified by incorporating a small glass porthole for him to see out of and two holes to stick his arms through, the protruding arms being sealed by some sort of watertight leather cuffs. He would crawl inside the barrel, position his head so he could see through the porthole and poke his arms through the leather cuffs. Then a very trusted helper would seal him inside by screwing on a wooden lid before lowering the strange contraption into the water on ropes attached to some sort of crane.

Whilst under the water, Lethbridge would lie on his stomach and just breathe the air that was already sealed inside the barrel, which must have been weighted in some way as it would descend to a depth of around twelve fathoms and stay underwater for about thirty minutes at a time. His helpers would then haul the barrel back to the surface, where they would pump more fresh air into the primitive machine via a special vent, with the used air being let out via another vent.

Apparently he made a fortune salvaging all over the world for the East India Company, and on his very first operation he recovered twenty-five chests of silver and sixty-five cannons! I thought he must have had nerves of steel, as well as total confidence in his helpers, to allow himself to be encapsulated in such a strange device and lowered beneath the ocean. If the ropes had snapped and he'd been left floundering on the sea bed, rescue would have been impossible and he would have suffered a slow and horrible drowning.

I imagined he must have had a short life expectancy; but

surprisingly he lived to the ripe old age of eighty-four and enjoyed his hard earned and well deserved wealth. It seemed to me to be a fascinating but little known story, which deserves to be more widely told and would make a very interesting film or television series.

The museum was packed with a tremendous range of local and maritime history, and we thoroughly enjoyed our visit. There was so much more of interest than could be described here, and I would thoroughly recommend it to anyone visiting the area. Modern day Charlestown isn't much different from how it appeared in the old photographs in the museum, and it would have been the icing on the cake to have seen the old sailing ships, especially now we knew about their filming connections.[24]

However, just as we were leaving the museum, someone told us they were just up the coast filming, and we wondered if we'd have enough time and energy to walk to the top of the cliffs to try and see them. Not wanting to miss the chance, we set off and the short climb proved to be well worth the effort. In the far distance we could make out two sailing ships tacking and turning about up the coast. Unfortunately they were too far away to clearly make out and we cursed ourselves for forgetting our binoculars. I thought Emm had them and she thought I did, but they were back in the motorhome where they were no use to anyone. We really would have to get the binocular carrying duties sorted out in future, as we never had them with us when we had something interesting to look at.

Anyhow, we were pretty sure the sailing ships were in the middle of filming as, even with the naked eye, we could make out quite a few people on the cliff top alongside the ships and were sure that some of them were operating cameras. We wondered what film they were making and whether we'd ever get to see and recognise it. We were tempted to walk further up the cliff path towards them and to get a better view, but it was late in the day and we had to find our campsite.

---

24 We went back the following year and all the tall sailing ships were in the harbour. A magnificent sight!

20

THE WRONG CAMPSITE

After our early start, long drive and Charlestown visit, we were rather tired and grateful that we'd made the effort to book our overnight stop. Following the simple directions in our campsite book, we effortlessly made our way back along the main road for a few miles then turned on to the B3273 Mevagissey road where we confidently expected to find our campsite on the left hand side. We didn't think for a moment we'd have any trouble finding it and thought we'd soon be having a hot shower and preparing our evening meal. How wrong we were!

We were definitely on the right road and saw three or four sites, including an enormous holiday park at Pentewan, but the one we'd booked into earlier was nowhere to be found. We drove from one end of the road to the other and went back again, more slowly this time in case we'd missed it, and were mystified as to why we couldn't find it. We turned round again and drove up and down the road once more, but to no avail. Exasperated, I thought we should give up as a bad job and just book into one of the sites we could actually see. After all, we hadn't paid in advance and the ones we could find were certainly nowhere near full.

However, both our stubborn natures got the better of us, and just to prove we weren't losing our marbles we had to find this particular campsite. Mind you, after spending forty-five minutes or so driving aimlessly up and down the road continuously stopping to look at the map, we began to doubt our sanity and started to get a teeny-weeny bit irritable with each other!

Eventually, we decided the only thing to do was phone and ask for directions so I stopped to look up the number and made the call. As I then listened to an annoying robotic voice telling me what key to press if I was enquiring about sales, static caravans, touring, or whatever, alarm bells began to ring. Then, having listened to all these annoying options, pressed the appropriate keys and eventually got to speak to a fairly pleasant sounding lady, she couldn't find a record of our booking and the alarm bells rang even louder. When I phoned earlier, I'd got straight through to a man with a distinctive Cornish twang and the directions this lady so patiently gave me bore no resemblance to where we were looking.

I was totally flummoxed until the penny suddenly dropped and I realised I was speaking to a totally different campsite to the one I'd booked into earlier in the day. However, although I'd phoned the wrong site, it was bizarrely the very one we'd been looking for as we drove aimlessly up and down the B3273. It all sounds so stupid now but, somehow or another, I'd made a right old balls up of this booking.

What had happened was that, as we wanted to stay near Mevagissey, we'd looked up a site in our book which was fairly nearby, i.e. the *Penhaven Touring Park,* which seemed to fit our requirements. And that was the site we had phoned earlier and booked into. However, adjacent to the entry in our book for the *Penhaven Touring Park* was *Par Sands Holiday Park* and, for whatever reason, we'd both got it into our heads that that was the one we'd booked into for the night. It turned out that *Par Sands Touring Park* was somewhere the other side of St Austell, so we could have driven up and down the B3273 for all eternity and still not found it. Don't ask me how we made that mistake; I still can't understand it today as I write this. It was a momentous senior moment that possibly could have happened to anyone at the end of a long tiring day, but judging by the way Emm went on at me about it anyone would have thought I'd done it deliberately!

Anyhow, thank goodness we finally understood why we'd been frantically driving up and down the road looking for a lost campsite we were never going to find. Also, and more importantly, we now realised the campsite we had actually booked into was no more than a few hundred yards away. So, doing my best to ignore Emm's continuous cryptic comments, I turned around and drove the short distance to the *Penhaven* campsite and, as I pulled up outside reception, was extremely relieved to meet a friendly man whose distinctive voice I instantly recognised from my first phone call earlier in the day. He was expecting us and I gladly paid him for our pitch for the night.

The campsite wasn't that busy so we had the pick of the pitches, which he showed me on a plan. After our shenanigans trying to find the wrong campsite I certainly didn't want to pick the wrong pitch, so I went and got Emm to help me decide. Or should I say, get her to choose so she couldn't blame me later for choosing the wrong one? After much deliberation, she decided on a space in the middle of the field, not too near the road and not that far from the toilets and showers, which seemed fine by me.

When the owner then told us to follow him to the pitch on his bicycle, I wondered how far away it was and how difficult it would be to find. However, I certainly didn't want to spend the next half hour driving round and round in circles looking for pitch number sixty-nine, or whatever it was, so gladly went along with his suggestion. We then went outside where he mounted his bike, waited for me to start my engine and signalled for me to follow him. This we did, and in no time at all were parked up on our allotted pitch, which was entirely to our satisfaction. We thanked him for his help and, with a cheery wave, he pedalled no more than twenty-five yards back to reception whilst, with much relief, we started to sort ourselves out.

Strangely enough, when putting this book together I looked up *Penhaven Touring Park* on the internet and was flabbergasted to see some of the comments other visitors had made about the site and, in particular, the owner. Several people had stated he was rude and one reviewer even reported that he'd been physically assaulted by the owner!

Apparently, this man had telephoned to make a booking and,

unlike us, paid in advance. When he arrived with his family it seems he didn't check in, probably because no one was in reception. The owner supposedly went to speak to them about this and some sort of argument ensued, during which the owner allegedly shouted at the wife. It's not clear whether the man was present during this incident, but it sounds as though he wasn't. He then went to the shop to have a word with the owner about it and was supposedly physically assaulted and forced out of the building for his trouble! The irate camper then called the police, before packing up and leaving with a full refund.

This was in August 2006, which was just a month before we went there. However, I have to say that on the same website there were also a fair number of positive reviews which rated the campsite very highly, as indeed we would. As I said, we both found the owner to be very friendly, as well as helpful, and not at all like the Basil Fawlty character portrayed in this particular review. Of course, there are two sides to every story and on these web pages people are far more likely to write and complain than they ever are about reporting good service. However, apart from not being able to find it in the first place, which was my fault entirely, I can only report having a good experience at this site and would definitely go there again.

Anyhow, by the time we'd got ourselves organised it was around six o'clock and we decided to walk around the site and check out the outdoor heated swimming pool, which was an unexpected bonus. The late afternoon sun was still shining brightly and we thought that if the water didn't seem too cold we might have a dip. Emm was dead keen and, after I'd appeared so wimpish when I refused to paddle at Porthcurno Beach the day before, I thought I might win back a few Brownie points if I plucked up enough courage to have a swim. We tentatively dipped our hands in the water and were both pleasantly surprised that it felt quite warm. It was also extremely clean and looked very inviting, especially as there was no one else using it, so we went back to the motorhome and quickly changed.

Surrounding the pool was a low wooden picket fence, to which we tied Monty's lead and he was perfectly happy to sit in a shady spot and watch us through the railings. It was ages since we'd been for a swim anywhere and the water looked very inviting. The pool was sheltered from the slight breeze by some trees and, as the sun shone down from the west, was still in full sunshine. Even so, once I'd stripped down to my bathing trunks, I started to have second thoughts. However, I couldn't lose face again, so made up my mind to just dive in and get it over with.

Then, once fully immersed in the clear blue water, although not as warm as I would have hoped, it was very enjoyable to be able to swim a few lengths up and down the pool. Meanwhile, Emm had gradually lowered herself into the water a bit at a time which, to me, is the worst way to get in and she eventually joined me in our own private pool. I thought that later in the autumn the pool could quickly get covered in leaves from the nearby trees, but for now the only foreign object in the water was a stag beetle which I'd noticed struggling to swim on the surface.

I swam over to it, scooped it up in my hand and deposited it in some bushes well away from the pool, satisfied in the knowledge that I'd probably saved it from drowning. We continued to swim leisurely for about twenty minutes or so before towelling ourselves down and taking Monty back to the motorhome. We then went over to the clean shower blocks, where we each had a refreshing hot shower and washed the chlorine out of our hair.

Whilst in the shower, I recalled when I first learned to swim way back when I was at primary school. I think we were in our last year before having to sit the dreaded eleven plus exam, and come rain or shine, at nine o'clock every Monday morning during the summer months, my whole class went to Fleet swimming pool for our lesson with Mr Robins, our form teacher. I can't remember how we got there. I have a hazy recollection we might have marched down there in a long line, but it was a fair old distance for ten-year-olds so maybe we went in a coach.

The swimming pool was privately owned and, unlike the pool on the campsite, was never heated. I'm not sure what sort of financial arrangement existed between the school and the owners of the pool, but in any case we wouldn't have given that a thought at the time. In the main, we schoolchildren were just happy to be able to learn how to swim, especially as it got us out of some of our more usual lessons.

Looking back now, it seems to me that most Monday mornings that summer were cold, overcast and often wet. Even so, we still had to go swimming and, more often than not, after changing in the wooden changing rooms we would shiver as we somewhat reluctantly made our way to the side of the pool to await Mr Robins' instructions. I seem to recall that after he blew his whistle everyone had to get in the water as quickly as possible, which we all did with a sharp intake of breath as the cold water hit our small bodies.

We must have been a hardy lot in those days as once we were in it was reasonably OK. That is, as long as we kept our bodies under the water, for any flesh exposed to the elements was quickly covered in goose pimples. I think Mr Robins did actually get into the water with us on some mornings, but only when the sun was shining. Usually, whilst we suffered in the cold, he would stand on the side of the pool fully clothed in his suit and tie shouting out instructions.

Despite these rather primitive conditions in which we learned to swim, we felt a rather privileged lot and most of us became reasonable swimmers. We started off by holding on to the edge and kicking our feet, then putting our heads under water without being afraid and holding our breath. Once we could confidently do all that, we graduated to doggy paddling ourselves across the width of the pool, after which we managed the breast stroke, crawl and swimming underwater.

As I dried myself after my invigorating shower I remembered that, after a freezing cold swimming lesson, such a luxury was completely unheard of and we always had to get changed as fast as we could and go back to school with cold, wet hair. As I said, we were a hardy lot in those days!

Even so, when we became reasonable swimmers, we all loved going to the pool at every opportunity. It cost six old pence (just two and a half pence in modern money) and I recall spending most days there during the summer holiday in 1959, just swimming and messing about with friends, most of whom I haven't seen since I left school. Also, I vividly remember a very young Cliff Richard's 'Travelling Light' being played over the distorted tannoy system, as well as a host of other hits of the day.

Feeling clean and warm after my hot shower, I was still thinking about those long ago days at Fleet swimming pool whilst I prepared spaghetti bolognaise, which we ate outside in the evening sunshine washed down with a bottle of rosé. Having then washed up, we were ready for our evening dog walk. We didn't plan to go far, just along the footpath by the stream, which ran by the side of the campsite, until Monty did his business and then come straight back.

If it hadn't been for the squadrons of midges, which swarmed all around us the moment the sun disappeared from view, it would have been a pleasant walk. However, there wasn't much we could do about them so we just had to do our best to ignore them, which wasn't that easy as dark formations of these pesky insects hovered over our unprotected heads and caused us to constantly scratch our itchy scalps.

Although not intending to go far, Monty didn't seem to be in a business mood and whilst we impatiently waited for him to perform we ended up walking much further than we really wanted. I reminded Emm that, earlier in the day, he'd been right in the middle of Charlestown and that maybe he didn't need to go again. Emm had scooped it up in a polythene bag, but we couldn't immediately find a suitable bin to dispose of it. We did see a large black refuse bin somewhere where we were tempted to put it, but when we saw a notice saying '*Not for Public Use. Depositors will be Prosecuted – CCTV Cameras Watching*', we thought better of it. We certainly didn't want to appear on *Crimewatch*, and ended up carrying it around for quite a while before eventually finding somewhere more appropriate to responsibly get rid of it.

Anyhow, I repeated that Monty probably didn't need to go again and suggested that we should just turn around, go back and get away from the menacing midges as quickly as possible. However, she wouldn't hear of it and pronounced that we must give Monty a fair chance to do what dogs do when they go for walks after meals. So we carried on a bit longer, during which time it must have been the midges' main mealtime as they became more and more annoying. Finally, after about ten more minutes Emm thankfully relented and gave us the go ahead to turn around and head back before we got eaten alive.

By this time, I was absolutely bursting for a pee and every step I took became more agonising than the last. I cursed myself for drinking so much wine before we went out and, as much as I tried, I couldn't put the ache in my bladder out of my mind. Monty then slowed down, started sniffing and looked as though he might perform after all. However, I was no longer bothered whether he relieved himself or not and was only concerned about my own predicament.

Much to Emm's delight he finally did what he had to do and after Emm picked it up I started to quicken my pace to get back to the campsite. Emm kept telling me to slow down and wait for her and Monty, but I took no notice and accelerated ahead as fast as I could, gritting my teeth with every painful step. I just about made it back to the toilet before I wet myself, and to my tremendous relief the pain in my bladder gradually subsided!

Time was getting on and once Emm and Monty caught up with me and we got back to the motorhome it was almost dark. We both read for a while, but Emm's book couldn't have been all that interesting as her head was soon nodding, her eyes were closing and by eight-thirty she was fast asleep, as was Monty. I eventually had to wake her up, so we could make up the bed and turn in for the night.

After another long, tiring and interesting day, I should have immediately fallen asleep, but Emm, who'd already had an hour's shut-eye, was unable to immediately drift off again and kept tossing and turning. What with that, plus the onslaught by the midges which caused us both to constantly want to scratch ourselves, it seemed an age before we finally succumbed to the land of nod. But once we had, we slept like logs.

21

MANIACS IN
MEVAGISSEY

For once, we didn't waste time dithering around trying to decide what to do with our morning and both agreed to go to Mevagissey. We did think about going to the Eden Project or the Lost Gardens of Heligan, which were both close by, but we'd been to both those major attractions before and knew we couldn't have done either of them justice this time around. However, neither of us had ever been to Mevagissey, and although it had been good to revisit some familiar places on this trip and stir up old memories it was also good to discover new places, like Trebah, Zennor and Charlestown for example, and create new memories.

I've always been more interested in social history than geography, and I'm embarrassed to admit that for years I thought Mevagissey was somewhere in Wales. I really don't know where I got that idea from. It's just my lack of geographical knowledge, but to me the word *Mevagissey* just sounds Welsh and I've always imagined the name being spoken in a Welsh accent, rather than a Cornish one. Likewise, another notable town I mentally misplaced for years was Pontefract, which most people would know is in West Yorkshire. However, until I had to occasionally drive up the A1 on my way to Harrogate when I was working in London, I always thought Pontefract was in Wales. Again, for no other reason than, to me, it just sounds Welsh.

I like to think that centuries ago small communities from the Welsh valleys resettled in these places and came up with the names, but in fact Mevagissey gets its name from two saints, St Meva and St Issey, and Pontefract means broken bridge. Now I know better, everybody with Welsh, Cornish or West Yorkshire origins, please accept my sincere apologies for my previous ignorance.

Anyhow, having packed up early, unlike the previous day, we knew precisely which way to go. We turned left out of the campsite, and even we couldn't go wrong as we made our way towards Mevagissey where the road terminated. We were soon at the outskirts of the fishing village keeping a lookout for somewhere to park. Then, seeing a large car park on our left, thinking there would be another closer to the village centre, we inexplicably drove past. However, we soon realised that that was a very big mistake!

Why we didn't just go straight into that car park, no matter what it cost or how far it was from the village, I'll never know. For in no time at all we'd both broken out into cold sweats as we found ourselves driving along winding and ever narrowing streets, which were never designed to cope with modern traffic, let alone larger vehicles like our motorhome. Not only were they extremely narrow and twisty, they were also part of a horrendously complicated one-way system, with some very acute angled turns to boot.

I was soon in a state of blind panic driving round and round in ever decreasing circles in what seemed like a futile effort to find our way out of the village and back to the car park, where we obviously should have gone in the first place. However, there just didn't seem to be any way out of this supposedly quaint and attractive Cornish fishing village which, as we struggled to get back to the main road, didn't appear to be anything like quaint or attractive to us. All the ever narrowing streets were edged with double yellow lines, which seemed to cover the whole street, and we felt as though we were following the yellow brick road around an impossible maze, with hardly a hope of finding our way out again.

Even though it was still quite early, there were a fair number of pedestrians around and this added to our misery and acute embarrassment. There were no pavements and people were nonchalantly strolling around the narrow streets, completely oblivious to the possibility that they may have to share them with idiotic drivers like us. Consequently I had to take even greater care and drive very slowly whilst Emm did her utmost to direct me. Not that I had very much faith in her directions. Several times she told me to turn right, for example, but when I turned the wheel in that direction I suddenly realised I was just about to go down a one-way street.

She would shout out that she didn't mean that particular turning but the one on the opposite side of the street, which was actually on the left hand side. As I've pointed out before, she really doesn't know right from left, so the directions she'd give me were more of a hindrance than a help, and it was just too dangerous to take much notice of them!

Anyhow, not having a clue where we were going or how we were going to get out of this mess, I gradually inched the motorhome down the narrow streets whilst disgruntled pedestrians scurried out of our way to let us to pass. Some of them had dogs, which were pulling on their leads, and others were pushing prams or holding toddlers' hands as they took what were possibly their very first steps. Some seemed to be struggling with dogs, prams and toddlers all at the same time, and none of them seemed best pleased with us maniacal motorhome motorists who threatened to mow them all down!

In order to avoid being run over or dragged along with us, they all had to squeeze themselves, their prams, dogs and toddlers into the minute gap between our motorhome and the adjacent shops and buildings, which unsurprisingly made them rather hostile towards us, especially as they also had to contend with breathing in our diesel fumes. However, there was absolutely nothing we could do but carry on regardless and hope we would soon put some distance between us and the angry mob.

Sitting high up in our motorhome, squirming in our seats and in full view of everyone, we both felt embarrassingly stupid and wished the earth would just swallow us up. Everyone was staring, or rather glaring, at us and we received the filthiest of looks. Not only that, we didn't need to be trained lip readers to understand what sort of unprintable things they were saying about us!

Unusually, we didn't start blaming each other for our self-inflicted predicament. We both subconsciously realised that if we'd started to argue about the situation it would have made matters far, far worse, and for once we silently accepted we were both just as stupid as each other and willingly shared the blame.

After what seemed like a very long hour, but in reality was more like ten minutes, manoeuvring the motorhome around Mevagissey's confined streets, squeezing past more and more sensible tourists and locals alike, we somehow found ourselves thankfully heading out of the village and back onto the B3273. It then wasn't long before I mercifully turned into the car park I'd earlier ignored and we both heaved spontaneous sighs of relief.

Wiping the sweat off our brows, we noticed that most of the spaces were occupied and that there didn't appear to be any vacant spaces large enough to park the motorhome. Emm said we should just cut our losses and go to the Eden Project or the Lost Gardens of Heligan after all, which I didn't want to do. I wanted to finish what I'd started and, in any case, felt we'd spent enough time in the motorhome for one morning and wanted to get out and stretch my legs as soon as possible.

We were on the brink of getting ratty with each another when a car park attendant approached and, speaking in a wonderful Cornish accent, told us to follow him. He seemed to be such a pleasant man that I obeyed him without question, and he was soon helping me reverse into a large space in a specially designated part of the car park for motorhomes. He obviously couldn't have known that we'd earlier ignored his car park and caused havoc during our disastrous mystery tour around Mevagissey's miniscule streets. If he'd realised, he surely wouldn't have been as helpful, friendly and courteous as he was and possibly would have run us out of town and told us never to come back.

Anyhow, at long last, we were all parked up in a motorhome

friendly car park on the edge of a motorhome unfriendly village and didn't want to waste any more time or be recognised by anyone. I can't remember what the car park cost, something like three pounds for two hours I think, but it wasn't excessive. And we both thought what utter idiots we'd been for not just pulling into it earlier and saving ourselves, and all the pedestrians in Mevagissey, a heck of a lot of hassle.

So if anyone reading this ever drives a motorhome or a car for that matter to Mevagissey, take my advice and head straight for this car park. Do not, under any circumstances, do what we did and drive past and end up in the town itself. You have been warned!

22

CLOUD CUCKOO LAND

Panic was over, we got ourselves ready to walk down to the village and see it from a different perspective, this time in a much more leisurely and relaxed fashion.

Before setting off and without making it too obvious to Emm, I tentatively edged my way around the motorhome on some pretext or other to check for possible damage or anything else untoward. I wouldn't have been all that surprised to have found the odd scratch where I may have got too close to one of the buildings, for example, or even the odd pushchair, toddler, dog or old age pensioner caught up on the bicycle rack having been dragged along behind us! Thankfully, my fears appeared groundless so, much relieved, we finally set off towards Mevagissey just like normal tourists.

In no time at all we were back in the small village centre and, even though we had to occasionally squeeze up close to the walls to allow a car to pass, we were enjoying ourselves much more than half an hour before. As we mingled with the other visitors and residents alike, we hoped we wouldn't be recognised as the maniacs who, not so long before, almost mowed them down with our motorhome.

When a delivery van approached everyone had to squeeze up close to let it pass and, as we almost choked on its exhaust fumes, it drove home to us just how moronic we were to have driven the motorhome down the same narrow streets that were originally designed for pedestrians and the odd horse and cart. As everyone around us coughed and cursed we kept our heads bowed as much as possible, avoided eye contact and tried to blend in and remain inconspicuous.

We even found ourselves giving the unfortunate drivers of passing vehicles the evil eyed stare, just like everybody else!

Although it was warm and sunny, we soon noticed a fairly strong easterly wind blowing in off the sea and funnelling down through the streets between the buildings. Consequently we were both pleased we were wearing long sleeved shirts with long trousers and not the T-shirts and shorts we'd been tempted to put on that morning. Even so, as well as the cold wind, the streets were largely in the shade which reduced the temperature even further and we both wished we'd worn our thick fleeces as well.

Nevertheless, I just wanted to get down to the seafront as soon as possible to explore the old fishing harbour and take in the scenery, but had to be very patient as Emm insisted on looking in virtually every shop we passed on the way. Admittedly there were plenty of interesting and unusual shops to look at and Emm was in her element.

She particularly wanted to buy a pair of leather sandals which I didn't think would be too much of a problem, there being a fair number of shoe shops with huge selections of them. She went inside each and every one, browsed through the vast quantities of footwear and tried on all the ones that took her fancy. However, she dithered as usual and just couldn't make up her mind as to which ones to buy.

So she then proceeded to try on all the ones that didn't particularly take her fancy as well, but still felt compelled to try on anyway. Unfortunately, just like Emm's old sandals, my patience started to wear thin as I stood outside with Monty waiting for her to make a decision. Also, the closer we got to the sea front where it was more exposed to the cold east wind, the colder I felt.

In order to warm myself up a bit I started to pace up and down the street, when an unusual old fashioned shop caught my attention and took my mind off the cold for a while. This shop had a wide frontage and large gold coloured capital letters on a jet black background spelt out the words 'CLOUD CUCKOO LAND'. Either side of a centrally positioned entrance were two large window displays jam-packed with vast quantities of fascinating memorabilia and paraphernalia.

Imagine an Aladdin's cave full of all the treasures you might have owned years ago, but have long since discarded and wished you'd kept, plus all the things you wished you once had, but could never afford or could never get hold of, then there was a chance that many of those treasures could be found in this shop.

What immediately took my interest, being a passionate fan of their music, were items relating to The Beatles. The centrepiece was four large glazed pottery busts of John, George, Paul and Ringo in their famous 1967 Sergeant Pepper guises. John was wearing his granny glasses, which he was photographed wearing for about the first time on the cover of the Sergeant Pepper's Lonely Hearts Club Band album (or LP as we called them in those days).

All four Beatles sported moustaches, which was a revelation at the time and triggered off a fashion for many youths to give up shaving their upper lips in an attempt to emulate them and impress their Beatle-mad girlfriends. Many of these lads were barely old enough to shave, but still persisted in their attempts to spout a moustache, *barely* being the operative word as only bum-fluff ever grew on most of them.

I remember someone actually applying black mascara (it might even have been black shoe polish) to his fluffy upper lip in a vain attempt to make his almost invisible facial hair stand out. I dread to think what his girlfriend thought, when after kissing him she looked in a mirror and saw black stains all around her mouth. Happy days indeed and no, it wasn't me!

I can't remember what these impressive figures cost, but knowing there's a good market for rare quality Beatle memorabilia I don't think they would have been cheap. To my inexpert eye they looked to be very good quality indeed as, unlike most Beatle souvenir figures I've seen, these were very finely detailed and were excellent likenesses of John, George, Paul and Ringo. There were also lots of other Beatle memorabilia, such as model cartoon characters from the *Yellow Submarine* film, including the Blue Meanies, which were all complete with their original boxes and again of excellent quality.

Other items that took my eye were similarly high quality figures of *Wallace and Gromit* and *Only Fools and Horses* characters, which may well have also been collectors' items. In the other window there were posters, original newspapers, including one with a report on the killing of Lee Harvey Oswald, autographs of famous people and much, much more. The whole shop was like a living museum with ever changing exhibits as the objects were sold and then replaced with more rare and interesting items.

Just looking in the window was like taking a nostalgic trip back to my youth and I would love to have gone inside to have a really good browse around, but unfortunately I couldn't take Monty in with me. I did think about tying him up outside somewhere, but there just wasn't anywhere suitable to do so. Even if there was I couldn't have risked it as I was aware that, even on a tight lead, he still would have been too close to the road and could easily have been injured by a passing vehicle.

Emm eventually emerged from whatever shop she'd been exploring and I reluctantly gave up the idea of stepping into CLOUD CUCKOO LAND, which was probably just as well. It would have taken me a fair old time to look around this fascinating emporium and I could easily have been tempted to buy something I regretted later. All the items looked fantastic together in a large display, but a solitary *Wallace and Gromit figure* or *Yellow Submarine* poster, for example, could never have looked so good at home in isolation.

Nevertheless CLOUD CUCKOO LAND fascinated me so much that I later looked it up on the internet where I discovered that it was owned by Paul Mulvey, who says he lives in cloud cuckoo land, and judging by what I saw he's not wrong there. Back in the 1980s he ran a shop in Carnaby Street where he sold clothes to the pop stars of the day. Apparently, he always had a photograph taken of him with his famous customers, which he would ask them to autograph. He would then display the signed photos in his shop, and when customers asked if they could buy them he realised there was a big gap in the market for autographed pictures and other mementos.

It's not clear when he left London, but at some point he moved to Mevagissey and started up his own CLOUD CUCKOO LAND, which is a brilliantly apt name for his shop. Goodness knows where he gets all his stock from, but he'd certainly amassed a very fine collection of fascinating and intriguing memorabilia. Apparently a Michael Jackson look-alike once turned up at the shop, or that's what Paul first thought. However, this exceptionally realistic look-alike turned out to be the real Wacko Jacko!

Paul must have been absolutely gob-smacked and even more so when he later received an invitation to Jackson's wedding! Unfortunately he couldn't go, which he must have always regretted. Just think of all the celebrity signatures and photos he could have acquired there!

He says that collecting has become big business all over the world and that not everything he's been offered to buy has been genuine. For example, I think most people are probably aware that there are huge numbers of supposedly genuine Beatle autographs in circulation, which were actually signed by their roadies. However, Paul was apparently offered a signed copy of *The Best of John Lennon* (which I assume was a vinyl long playing record, as it would have been a bit early for CDs), but was quick witted enough to remember that that particular collection of Lennon greats was issued in 1981, whereas the great man himself was murdered by a deranged Mark Chapman on 8th December 1980!

As I said, I would love to have gone inside the shop and had a really good browse around, and resolved to come back to Mevagissey sometime in the future and spend more time there. However, whilst writing this, I found out – again from the internet – that the CLOUD CUCKOO LAND shop had closed down so I really do wish I'd taken the opportunity to explore it further when I had the chance. Paul continued to sell his wares for a while from cyberspace via his own website, but sadly that seems to be no more and I have no idea what became of Paul and his CLOUD CUCKOO LAND nostalgia business.

Anyhow, we eventually made it down to the harbour front where the wind really started to bite. Emm immediately spotted yet another shop selling leather goods, funnily enough called *The Leather Shop*, and before I knew it had vanished inside.

I stood outside for a while feeling pretty fed up, and between pacing up and down in an attempt to keep warm kept peering in and asking how much longer she was going to be. The shop owner obviously saw me and, sensing the loss of a potential sale, came out and told me I was welcome to come in with Monty. I must admit I was reasonably happy to do so and once I'd stepped inside immediately felt much warmer.

23

BREAKING A LEG & PAINFULLY PEEING IN BED

Emm was right down the far end of the shop, which was deceptively larger than I imagined, surrounded by umpteen pairs of genuine leather sandals she'd been trying on. She asked me which ones I liked best and, hoping she'd get a move on, I picked some out which looked all right to me. Rather than being imported from a Far East sweat shop, they all appeared to be locally made and of high quality, so were a bit more expensive than their foreign imported counterparts. However, to me they all seemed to represent good value for money and I encouraged her to buy a pair. Any pair, just so we could get out of the shop and see some more of Mevagissey before our parking ticket ran out!

In the end, though, it was my patience which ran out as she continued her dithering. Exasperated, I left her to it and wandered off to look around the shop on my own. Holding Monty on a tight lead, I constantly kept an eye on him to make sure he didn't cock his leg on the carpet or any of the goods which were at ground level. Luckily he behaved himself and I needn't have worried, but if he had disgraced himself in such a way it wouldn't have been the first time.

At the other end of the shop from Emm I spotted loads of leather moccasin style slippers, and as mine were wearing a bit thin decided to have a closer look. I picked out a pair of size 9s in navy blue and tried them on. They fitted. The price was right. So I bought them, and my shopping completed was eager to carry on down to the harbour.

I've worn similar moccasins ever since I was in my prime as a twenty-year-old. I was lying in hospital with a broken leg, the result of a very painful football injury. I'd cut in from the left wing and put over a perfect right footed cross into the opposition's goal area, and as my leg followed through a clumsy defender swung his foot in my direction in a very late attempt to get the ball.

I'm sure it wasn't deliberate, but his clumsy tackle was very, very late and the combined momentum of my follow through, plus his size ten foot striking my leg just above the ankle, resulted in me collapsing to the ground in absolute agony. Everybody could clearly hear the sickening sound of my tibia and fibula bones in my right leg snapping cleanly in two, which was a blessing, I suppose, as it would have been much worse if it had been a compound fracture.

The pain was awesome. It was one of those moments when I thought, then hoped I was dreaming. I tightly closed my eyes, and then opened them again hoping I'd find myself tucked up safely in bed. But, of course, I didn't. Then, as I foolishly tried to lift my shattered limb off the ground, I saw the stomach-turning sight of the lower part of my leg bent over at a gruesome angle. An even sharper, more agonising pain shot through my body and I immediately knew I wasn't dreaming. I was lying in the mud surrounded by concerned team-mates, plus a few unconcerned opponents telling me to get up and get on with it. It was very real indeed and I realised I wouldn't be playing football again for quite a while, nor would I be doing much else for that matter.

An ambulance came and took me an excruciatingly painful five miles to the now defunct Cambridge Military Hospital in Aldershot. Every single movement the ambulance made was magnified a million times, as every judder, bump and vibration transmitted itself from the nerves in my shattered leg to whatever part of my brain it is that detects pain. I don't remember much more about it until after I woke up in bed and found my right leg encased in plaster from my heel to the top of my thigh. It was agonising to move and I ended up in my hospital bed for the next two weeks which, needless to say, as well as being very painful, was pretty boring.

Anyhow, if you are wondering what relevance this tale of woe has on me wandering around a leather shop in Cornwall it's because, as I lay in hospital all those years ago with nothing to do but grow my beard for the first time and read, a lady came round with various ideas for what she called *occupational therapy*. I can't remember all the various therapeutic activities she thought might keep us bedridden patients occupied, except that it was the real leather moccasin making kit that caught my eye and I ended up buying.

I subsequently spent a few hours propped up in bed happily stitching various bits of leather soles and uppers together with a large needle and strong waxed cord, all of which were supplied with the kit. Once completed they made a superb pair of footwear which I was rather proud of, the irony being that I knew I wouldn't be able to wear them as a pair for at least three months until my broken bones healed and the plaster was removed.

Apart from stitching together the moccasins I passed the time reading loads of Dennis Wheatley novels for the second time, but this time in the right order. These days Wheatley's books seem to be out of favour, but way back then everyone I knew was reading them. He was a prolific author who was probably best known for his black magic tales, but was much more than just a supernatural story teller. He had a couple of special heroes, namely Roger Brook and Gregory Sallust, who were both spies during the Napoleonic and Second World Wars respectively. There were about twelve books in each of these series and I'd read them all before but, as Eric Morecambe once said, *'not necessarily in the right order.'*

Now, with my enforced confinement, I whiled away the hours re-reading as many of the Sallust sagas as I could, this time in chronological order. Consequently I gained a pretty good knowledge of the Second World War from Dennis Wheatley's incredible tales, which were complete fiction inter-woven with fact. However, after reading nearly all day and every day during that time, I ended up much more short sighted than I was before and started to wear glasses virtually all the time.

Anyhow, it wasn't too bad in hospital and could have been much worse. The food was reasonably good and, as I was there during the coldest two weeks of the year with sub-zero temperatures most of the time, I was warm. Although I had a broken leg and was in a lot of pain, there were others far worse off than me who were confined to bed for months on end with multiple injuries and shattered bodies. So, even though I knew I wouldn't be playing football for a while, I acknowledged I was much better off than many of the other patients who'd been involved in horrific road accidents and suchlike.

The only real problem I had, apart from the pain of course, was that I couldn't pee in a bottle under the bedclothes! I remember coming round from the anaesthetic in the early evening after my leg had been set and, as I drifted in and out of consciousness for the rest of the night, a male nurse asking me at regular intervals if I'd passed water. I hadn't, and he gave me a papier mache bottle to pee into when I needed to go.

Eventually, I did need to go and needed to go very badly. I fumbled under the bedclothes to adjust the hospital pyjamas and position the bottle where it needed to be positioned. But, nothing happened. Try as I may, it seemed so unnatural to actually pee in bed. It appeared that, right from when I was a toddler trying not to wet the bed at night, my brain had been programmed to never allow me to urinate in bed ever again. And I just couldn't do it.

The nurse seemed to get more and more concerned with my lack of action. But the more he asked if I'd passed water, the more my urinary stopcock seized up and, no matter how hard I tried, I couldn't expel a single drop from my overfull bladder. This unsatisfactory state of affairs carried on until early the next evening, when I started to get extremely desperate. After all, more than twenty-four hours had passed since I'd last passed water. But I still couldn't go!

My predicament was made worse by the fact that it was now visiting time, and although no one came to see me there were loads of people in the large old fashioned open-plan ward, some sitting on chairs right next to me talking to their loved ones in adjacent beds. I knew there was just no way I'd ever be able to lie in bed next to these strangers and fill the bottle under the blankets. Also, I was afraid that if I did somehow force myself to start I wouldn't be able to stop, and the bottle wouldn't be big enough to hold the full contents of my ever expanding bladder.

Looking back now, it's strange to think that when I was twenty I could drink six pints of beer a night and still not need to take a leak. Now, as I write this in my early sixties, if I drink a pint I pee a quart every half hour or so. Nevertheless I haven't yet reached the stage where I pee in bed, intentionally, or otherwise!

Anyhow, by this time all thoughts of pain from my shattered bones were completely overshadowed by the unbearable agony emanating from my swollen and pressurised bladder! Visitors were still milling about completely oblivious to my predicament and the next time the nurse asked if I'd been, I more or less pleaded with him to somehow get me to a toilet before I exploded.

He rushed away and in no time at all returned with a wheelchair. Then, carefully cradling my plastered leg, he eased me out of bed, sat me in the chair and gently rested my shattered leg on a special leg rest built into the chair. As he then wheeled me down to the end of the ward, I winced as I imagined him bumping my protruding leg onto a bed or other solid object. Luckily he was skilled in wheeling wheelchairs around and soon had me backing into a WC cubicle. There being no way I could stand up in the state I was in, he then manhandled me out of the chair and onto the toilet seat, with my plastered leg stretched out straight before me resting on the chair.

He left me to it, and as a fast flowing stream of beautiful yellow urine poured from my pain racked body into the pan the relief was mind blowing. Talk about out of the frying pan into the fire – this was more like out of the fire in my hot and burning bladder into the toilet pan. I don't suppose the most cocaine dependent junkie has ever felt as much instantaneous pleasure in administrating a fix as I did during that moment. Actually it was more than a moment, as I seemed to be peeing for an inordinate amount of time and thought I'd never be able to stop. It really was just as well I didn't finally manage to under the bedclothes. The bottle would have surely overflowed and soaked the bed!

When the nurse returned and wheeled me back to my bed, he seemed almost as pleased as me that I'd finally done what my bladder had been screaming out at me to do for so long. After that I usually got a nurse to take me down to the toilet in the wheelchair, but unless surrounded by visitors I did manage to use the bottle when I really had to. However, I was greatly relieved I never had to use a bed pan.

Towards the end of my stay in hospital when my bones had started to knit together, I managed to hobble unaided down to the toilet on a pair of crutches with a shiny new leather moccasin on my left foot.

Then, after I was discharged I wore my new left moccasin virtually all my waking hours both indoors and out. With my right leg and foot encased in plaster and only my toes sticking out, it was impossible to wear any sort of shoe on that foot, and in order to keep my exposed toes warm I would pull a thick walking sock over my plaster covered foot as best I could and fix it in place with a large safety pin.

I couldn't go to work and hated just sitting around at home all day stagnating, so would try and do as much exercise as possible by walking, or rather hobbling, up to town every day on my crutches. Sometimes I'd go to the library, but almost always ended up in the pub where I'd sit in the corner reading whilst enjoying a couple of pints of *Double Diamond*, which always worked wonders.

My shoulders got broader and my arm muscles stronger, as did the muscles in my left leg. However, being inactive all this time, the muscles in my right leg rapidly withered away and the plaster became decidedly loose. After six weeks, my broken bones had fused together enough to allow the plaster to be removed and replaced with another, this time with a heel built into the foot. With my leg encased in this new plaster I could put some weight on my bad leg and, once I realised it wasn't going to snap under me, gradually disposed of my crutches and walked, or rather limped to the pub every day.

Then after three months of being plastered, the big day arrived when it was removed to expose my matchstick thin leg, which was obviously going to need building up before I kicked a football again. However, even though it might have looked a bit strange compared with my well-worn and faded left moccasin, at least I could wear my shiny virgin right moccasin at long last.

Nevertheless right up until the time the left one finally disintegrated, I still wore them. Then I made another pair from a kit I bought from a craft shop in Aldershot. When they wore out I made another, and when the craft shop closed down I bought some through the old *Exchange and Mart* magazine. Later on it became impossible to buy the kits, so I'd get ready made ones which were never as good as the real leather ones, but just as comfortable. Anyhow, ever since that painful stay in hospital I've always had a pair and now, almost forty years later, there I was in Mevagissey buying more moccasins and being reminded of breaking my leg and painfully peeing in bed.

Anyhow, I went back to see if Emm had finally managed to pick some sandals she liked and again pointed out several pairs I thought would do the job. However, they were all too tight, too loose, too wide or too thin. Or she didn't like the buckle, the heel or the colour. In the end she told me she'd *leave it for now* and *think about it* and she left the shop empty-handed.

So we finally made our way down to the harbour, which in many ways was similar to Charlestown insomuch as there was an inner and outer harbour. It was easy to understand why the sanctuary of an inner harbour was required in this part of Cornwall and the contrast between the two harbours was very pronounced. Numerous fishing boats bobbed up and down within the confines of the harbours, with the boats in the outer harbour bobbing up and down far more than those in the inner harbour.

We walked past the relatively calm inner harbour before finding ourselves facing the full force of the wind by a slipway which was directly opposite the outer harbour entrance. There was no shelter from the strong easterly wind and we were mesmerised by the huge waves that raced in from the rough sea, smashed against the high harbour walls and sent spray high up into the air all around us. Mevagissey seemed even more exposed to easterlies than Charlestown, and the water in the outer harbour was very rough indeed. We certainly wouldn't have wanted to lose our footing and slip down the slipway into the turbulent sea, so we beat a hasty retreat.

We carried on to the lighthouse at the end of the exposed outer harbour wall, where we stopped to admire the view back towards the village. Multi-coloured cottages, built on different levels adorning a rocky hillside, presented a very picturesque view against the turquoise sea and the bright blue, almost cloudless sky. Conversely, the lucky people who lived in those elevated cottages would have enjoyed enviable views over the harbour and out to sea.

Just like Charlestown and many other Cornish villages, hardly any modern building work or development had taken place and, with the exception of several cars and vans which were parked on top of one of the high harbour walls, nothing much had changed in the last few hundred years. There were no railings or barriers of any kind on the wall, and if any of the vehicle owners had been unfortunate enough to lose their concentration there was absolutely nothing to prevent their vehicles from going over the edge and into the sea.

I thought it was a good job we didn't inadvertently get as far as the harbour whilst on our harrowing motorhome tour of Mevagissey and been tempted to park where those vehicles were. If we had somehow managed to manoeuvre the motorhome onto the very narrow and slippery wall, I dread to think what could have happened if we'd had to perform a three point turn or reverse back along it!

Thinking of parking, I checked my watch, remembered we'd only paid for two hours in the car park and realised our time was almost up. Consequently we made our way through the narrow streets, passing all the shops, and back to the car park as fast as we could. After we'd climbed aboard the motorhome and I'd started the engine Emm said she wished she'd bought a particular pair of sandals after all. As I pulled away and gave the friendly car park attendant a wave, I told her to belt up before heading up the main road without saying another word!

24

GOING TO LOOE
WITH THE GIRLS

Sadly, we were almost at the end of our holiday and wanted to make the most of the remaining time before going home to rejoin the rat race. We both thought it would be good to take another trip down memory lane and stay for our last night near Looe at *Tencreek Holiday Park* where we'd spent a couple of holidays many years before.

The first time was in 1978 when we stayed under canvas with a fifteen-month-old Joscelin who was still in nappies, and Rowena hadn't even been thought about. We'd driven down to Cornwall from Lee-on-Solent, where we lived at the time, in our old Fiat 850 which was a small Italian saloon car that had its engine in the back and the boot in the front. Fiat had obviously designed this model, as well as their other models at the time, for the warm dry Mediterranean climate and several years exposed to the damp British weather quickly reduced the thin metal bodywork to a mass of proliferating brown rust.

This was the second Fiat 850 we'd owned. Emm had bought the first one (in which we drove to Cornwall for our first camping holidays) before we were seriously courting and that car was in a particularly bad way. As she proudly showed me her new acquisition I was horrified to see that a huge area of the floor, which should have been solid metal, was rapidly being eaten away by the dreaded rust bug that plagued most cars of the time. Even so, the car was Emm's pride and joy, and during the early days of our relationship I realised that, if I allowed myself to get too serious with this girlfriend, I'd inevitably end up spending many hours touching up her bodywork.

Needless to say, true love won the day and throughout the years we owned the car I fought a never ending battle sandwiching the rusty floor between layers of fibreglass and, somehow or other, this rust-bucket of a car still managed to pass its annual MOT test. That is, until the lenient MOT tester at the Fiat garage where Emm bought the car left his employ and a much stricter tester condemned it to the scrap heap.

I certainly couldn't argue the point. Deep down, I had to admit the car was a potential death trap and that if it was ever involved in a collision with a more solid vehicle (or in other words, *any* vehicle) we wouldn't have stood a chance. So the faithful old Fiat was finally sent to the breaker's yard and replaced by a slightly newer, much less rusty Fiat 850 we bought quite cheaply from a *careful lady owner*.

Thinking about it now, the logic behind buying the same model again may seem slightly flawed. However, back then we had little spare money to spend on another car, and knowing exactly where to look for the dreaded rust-bug, I gave it a thorough going over before agreeing to buy. To my surprise it was pretty much free of rust and had obviously been well looked after. Also, I realised we had loads of spare parts that just needed to be stripped out of the condemned car, which by the time the scrap man came to collect was just an empty shell resting on bricks.

For example, I kept the wheels which were fitted with good tyres, engine, gearbox, dynamo, shock absorbers, headlights and virtually everything else that was removable and stored it all in our garage. Even though the scrap man wasn't all that happy about leaving this valuable stock of spares with me, he still took the body away to the crusher without charge. Maybe he just took pity on me having bought another Fiat 850, but those spares kept our newer model on the road for quite a few more years to come and kept its cost of ownership down to an absolute minimum.

Having endured (I really mean *enjoyed*) those earlier long haul camping holidays down in Cornwall courtesy of our old Fiat 850, we decided that baby Joscelin was now old enough to be introduced to the pleasures of camping. We splashed out on a larger tent, and realised that with a baby on-board we'd need far more camping gear than we could possibly squeeze inside the car. Consequently we invested in a roof rack, onto which we'd strap the tent and all the other larger equipment, such as the essential McClaren baby buggy, a wooden playpen, plus a couple of suitcases crammed full of baby clothes and nappies, as well as a minimum amount of spare underwear and a few odd T-shirts for us.

In order to try and keep everything dry in case it rained, which it usually did whenever we went camping, we covered all this gear with a large polythene sheet which I held down with several of those elasticated thingamajigs with hooks on the end. Great care had to be taken when fixing them, as without warning they could fly back and punish such carelessness with a vicious whack in the eye!

After I got everything safely strapped down on the roof rack, every available space inside the car then had to be utilised to carry everything else, like the nappy sterilising bucket, water containers, baby bath, toys, sleeping bags, pillows, mattresses, cooking stove, pots, pans and tins of food. And after all that was crammed in, there hardly seemed to be any room left for the three of us to fit inside the car. But somehow or other we wedged ourselves in and were ready to set off on our first truly family holiday.

It was a fairly good summer, although not nearly as hot as the heat wave of 1976, which was probably just as well, and we could see no practical reason why we couldn't cope and still have a good time camping with a baby. Indeed, we did have a super time touring around Cornwall, but disaster struck on the last night of our holiday whilst camping at Tencreek.

We'd spent the day on the beach at Looe, right next to the banjo pier, and Joscelin had really enjoyed herself playing in the sand and paddling in the shallow waters whilst we held her up. We still have photographs of her grinning from cheek to cheek and wearing a sun hat whilst playing on the beach with a toy watering can. Up until then we'd had a really good week with no problems whatsoever. The car hadn't played up, the weather had been kind and we'd managed with all the baby food, nappy sterilising equipment and baby bathing out in the open air.

We may have used the odd disposable nappy, but we certainly stuck to the traditional terry nappies most of the time. I can't recall how we managed to wash them – I suppose we must have used campsite launderettes – but I certainly remember having to be extra careful not to knock over the nappy sterilising bucket which we left outside the tent.

Anyhow, we'd had a good last day to conclude a good week's holiday and were due to drive back home the following morning. We'd all settled down for our last night in the tent, but were woken up in the very early hours of the morning by baby Joscelin's constant crying. She sounded in some distress, to say the least, and the reason for her discomfort quickly became clear.

To say she needed changing would be a gross understatement and I'm sorry to say that the contents of her nappy were quite appalling. It was no wonder she was in such a state, as everything had oozed out all over her Babygro and onto her bedclothes. It was a horrible bright yellow slimy mess, which gave off the most obnoxious odour I've ever had the misfortune to experience and, trying our best not to breathe, we cleaned everything up by torchlight as best we could and changed her nappy, Babygro and bedclothes.

Once she was cleaned up, she calmed down a bit and we hoped she'd go back to sleep, which she did for a bit. But then the same thing happened again. It seemed as though the poor little thing was suffering from a bad bout of food poisoning, and if we'd known where the nearest hospital was we would have immediately taken her there.

I tried to reassure Emm that everything would be fine once Joscelin got it all out of her system, but I was just as worried about our precious daughter. She didn't seem to improve at all, and as soon as we changed one nappy, it needed changing again. We felt extremely guilty about taking her camping, but still couldn't understand what it was that could have caused her to be so ill. We'd been as meticulous as we could with her hygiene and she'd been a perfectly healthy and happy little girl up until then.

It must have been about two o' clock in the morning when we both realised we couldn't stay in the tent any longer, and decided to pack up as quickly as possible, make our way home and seek medical help. As I said, we would have headed for the nearest hospital but didn't have a clue where it was, and at that time of the night there was no one around to ask. Luckily it was a calm moonlit night and, in record time, we took the tent down, got all the camping gear strapped onto the roof-rack and squeezed everything else into the car, where there was just enough room to strap Joscelin into her baby seat in the back.

The road was unbelievably clear and Joscelin soon settled down as the motion of the car sent her to sleep. I don't think we saw more than a dozen vehicles on the frantic journey home and although I couldn't be accused of speeding – after all our tiny Fiat with its low powered 850 cc engine could only go so fast – we made incredible time. I seem to recall we only stopped once to change her nappy again which, to our great relief, was almost clean compared to the previous times. Even so, with the windows wound down, the stench in the car was still pretty vile.

We got back home without further incident, and by the time we managed to see the doctor first thing in the morning Joscelin appeared to be back to normal. Fortunately, having lost so much fluid from her tiny body, we'd had the foresight to give her as much water as possible to drink and she didn't get dehydrated. Looking back, we deduced she'd probably put something nasty in her mouth when we were on the beach in Looe, possibly some sand a dog had peed on – or worse.

However, she lived to tell the tale and it obviously didn't put her off camping. She's always enjoyed life under canvas, firstly with us, then with the Girl Guides and later with her boyfriend and future husband. They recently camped with their baby, but had to pack up and go home in the middle of the night after a stream suddenly started to flow through the middle of their tent during a very stormy night in the Lake District. Luckily, they didn't have too far to travel back home, but that's another story and not mine to tell.

Anyhow, almost a decade later, we went back to Tencreek as a family but this time stayed in one of their static caravans. We still had our own static at Durdle Door, which we all absolutely loved and never tired of, but after our holidays at Kennack Sands we decided to splash out on hiring a caravan somewhere else to give us another change of scene. Joscelin would have been about ten and Rowena eight and we all had a great time.

For a family holiday with young children Tencreek was ideal and we all enjoyed it immensely. We wandered around Looe, explored the surrounding countryside and walked along the beautiful cliff tops, but the best thing about it was the varied family entertainment which was laid on each evening. As well as disco music, different live groups played every night and we all enjoyed dancing – especially me with the girls after I'd had a couple of beers, even if they were embarrassed and I had to force them onto the floor.

Also, for three nights of the week at six o'clock, different entertainers performed for the children. I can't remember what they all were, but seem to recall Punch and Judy and vividly remember Uncle Ken's Magic Show, which was very good indeed. The girls loved it and we bought Uncle Ken's magic book for them which we still have at home somewhere. At the following family Christmas party I actually performed some of the simple tricks he described in his book and, even if I say so myself, baffled the girls with my trickery.

What with the varied free entertainment being such a huge bonus, we all particularly enjoyed that holiday and decided to go back the following year. However, that proved to be a huge mistake! There was no children's entertainment laid on whatsoever, and the family entertainment was exactly the same each and every night with just one man playing an organ. For the price we paid I guess it was fair enough, but as we'd been totally spoiled by the previous year's varied entertainment programme it was hugely disappointing by comparison.

In retrospect, I suppose going back to a place where we'd had such a good time before could never quite live up to expectations second time around, and so it proved on that particular family holiday. Nevertheless, after our drive from Mevagissey, Emm and I found ourselves in the reception at Tencreek Holiday Park asking if they had a motorhome pitch for the night. They had plenty of vacancies so, for old time's sake, we booked in for the last night of our motorhome tour.

We got the impression that since the last time we'd been there the site had been taken over by a large caravan and camping holiday chain, which indeed it had. Nevertheless, our needs now were entirely different from when we went there with our young family and this time we weren't at all bothered about any on-site entertainment or children's facilities.

We were just passing through and only wanted somewhere to pitch up for the night and take the opportunity to have a few nostalgic hours in Looe. As long as the showers were hot and the toilets clean, we'd be happy enough. For now, all was right with the world and we decided to make the most of what remained of the afternoon by walking into Looe in the sunshine.

25

HIGH TIDE, STRONG WIND & QUEUEING IN LOOE

We locked up, turned left out of the campsite and, just before the busy main road, took a right turn down a quiet country lane where we'd earlier seen a signpost for the town centre. At first the path seemed to be straightforward enough and we found ourselves walking past fields and farmland. Then, after about twenty minutes or so, we came to a junction where there was no signpost to indicate which direction we should take.

I wondered why signposts on some roads or paths often lead to junctions such as this one where a further signpost is conspicuous by its absence, and the unwary walker or motorist doesn't have a clue which direction to take. Is it some sort of sadistic ploy, which local authorities delight in to confuse unsuspecting strangers? Were there a couple of local yokels, like those that used to be portrayed by the Two Ronnies, hiding in nearby bushes suppressing fits of laughter as they watched us in our confused state arguing about which path we needed to take?

And although neither of us were completely confident about which path led to Looe, were they disappointed that, more by luck than judgement, we eventually followed the left hand path, which luckily proved to be the right path? However, at the time we didn't know that for sure and, as we seemed to end up walking some considerable distance and still couldn't see the sea, further doubts crept into our minds and we thought we might have been going round in circles.

We were on the verge of giving up and doubling back to Tencreek when we saw signs of civilisation ahead and then distant glimpses of blue sea. Although we tried to convince ourselves it couldn't be much further, we were genuinely more optimistic when we found ourselves walking down a very pretty Cornish lane with exceedingly picturesque cottages either side of us. When I say walking *down*, that's exactly what I mean, as we were indeed making our way down a very steep hill towards the sea.

Every cottage was adorned with colourful late summer flowers and it was clear that everyone who lived here took much pride in their homes. Some of the cottages were probably second homes or holiday lets, but I got the impression that most of them were permanent homes, and I envied the lucky people who lived there. Mind you, we were seeing it on a sunny day and, on reflection, I'm not entirely sure it would have held quite the same attraction on a cold winter day with a gale howling in off the sea, especially if having to walk up the steep hill in the dark.

Anyhow, now we knew for certain we were going in the right direction, we put on a bit of a spurt and thankfully soon found ourselves in West Looe down by the river which separates East and West Looe. We went past a cottage where we knew Babs Atkins once lived. Babs and her sister, Evelyn, used to own Looe Island, just off the coast to the south from where we were standing. The sisters followed an impossible dream and back in 1965 incredibly bought the island lock, stock and barrel.

Their fascinating story is told in two excellent books, *We Bought an Island* and *Tales From Our Cornish Island,* both by Evelyn Atkins. They are well worth a read and tell how the sisters gave up their suburban life in Surrey and came to own and live in isolation on their own tiny island. They carried on living there, all on their own, right up until the time they died, Evelyn aged eighty-seven in 1997 and Babs aged eighty-six in 2004.

How those old ladies managed to cope on their small island with no mod cons almost defies belief. Even though during very low tides it's possible to walk to the island from the mainland, the only practical way to get there and back is by boat. However, the sea is often too wild and stormy for boats to make a safe crossing and the island is inevitably cut off from the mainland for long periods of time.

When the sisters made their extraordinary brave and life changing move Evelyn had just retired, but Babs, who was a few years younger, still had to work for a living. She was a school teacher in Surrey, and by an enormous stroke of luck there was a teaching vacancy at the local school which she successfully applied for. However, it just wasn't possible to commute from the island each day, so she had to have a base in the town where she could stay during the week and it was this very cottage we were now standing beside. And very nice it was too.

We'd visited the island on the camping holiday when Joscelin was a toddler and had met both the extraordinary sisters. We bought a copy of Evelyn's first book, which had just been published at the time, and whilst making a great fuss of Joscelin she signed it for us. Ever since then we've always wanted to go back for another visit but have never been able to manage it. Neither would we have time to do so on this trip. In any case, dogs aren't permitted so we'd have needed to find a local kennel for Monty. So, the island is still on our long list of places to revisit in future and we still look forward to that trip sometime soon. The island is now managed as a marine nature reserve by the Cornwall Wildlife Trust, to whom the sisters bequeathed the island, and they organise trips in the Trust's own boat, ironically called *Islander*.

As we approached the sea, or more strictly speaking the river that divides East and West Looe, we suddenly noticed that there was a very strong and cold south easterly wind blowing. Why this surprised us, I don't really know. After all it was just the same earlier in Mevagissey, but now the wind seemed to be even stronger and much more menacing. During our walk we'd been sheltered, firstly by tall trees and then the cottages, but now as it blew in off the sea and funnelled up the river we were fully exposed to the full force of the strong wind.

No matter, it was the last day of our holiday and we weren't about to let a bit of wind spoil it. I'd promised Emm a boat trip, which so far we hadn't managed, and before us was a boat trip opportunity not to be missed. So without hesitation I decided to treat her to a mini boat cruise and at the same time save our weary legs from having to walk further up river and cross the bridge into East Looe.

The boat was just approaching us from the other side of the river so I knew we wouldn't have long to wait and, after its skipper had tied up and its passengers disembarked, we climbed on board the small ferry boat with a few other people. It only cost eighty pence for the two of us plus Monty, which I thought was an absolute bargain for a river cruise – albeit a short one.

Mind you, it was a bit hairy as the exceptionally strong current was surging up river from the sea at what seemed to us an incredible rate. The ferryman had to skilfully aim the boat almost at right angles to the landing stage on the opposite bank where we were heading, and virtually pointed the bow right into the fast moving current. It was a good job the boat had a powerful motor and that we didn't have to be rowed across otherwise we surely would have been swept way up river. Even so, the ferryman must have been extremely proficient at setting the right course and, after only about five minutes, our *river cruise* came to an end as we safely stepped out of the boat at the correct place on the opposite side of the river in East Looe.

We both commented that the water level was much higher than we'd ever recalled seeing it at Looe. Usually when we'd been there, the tide had been a long way out and the river a virtual trickle with boats resting on a sea of unsightly mud. However on that particular day, as well as fast flowing, the water level came up to just below the level of the concrete path we were walking along, so we assumed the tide was at its highest point and about to turn.

We headed towards the nearby shops (where else?) and were alarmed to see loads of sandbags stacked up outside, which gave us a bit of a clue that trouble was expected. Even so, everyone seemed to be going about their business as usual and if it hadn't have been for the strong wind, high tide and fast flowing water, everything would have appeared to be normal in the bright sunshine. Consequently we didn't think too much about the sandbags for the moment and I found myself waiting outside a shop with Monty, whilst Emm disappeared inside to browse and try on flip-flops. It was decidedly chilly standing still in the cold wind so I started to pace up and down the promenade to keep warm.

I noticed more sandbags, some of which had already been piled up against the doorways of shops and other premises. I then saw notices displayed on many of the doors and, having nothing much else to do for the moment, I ventured closer to read them. They informed me that *'Due to the expected high tides on Thursday and Friday nights, these shops will be closed for the day'*. Well today was Friday and I wondered if there'd been problems the night before.

Pinned up in one of the shop doorways was a tide table which informed me that high tide was much later in the evening, which surprised and alarmed me. It was now around three-thirty and, to my inexpert eyes, the water level already appeared to be as high as it could be without flooding into adjacent premises. High tide was still six hours away, so it was no wonder shop owners were stockpiling sandbags!

What with the present height of the water, plus the very strong wind blowing in from the sea, even a landlubber like me could see it was highly likely that the river would breach the limited sea defences and flow into the nearby buildings. Suddenly, all these picturesque Cornish coastal villages didn't seem quite such attractive places to live after all, and I hoped Looe and all the other places along the coast would escape the threatened floods.

Even so, apart from the sandbags and a few closed shops, life seemed to be carrying on as normal. I went back to the shop to wait for Emm where some striped cotton fishermen's shirts in the window caught my eye, especially as they were at reduced end of season prices. When Emm reappeared without having bought anything, I handed her Monty's lead and told her I was just popping inside to try on a shirt.

I went in, picked up the one I wanted from the rack and took it straight into an empty cubicle to try on for size. As I pulled the fleece I was already wearing over my head, it annoyingly caught on my glasses so I took them off and carefully placed them on a stool in the corner of the cubicle. I then put on the shirt, had a quick glance in the mirror to check it fitted, did a twirl and, without hesitation, decided to buy it. Having taken it off again, I put my fleece back on and went to join a short queue to pay.

I could see Emm waiting impatiently outside waving her arms about and mouthing for to me to hurry up. No doubt she was feeling the cold, but it was embarrassing waiting my turn in the queue and I turned away and made out I didn't know her. In no time at all though, the young lady assistant had folded the shirt and placed it in a bag before asking me to put my debit card in her machine and key in my PIN. However, when nothing happened I realised that only three numbers had actually registered, so had another go.

The same thing happened again, which made me realise that one of the numbers on the keypad was a bit temperamental and that I needed to press harder. The assistant told me to do it again, but this time more slowly and more firmly. I did as she asked, took my time and pressed down on the dodgy digit with just a little more pressure. This time our transaction was completed satisfactorily so I removed my card and slipped it back inside my wallet, along with the receipt.

Apologising for the delay, I rejoined a shivering Emm and we hurried towards the beach, where we were sure Joscelin had caught her bad bout of food poisoning all those years before. We were almost there when I suddenly realised I was no longer wearing my glasses. In my haste to buy the shirt, I must have left them in the changing cubicle back at the shop, so I gabbled out an explanation to Emm and ran back to the shop as fast as I could.

Breathing heavily after my short sprint, I interrupted the assistant and asked if anyone had handed them in. They hadn't, and I imagined someone sitting on the stool where I'd left them and damaging them beyond repair. Either that or they'd dropped to the floor and been crushed by someone's size ten shoes. I pushed my way through the customers towards the back of the shop and hoped beyond hope that my fears were groundless. I hadn't had them long and they'd cost a small fortune.

Luckily the cubicle wasn't being used and, half expecting to find fragments of clear plastic and bent wire ground into the floor, I was incredibly relieved to see my glasses on the stool where I'd left them. Considering that the shop was so busy, I'd imagined that any saving made on my bargain shirt to have been wiped out by a huge bill for replacement specs and I was extremely thankful to have been so fortunate.

After putting them back on, I ran straight back to Emm who, like me, had expected the worst. However, even though she was also thankful I'd got away with my carelessness, she kept telling me what an idiot I was to have left them there in the first place. However, I didn't need to be told over and over again, so did my best to ignore her as we carried on to the beach by the banjo pier.

Considering the wind strength, there were loads of people on the beach, virtually all of whom were sheltered behind wind breaks which must have been hammered in really hard otherwise they would have blown away. Everyone seemed to be looking at what must have started out as a dinghy race, and we saw loads of serious sailors floundering in the water alongside capsized dinghies.

In fact, there seemed to be more dinghies lying on their sides in the water or, worse still, completely overturned, than there were upright dinghies. And even the upright dinghies were no longer racing, but just making their way back to shore as carefully as possible with lowered mainsails and jibs violently flapping from side to side. A rescue motor boat was buzzing about amongst all this mayhem and its crew was extremely busy making sure everyone was alright and towing capsized dinghies ashore.

I'd done a bit of dinghy sailing myself, but even with a most experienced helmsman there was no way I would have even considered venturing out on the water in such strong winds. Either these guys were very skilful sailors, which I'm sure they were, or else they were very foolish to even think about going out in such conditions. Any official race had clearly been abandoned and luckily everyone seemed to be none the worse for their experience. We'd missed most of the excitement, but the crews we saw coming ashore looked as though they'd enjoyed any adrenaline rush. So no harm done – we hoped.

We started to feel very cold just standing there in the strong wind, the force of which whipped up the fine sand from the beach and almost sandblasted the skin off our faces. We decided to make our way to the town centre which, I have to say, appeared to be much tackier than when we were there some years before.

There seemed to be many more fast food shops, and loads of takeaway litter was strewn all around. With such a strong wind funnelling down the streets, it was difficult to stand or walk in an upright position and bits of paper, takeaway containers and other assorted litter blew all around us. However, to be fair, we realised most of this unsightly rubbish would have been blown there, rather than thrown there, such was the strength of the wind which seemed to swirl around the inside of all the rubbish bins like mini tornadoes and send the lightweight contents hurtling high into the air.

The sight and smell of all the takeaways made us think about what we could eat that night and we were slightly tempted by fish and chips. However, we didn't relish the thought of eating them outside in the open air amongst all the litter and flying sand. Anyhow, it was our last night and our last chance for some time to eat one Cornwall's finest delicacies. So we followed our noses to the pasty shop and, leaving Emm outside with Monty, I went inside to buy our dinner.

There were about three or four customers in front of me, so I didn't expect to have to wait long, especially as they were being served quickly enough. Nevertheless, I could see Emm again getting agitated having to wait outside. Like me, she hates waiting around and is never that patient at the best of times, but now she was tired, hungry and, worst of all, standing in a cold, shady and windy spot with that pained hurry up look on her face. However, in no time at all there was only one customer in front of me so I confidently indicated I wouldn't be long.

I then heard that customer place his order. I can't remember now exactly what he wanted, but it was a big confusing order for twelve various flavoured pasties, and I grimaced as I heard him ask for three steak and stilton, two cheese and onion, three chicken tikka, two cheese and sweetcorn, one tomato, one cheese and basil, one vegetarian, one tomato, one potato and one onion. Or something like that!

The shopkeeper rummaged around his counter, but clearly didn't have all these varieties readily available. So, after spending a few minutes searching for a pen and paper, he then reconfirmed the order and wrote it down. The customer then changed his mind about one of his choices, forcing the shopkeeper to amend his list before he disappeared to the back of the shop leaving one extremely hungry customer, me and a couple of others waiting for what seemed like ages. He took so long that I imagined him planting the seeds for the vegetarian pasties, butchering the meat for the steak ones and then making the pastry.

I was acutely aware of Emm waiting outside waving her arms around as she paced up and down the street. She kept pointing to her watch and mouthing at me to give up and come on out, but I convinced myself the shopkeeper couldn't be much longer. In any case, now that I was next in line to be served, I didn't want to cut off my nose to spite my face and leave the shop empty handed. I just knew that if I did leave the shop, then the greedy customer in front of me would be immediately dealt with and it would have been my turn. In any case, I didn't want to end up with Emm's speciality tuna delight and rice, which was about all we had left to eat.

The time slowly passed, Emm got even more impatient and I became even more resolute in my determination to have pasties for dinner. A slightly older looking shopkeeper finally emerged with a sack-like bag of Cornwall's finest, which I assumed the customer was going to share with eleven of his mates. Mind you, judging by the size of him, I cruelly thought they could *all* be for his own supper.

He then went to pay his £25, or whatever they cost, and proceeded to frustrate me and everyone else in the queue even more by rummaging through all his pockets to find his cash. Why he hadn't used the extensive waiting time to sort out his money was totally beyond me. He acted as though he had all the time in the world, and was rudely oblivious to the growing queue of impatient customers behind him. At long last he managed to find the means to pay before waddling out of the shop, and mercifully it was my turn to be served.

I asked for a traditional and a vegetarian, both of which I could see were readily available, handed over the right money, which I'd had more than enough time to work out and get ready, and left the shop to rejoin Emm as fast as I could. Of course, having to wait so long she was cold and weary, as well as a bit ratty, but at least I could now assure her we wouldn't have much cooking to do.

We'd originally planned to walk back the way we came, but had to admit it was considerably further than we first thought. In any case, it was now gone five o'clock and we were both tired, our feet ached and neither of us fancied the plod back up the steep hill out of West Looe. We hoped there would be a bus that would drop us off right outside Tencreek, where we remembered seeing a bus stop. We knew the bus stopped in Looe just past the bridge and, having no idea what time the buses went or how frequent they were, we hurried off in that direction.

We passed the Tourist Information Centre where we thought we'd ask about the buses, only to find it was closed, but then we then spotted a timetable outside on a notice board. Knowing our luck, we thought we'd have a very long wait or, even worse, have missed the last bus and would have to walk back after all. However, we were being too pessimistic and there was one due to leave at five twenty-five and it was now five-fifteen. That was perfect, so we gratefully made our way the short distance up to the bus stop where we joined a few other waiting passengers.

The bus was dead on time and we were extremely happy to pay our fares, flop into our seats and take the weight off our aching feet. As we crossed the bridge we saw that the river level was incredibly high, which was very alarming as high tide was still almost five hours away![25] The combined forces of the high tide and the strong wind were forcing the water to rapidly flow upstream and again we feared the worse and hoped the river wouldn't burst its banks and flood the adjacent buildings. There wasn't much anyone could do about it and, apart from the few closed shops and the sandbags we saw in the town, the locals didn't seem all that outwardly perturbed, so we settled down to try and enjoy our short bus ride.

Monty had never been on a bus before and we couldn't remember the last time we had either. In Chiselborough where we lived we did have a regular bus service. It came regularly once every day, except on Sundays. Like most people living there we always relied on the car, so this bus journey was a bit of a novelty. As the bus climbed the steep hill out of Looe we had a great view of the surrounding countryside, and not having to concentrate on driving I could really look around and appreciate the scenery.

I wished we'd gone upstairs where we'd have enjoyed an even better view, but before we knew it we were thanking the driver and stepping off the bus right outside Tencreek Caravan Park. What had taken us over an hour to walk across the back lanes, had taken just ten minutes by bus and, after an exceptionally long and tiring day, we were grateful to get back to our motorhome.

We were starving hungry, so simply popped our pasties in the oven and heated up tinned potatoes and baked beans in a saucepan. The pasties were delicious, which we knew they would be, and went down really well with a bottle of cheap red wine. After clearing up and taking Monty for a short walk, we did think about going to the clubhouse to take advantage of the evening entertainment, which we would have

---

25 There's a video on You Tube showing the high tide in Looe on 9th September 2006, which was when we were there.

paid for in our site fee. But all the fresh air had taken its toll and we were feeling far too tired to even think about going, so ended up having another early night.

Tencreek is quite high up and rather exposed and during the night we woke up to the alarming sound of a howling gale blowing all around us. Our motorhome rocked violently from side to side and sleep became almost impossible. Hardly daring to look, we nervously raised the blind and peered out into the darkness. Luckily there didn't appear to be anyone camping in tents, just a few motorhomes like ours and some touring caravans, plus plenty of static caravans in an adjacent field, most of which seemed to be unoccupied.

However, some of the tourers had large awnings which were in a semi collapsed state, flapping furiously in the strong wind and noisily beating on the sides of the caravans they were attached to. We gave thanks it was just the two of us in a relatively solid motorhome, rather than our old tent with a baby like the last time we were at Tencreek, and hoped the storm would soon peter out. We were also mindful of the night's high tide and thought that some flooding in Looe, as well as elsewhere along the coast, must be inevitable.

We remembered the great storm across southern England during the night of 15/16th October 1987, when the winds reached over ninety miles an hour and eighteen people lost their lives. Incredibly, fifteen million trees were upended, roofs were ripped off buildings, hundreds of thousands of homes were without electricity for over twenty-four hours and the cost to the insurers was around a billion pounds. I wouldn't have believed that there were actually fifteen million trees in the whole of the country, so to actually lose that amount across southern England alone was quite staggering!

We were living in Farnham at the time and actually slept through all this destruction, which happened to a lesser extent all around us. For some reason or other, on the day after the storm, which was a Friday, I had a day off work and had volunteered to take Rowena to school. As we walked up the road it seemed eerily quiet and I was surprised to see loads of bits of broken branches strewn across the road, which gave me a bit of a clue that it must have been fairly windy during the night. I was then flabbergasted to see a large tree, completely uprooted and leaning at a forty five degree angle against a house.

I'd never seen anything remotely like it before, and was even more flabbergasted when we arrived at school to be met by a very perturbed headmistress who told me and all the other dazed parents that the school was closed for the day. She didn't really have to explain the reason why as, even with our rather disbelieving eyes, we could all see an even larger mature tree completely uprooted and lying on its side across the school entrance.

When we returned home and told Emm, she initially didn't believe what I told her, but when we turned on the television the full story of a massive disaster slowly unfolded. Horrific footage was being shown of terrible destruction all over southern England. Trees lay scattered like matchwood, their roots just torn out of the ground by some unimaginable force. Many had fallen on cars, totally crushing them as though they were just discarded tin cans. Countless roofs had been stripped of their tiles and caravan sites all along the south coast had been totally devastated by the hurricane force winds. As I said, we'd somehow slept through this terrible destruction and just couldn't comprehend it at first. However, once it had sunk in we became concerned about our caravan, which wasn't insured, at Durdle Door.

The caravan site had officially closed for the season on the Wednesday before the storm and we'd been there over the previous weekend closing everything up ready for the winter break. Fearing the worst, we kept phoning to find out what the situation was and whether our caravan had been damaged or not. But the phone lines were dead. Therefore, on the Sunday after the storm, which was a fine calm sunny autumn day, we drove down to Dorset to find out for ourselves.

It was utter devastation, unlike anything we'd witnessed before or since, or ever want to see again and looked like the site had been hit by an almighty bomb blast. We shouldn't have been that surprised, as similar scenes all over the south coast had been portrayed in all the newspapers and on television. But to actually witness it for ourselves sent a chill down our spines.

Static caravans, especially those in the prime spots overlooking the sea, had received the full force of the storm and the vast majority were completely blown away. Nothing remained except their chassis, which were still chained down to their concrete bases. The walls, roofs and all their contents were scattered far and wide around the site, along with evil looking shards of broken window glass, some of which had embedded itself into the sides of those caravans that were still standing. The whole scene was eerily surreal and looked like the aftermath of a war zone or a shot from some Hollywood disaster movie.

Unbelievably, amongst all this devastation, our old caravan was completely unscathed with not even a scratch to blemish its newly polished paintwork.

We met a retired couple who were asleep in their caravan whilst all this devastation went on around them. They shouldn't have been there, as the day before the storm the site had officially closed for the winter. They told us they'd been given special permission to stay on until the weekend and that the storm had been worse than the London blitz which they'd lived through.

When they looked out of their window during the night, with their caravan being buffeted by the hurricane force winds, they couldn't comprehend what was happening. Seeing sturdy caravans literally being blown apart and debris hurtling all around them at tremendous speeds, some of which slammed into their own caravan, they must have thought they were back in wartime London. Either that or they were having a nightmare. However, once they realised it was for real and that they were alone in this horrendous situation, they were virtually paralysed with fear. They then ran for their lives to the relative safety of the brick built toilet block, where they failed to get a wink of sleep during the nightmarish remainder of the night.

All these unsettling thoughts of 1987 went through our minds as we again drifted off to an uneasy sleep in our motorhome. Later on, we woke up yet again as we felt the motorhome being buffeted about even more. Apprehensively, we looked out and saw a few caravan awnings, which had been totally torn away from their fixing points, blowing crazily about in the wind. Again we thought about the possible combined effect of the high tide and strong winds on all the homes and buildings which were at risk along the coast. We imagined some sort of flood damage to be almost certain and our hearts went out to all the owners who could be affected.

When we woke from our uneasy sleep in the morning the wind had mercifully died down and, as we peered through our window with half closed eyes, we were relieved to see that none of the caravans or motorhomes appeared to be damaged; the only evidence of the night's strong winds being just a few caravan awnings lying lifeless on the ground.

Later on we found out that, although there was some coastal flooding at Looe and Mevagissey, there thankfully didn't appear to be any extensive damage to property. However, knowing what happened during the great storm of 1987 which resulted in so much destruction and even loss of life, I must admit that it was quite a scary night at times and easy to let our imagination run away with us.

I counted our blessings and shuddered to think what it must have been like for the elderly couple who illicitly stayed in their caravan at Durdle Door during the October 1987 storm. They must have been scared witless! If the caravan site hadn't officially closed down just a day before, or the storm had occurred a week earlier, many, many more people would have been staying in their caravans during that great storm – including us. And that just didn't bear thinking about…

26

WOEFUL WASHROOMS & PARKING IN POLPERRO

It was the last morning of our first motorhome holiday and we were surprised that the week had passed so quickly. After a miserable start we'd gradually got used to the motorhome way of life and were not in a hurry to go home. Nor were we looking forward to going back to work. Unless there were unexpected traffic hold ups, our journey home would only take a couple of hours, so we decided to make the most of our time and spend the morning in nearby Polperro where we'd previously spent some enjoyable days out.

After a quick breakfast, I went over to the washrooms which were a bit run down and in need of updating. Just like many campsites we'd been to in the past, the majority of basins had no plugs, and I cursed all the idiots who find washbasin plugs to be so attractive that they just can't keep their sticky little fingers off them.

It seems that most site owners have got so fed up with the disappearing plugs that they just don't bother to replace them anymore. That certainly wasn't the case at the magnificent Ayr Holiday Park in St Ives where the plugs were of the most modern, up-market, non-removable type. But at other places we stayed that week I'd noticed some men carrying plugs around in their wash bags, and couldn't help wondering whether they'd stolen them from some campsite washroom. After all, someone does!

However, they mostly looked like model citizens, so I mentally gave them the benefit of the doubt and assumed they were seasoned campers, motorhomers or caravanners who'd learnt from experience and had legitimately bought them as an essential part of their campsite washing kit.

The other thing I specifically noticed was that there were different types of taps on the basins. Some were the normal *turn-on, turn-off* type, which were fine. But others were the type where the top of the tap has to be pressed down in order to turn it on. The washrooms were busy and the few basins which did still have plugs were being used. So I ended up having to shave in a plug-less basin, which also had *press-down* taps.

Just to be clear what type of tap I'm referring to here, I mean the type of tap that, when pressed, expels a high pressure jet of water similar in force to a mini Niagara Falls; the type of tap that can't then be turned off, until it's made up its own mind to do so; and the type of tap from which water cascades onto the bottom of the basin with so much force that it splashes out over the sides, soaking the floor and the unfortunate person using it. Of course I know why they're used in such places. It's to save water!

Anyhow, I needed a shave so persevered. But each time I had to wash the foam and bristles out of my razor, a simple operation usually accomplished in just a few inches of water in the bottom of the basin, even though I tried not to press very hard, I instigated a powerful jet of fast flowing water which splashed over the top of the basin all over my trousers. I must have wasted gallons during my shave and, what with that and the fact that I cut my lip, for future motorhome holidays I considered either growing a beard or, even if it did mean all the plug-less men in the washrooms would suspect me of being a plug pilferer, spending a few pence on purchasing my own personal plug from a plumber's merchant.

After finishing my morning ablutions, I went over to the washing up area to sort out the breakfast dishes. The water was piping hot, the sinks were huge and there were ample stainless steel draining boards. There were even plugs in the sinks. Unfortunately, there were also large dollops of spaghetti, bits of carrot, teabags and other various unidentifiable and unsavoury foodstuffs languishing there. So much food in fact, that a starving third world family would be grateful to have an opportunity to gather it all up and make a substantial meal from it all.

Decent washing up facilities and washrooms were the two things which, as far as I'm concerned, can make or break a campsite. Most of this site's business would have come from their static holiday homes, which all had their own self-contained bathrooms and kitchens, and it seemed to me that now the school holidays were over they hadn't made much effort with their cleaning. Mind you, it wouldn't be entirely fair to blame the site operators for the foul bits of food left in the communal washing up sinks or the missing wash basin plugs. After all, they didn't leave the leftover food there or pilfer the plugs.

It would have been a small number of irresponsible ignoramuses staying in tents, touring caravans or motorhomes who, without a thought for the majority of responsible campers, left their waste in the sink and stole the plugs. They were probably the same sort of pea-brains who always leave *turn-on, turn-off* type taps turned on, thereby wasting vast quantities of precious metered water, the cost of which has to be absorbed into everyone's site fees, as well as forcing site owners to inflict *press-down* taps on the rest of us. They probably let their dogs foul anywhere they want and never pick it up; or if they do pick it up, throw it in a hedge rather than put in a bin.

Anyhow, at nine o'clock precisely, I was easing the motorhome into the huge Crumplehorn car park on the outskirts of the pretty fishing village of Polperro. We knew this was the only place to park and certainly weren't going to repeat the mistake we made the previous day in Mevagissey by venturing any further! In any case, if my memory serves me correct, there's a huge sign informing unwary motorists that there was *No Vehicular Access to the Village*. We knew it was no exaggeration as the roads in the heart of Polperro are little more than footpaths between the buildings and impassable by car, let alone a motorhome.

Whether they arrive by car, motorhome or by the coach load, the car park is essential for the hordes of visitors who descend on Polperro. It covers a huge area, maybe the size of several football pitches, and didn't seem to be overly expensive. It's about half a mile from the village centre and people who aren't particularly able-bodied, just plain lazy or want to enjoy the novelty of a leisurely ride can, for a small fee, travel on down by horse and carriage, electric trolley bus or minibus. So, all in all, the people of Polperro seem pretty well geared up to welcome the multitude of visitors who descend upon them throughout the year.

The car park was practically deserted at that time on a Saturday morning and I drove straight into one of the nearest spaces to the entrance, paid for three hours and locked up. Then, as we were walking out towards the entrance and looking forward to seeing Polperro again, we heard a loud Cornish voice shouting out to us.

It was the car park attendant who gruffly repeated that he hoped we'd paid for two spaces. Puzzled, I asked him what the problem was as we'd only used one space, and he rudely informed me that the back of the motorhome was slightly protruding over the designated space behind it. Although I couldn't dispute this, I told him there was still plenty of room for a reasonable sized car and that I could move forward a bit if he wanted me to. Unfortunately, he must have got out of bed the wrong side that morning and told me that unless I paid double, I'd have to move the motorhome down to the very far end of the car park where the spaces were slightly larger.

By then I was getting rather irritated, especially as we'd already paid and were wasting valuable visiting time, and if it hadn't been for Emm's calming influence I would have argued my case further. However, before I could say another word to this jumped up *Jobsworth*, she interjected and told him very politely that it wouldn't be a problem for us to move to where he suggested. Through clenched teeth I told her not to be so stupid and that we should stand our ground. But knowing Emm as I did, I had to admit it would be easier in the long run to agree with her. So, muttering under my breath about the absurdity of it all, we climbed back in the motorhome and I drove about four hundred yards right down to the far, far end of the huge, deserted car park where we found the spaces to be no bigger than the one we'd just been evicted from.

Of course, now we were surrounded by vast numbers of empty spaces to choose from, it took a ridiculous amount of time for us to agree between ourselves which one to actually park in. After trying a few out, we finally (or rather Emm) decided, and with her help I carefully backed into her chosen space so that the rear of the motorhome was virtually touching a six foot wooden fence. Satisfied I could back up no further and that not one inch of our vehicle encroached over the white lines, I locked up and we headed off to Polperro.

When we'd got about three quarters of the way to the car park exit, I couldn't help feeling I'd forgotten to lock the motorhome. I wasn't certain; it was just a niggly feeling that wouldn't go away. I was acutely aware it was parked all on its own down the far end of the gigantic car park and that, what with it being a Saturday and a change over day, most visitors would be travelling to or from their holidays rather than visiting Polperro on that particular morning.

Consequently I thought it unlikely that any other driver would willingly choose to park so far away from the entrance, and that our motorhome could be vulnerable all on its own. I imagined some villain not believing his good fortune if, as I feared, I'd not locked up. Not only would he have had an open invitation to ransack all our belongings and walk off with anything he wanted, the alarms wouldn't have gone off and no one would have been any the wiser.

I got more and more paranoid as I also couldn't remember whether I'd left the parking ticket in a prominent position or not, and I imagined the officious car park attendant wandering down to our vehicle with a tape measure to ensure I hadn't encroached by a single inch over the adjacent parking spaces. I then envisaged his disappointment that I'd managed to squeeze into one space followed by his delight that, even though he'd seen me purchase one, I hadn't displayed a valid ticket.

I kept thinking I *must* have locked up and *must* have displayed the ticket, but the lingering doubts just wouldn't go away and my imagination ran away with me. I just knew that if I took the time to go all the way back to the far, far end of the gigantic car park, I was bound to find everything in order. But on the other hand, if I didn't check, sod's law was bound to operate and on our return we'd surely find we'd been ransacked and have to pay a hefty parking fine to boot!

There was just no way I could risk it, so had no choice but to go all the way back and put my mind at rest. I told Emm of my fears and just about heard her groaning as I turned on my heels and started to jog back as fast as I could. Of course, when I got there the motorhome was securely locked with our ticket prominently displayed.

Relieved, but also annoyed that after our early start we'd managed to waste so much time, I ran back to Emm who'd been waiting by some shops near the car park entrance. When I regained my breath and told her everything was all right, she audibly sighed as though I'd gone all the way back to the motorhome for my own amusement and to keep her from the Polperro shops for as long as I possibly could.

Anyhow, at long last we were ready to make our way on foot to the village centre, and as we walked out of the car park I'm sure I saw a satisfied smirk on the face of the most unwelcoming car park attendant we'd ever had the displeasure to meet. His whole attitude was so confrontational and so different from the kindly, helpful man who'd helped us reverse into a dedicated motorhome space in Mevagissey the previous day.

The Polperro car park is far larger than the one in Mevagissey, so why can't they also mark out a few larger spaces especially for motorhomes?

Later on I found out about the history of the car park. Apparently, during the late 1940s a certain Jim Beddoes and his wife, who were virtually penniless at the time, came to Polperro where they set up home in an old rented gypsy caravan which was parked in a nearby disused quarry. Being a brass founder by trade, he rented an old forge where he scraped a living making brass souvenirs, such as piskies and donkeys, which he sold to the tourists.

He must have been an exceptionally hard worker as he soon made enough money to enable him to take on a couple of helpers and buy the forge outright. Leaving the old caravan, he and his wife then took up residence in a rough and ready loft conversion which he constructed above the forge. All his hard work paid off and his business continued to expand, enabling him to buy a property in Polperro which he converted into flats and a shop where, presumably, he sold his brass souvenirs.

Then, in 1956 or thereabouts he had the foresight, as well as the money, to buy a meadow at Crumplehorn for the princely sum of six thousand pounds. This meadow was being used as an overspill car park for the ever increasing number of visitors, but the local council, who wanted to stop coaches driving further down towards the village, didn't think it would be profitable to buy for that figure. However, having turned down the chance to purchase this future goldmine, the same council still had the cheek to ask Mr Beddoes to use his newly acquired land as a permanent coach park!

But full credit to Mr Beddoes who, with the help of a man he met on a train, purchased more of the adjoining land which resulted in the present 4·36 acre car park, with over 550 car spaces, 20 dedicated spaces for coaches, 25 lock-up garages (which, I presume, are rented out to residents as well as visitors), a three bedroomed house and a timber boarded shop. All in all, a veritable gold mine which, even though the council didn't think so, could hardly fail to make money from the ever increasing throngs of motorists and coach operators who flocked to Polperro and had to park in the one and only car park at Crumplehorn.

Sadly Jim Beddoes died in 2006 and the following year his car park, complete with lock-up garages, shop and three bedroomed house was put up for sale with an asking price in the region of £3,000,000, which makes me think that the council's decision not to buy the land to be almost on a par with the man from Decca Records who turned down The Beatles!

Mind you, Mr Beddoes certainly wasn't just motivated by personal profit. Having worked extremely hard to build up his businesses, he was most benevolent towards the local community and is still highly thought of. He represented Polperro as a Liskeard Councillor for many years and was largely responsible for getting the street lights extended up to the village; he used his own money to provide seating areas by the beach, and to create an Age Concern room in the village hall; and, as a final gesture towards the village he loved, he contributed £25,000 towards the upgrading of the public toilets at Crumplehorn, for which I, for one, was grateful.

He supposedly stated that *'his car park customers were the ones who needed this vital facility, so it was his responsibility to fund it'*. He was also quoted as saying that *'when you have nothing, you risk losing nothing'* – true words of wisdom indeed. It's just a shame that the car park attendant didn't feel that benevolent towards us motorhomers on the day we parked there and seemed to go out of his way to be awkward!

27

POLPERRO

Determined not to allow *Mr Jobsworth* to spoil our last day, as soon as we reached the old mill on the edge of the village our moods changed for the better. We resisted the temptation to hop aboard a waiting horse and carriage and by the time we'd completed the therapeutic ten minute walk to the centre of one of Cornwall's most picturesque villages we'd forgotten all about the pompous car park attendant and the problems he'd caused us.

Polperro is squeezed into a steep sided, twisting valley and made up from a jumble of old whitewashed fishermen's cottages which are built on various levels within very narrow streets. It was originally a major fishing port where almost everyone made their living from the sea. The main catch was pilchards, which were once abundant in this part of the world, and huge numbers would have been caught and brought ashore in the pretty harbour. The catches were so great that even though pilchards would have been the staple diet for all the locals, there were always plenty left over to sell on. There being no refrigeration in those days, the fish would have been preserved in salt, then pressed and sealed in barrels ready to be exported to many parts of Europe. Additionally the oil, which was squeezed out in the pressing, would have been an essential by-product to be used for heating and lighting the tiny cottages.

Alas, the once abundant stocks of fish are no more. They started to diminish about a hundred years or so ago and pilchard fishing in this part of the world virtually ceased in the 1960s. In its heyday there were scores of fishing boats, but now only about twelve still commercially operate from Polperro and these look to catch scallops, crabs, monkfish, ray, pollock, bass and cod. Much of these supply the local restaurants that specialize in gloriously fresh seafood dishes which, as I write this, the very thought makes my mouth water. On several of our previous visits to Polperro we've treated ourselves to cod and chips from the local chippie which, bearing in mind its position overlooking the harbour, has one of the most apt and wittiest names for a fish and chip shop I've ever come across, i.e. *Chip Ahoy*.

It appears to be the only fast food outlet in the village and we certainly saw no American burger chains, dubious kebab takeaways or the like. Consequently we noticed a corresponding absence of discarded fast food litter to ruin the ambience of the village and, despite the previous night's strong winds, there was a marked lack of old fish and chip wrappings in the streets. It seems that Polperro's visitors fully appreciate and respect their surroundings and act accordingly by putting their litter in a suitable bin or taking it home with them.

We were too early for fish and chips, but I remembered treating ourselves in the past and walking a short way up the cliff path to sit in the sun, enjoy the view and eat our freshly cooked, piping hot meal straight out of the paper. Absolutely delicious and, for me, far superior to anything the modern fast food companies could even dream of serving up. In my view, fish and chips always taste better by the sea, especially when eaten out of the paper, and the ones served up from Polperro's chippie must rank right up there near the very top.

Mind you, fish and chips aren't that cheap any more, and considering the shortage of fish in the seas these days I suppose that's not too surprising. Even though fishermen have to adhere to strict fish quotas, the remaining fish stocks are in danger of being pretty much exhausted, just like the once plentiful pilchards. That wasn't the case at the end of the 19th century when fish supplies were much more abundant than today and low cost fish had no market value. Consequently much of it was simply thrown back into the sea.

However, the coming of the railways allowed this previously

discarded fish to be rapidly transported inland and delicious cheap fried fish with fried potato chips soon became the staple diet of working class people. Then with the ever growing railway network (and later charabanc trips), working class day trippers poured into coastal towns for a deserved respite away from the factories, still wanting their economical fried fish meal. Consequently in order to satisfy this insatiable demand, fish and chip shops sprang up in all the holiday resorts wherever there was a railway station.

Traditionally, they would have been served up in the previous day's newspaper, but hygiene regulations nowadays prohibit that practice and special white paper and polystyrene containers have to be used. There were concerns that the newsprint could contaminate the food and eventually poison fish and chip gourmets. Also, as most of the newspapers were donated by customers, nobody could ever be sure where they'd been and what germs they could be harbouring. Even though it was a good way at the time to recycle old newspapers, I suppose the decision to outlaw this practice was probably right and it died out by the end of the 1980s.

Even so, I'm not aware of anyone suffering adverse effects after eating their favourite takeaway food in the traditional way. As far as I recall, the fish and chips were never in direct contact with the newspaper, there always being a sheet of greaseproof paper between the food and the actual newsprint. However, progress is progress and I suppose that nowadays we should be thankful there's no danger of anyone's old newspapers being donated to the local chippie after first being read in the lavatory, stored in mouse and rat infested sheds or used to line pussy's litter tray!

Apart from fishing, the other major industry in this part of the world was smuggling, with much money being made by gangs illegally bringing goods in from Guernsey where taxation was exempt by the British government. Ever since the 12th century when Polperro first became a port, smuggling was a way of life. This unlawful, but profitable, trade reached its peak at the end of the 18th century when the costs for Britain's wars with France and America spiralled out of control. The government responded by continually increasing taxation on imported goods, thereby making smuggling even more profitable for the gangs who were prepared to take enormous risks.

One man, a certain Zephaniah Job, brought much prosperity to Polperro during that time and virtually legitimised this illegal duty free import trade. He arrived in Polperro a virtual fugitive from St Agnes, where it was rumoured he'd killed a man, and being educated he became a schoolmaster in the local school where he taught reading, writing and arithmetic.

However, there wasn't much call for such learning in a village relying solely on fishing, so he wangled his way into looking after local boat owners' bookkeeping and financial affairs, thus relieving them from hours of tedious paperwork. Of course, generations of Polperro fishermen had supplemented their meagre fishing income by bringing in contraband, and when the duty was increased even more to fund the Napoleonic wars brandy, tobacco, gin and suchlike became increasingly more expensive and virtually unobtainable. There was already a small legitimate trade between Polperro and Guernsey, which were only a hundred miles apart, and Zephaniah somehow became an agent acting on behalf of both the Guernsey merchants and the Polperro smugglers. And in no time at all he made himself a considerable fortune from such dubious and unlawful activities.

The Polperro smugglers must have been cocking a snoop at the government, as Zephaniah incredibly set up accounts with six Guernsey merchants whose goods were brought over from St Peter Port. A favourite landing place was at nearby Talland Bay, where the contraband would be taken to remote caves and other ingenious underground tunnels before being distributed far and wide.

Between 1788 and 1804 the sums he collected on behalf of just three Guernsey based companies was almost £100,000, which in those days would have been an immense fortune. He became known as the *smuggler's banker,* and bizarrely set up his own bank to deal with all the smuggling transactions, even issuing his own Polperro bank notes! These were printed by his London agent, who also handled the transfer of money to the Guernsey merchants for the contraband they supplied to the Polperro smugglers.

During times of war the government actively encouraged the seizure of enemy ships, a practice known as privateering, and Zephaniah also turned this to his advantage. He initially dealt with all the required documentation on behalf of the privateering ship owners. But later obtained his own privateering vessel, the Swallow, an impressive three masted lugger with a fifty man crew, which eventually captured six French vessels, thus further increasing Zephaniah's already vast fortune!

He must have been a really big bigwig in the community and had a great deal of influence with people in high places. For example, he was instrumental in having the death sentence of one of the smugglers revoked. He attended the poor man's trial where he spoke up for him and then went to considerable lengths to seek a royal pardon from the Home Secretary. The smuggler was reprieved but ordered to serve in the Royal Navy which, although not an easy life, would have been a far more lenient punishment for a seafarer than an appointment with the hangman. Zephaniah also organised lawyers for smugglers unlucky enough to be caught, as well as sending money to the families of those unfortunate enough to be apprehended and sent to prison.

Despite the risks involved, it seems the smugglers usually had an advantage over the Customs and Excise men, who could never have been as familiar with the secret coves or numerous caves and other obscure hiding places where the contraband would be unloaded, then surreptitiously stored. When the gangs decided it was safe to do so, they would load the illicit goods onto horse drawn carts or donkeys and whisk them away across Bodmin Moor en route to London and other faraway places.

These days, even though we all grumble about having to pay any of our hard earned money to the government, be it import duty, VAT, income tax or any other form of taxation, if we're honest about it, most of us can afford to pay our fair share. However, in those days ordinary folk certainly couldn't afford to pay the ever increasing duty and gladly accepted the risks associated with profiting from the illegal smuggling trade. In most cases it was either that or starvation, and they must have thought that Zephaniah Job was a great man, and in his way I suppose he was.

There's a small museum in Polperro dedicated to the history of fishing and smuggling which we've unfortunately never taken the time to visit, nor would we do so on this trip. However, when we're down that way again I fully intend to pay my entrance fee and find out more about Polperro's old fishing and smuggling industries, especially about Zephaniah Job.

As we continued our walk down the narrowing traffic free streets towards the harbour and listened to the seagulls screeching overhead, it was easy to imagine the same scene a few hundred years before, with huge numbers of fish being unloaded from countless fishing boats. Likewise, I could visualise the same scene at night with barrels of brandy, gin, tobacco, tea and other illicit goods being squirrelled away by lantern light to the various hideouts from where it would be moved on and sold for substantial profits with not a penny going to the government. The cottages and streets have hardly changed since those times and the fact that vehicles are largely prohibited greatly enhances the illusion.

However, now that the fishing industry is greatly reduced from what it once was and smuggling is no more *(or is it?)*, most of the present day villagers make a living from a modern and completely legal industry which would have been undreamed of all those years ago. I mean, of course, the tourist trade, which they seem to be rather good at.

Years ago, the only outsiders coming to these remote parts would have been the most unwelcome and hated militia or customs and excise men trying to catch the smuggler gangs, who would have suffered severe penalties if caught. Luckily for the smugglers, however, the militia would have been largely unfamiliar with the wild terrain, remote caves, tunnels and other secret hiding places and would have been at a distinct disadvantage in their quest to catch the smugglers red handed. Nor could they expect any co-operation from the villagers, who were all in on the act and benefiting in some way from the revenue these activities brought to these poor communities. Also, if any local should have been tempted to betray the smugglers, it would have been a pretty safe bet that he (or she) would subsequently be found out and ruthlessly dealt with.

Consequently, more often than not, the authorities would have been unsuccessful in their missions and, much to the relief of the villagers, eventually leave the area despondent and empty handed. If this wasn't the case, then surely Zephaniah Job couldn't have prospered as he did. His part in Polperro's history deserves to be more widely told and, in my opinion, would make a superb film or television series. However, such a film would probably seem too far-fetched to appear credible and maybe that's why, to my knowledge, such a film has never been made?

Nevertheless, an excellent portrayal of Cornish smuggling gangs was seen in the *Poldark* TV series where, for a large sum of money, Ross Poldark turned a blind eye to contraband being unloaded onto his private beach. However, the militia were tipped off and he missed capture by the skin of his teeth. Some of the smugglers were not so lucky, with some being shot and killed during the mêlée on the beach and others captured. The wretched informer was found out, confessed and very severely dealt with by members of the gang by being pushed over a cliff to his death.

Unlike the militia men in days gone by, the thousands of day trippers and holiday makers who come from far and wide to modern day Polperro are welcomed with open arms. The majority of residents are reliant in one way or another on the influx of visitors to make their living and the whole village is geared up for tourism. Although not appearing to have changed that much in the last few hundred years, a fair proportion of the once modest fishermen's cottages have been converted into souvenir shops, tea rooms, restaurants, holiday cottages and guest houses, all of which are contrived to tempt the tourists to part with their money.

Although catering for all pockets, there are no brash amusement arcades or, as already mentioned, American fast food outlets and suchlike. Without being disrespectful to such places, Polperro is no Blackpool or Southend-on-Sea which successfully cater for a different type of tourist. Visitors to this part of the world will enter a quieter, more soothing, virtually stress free haven, where they can relax and soak up the olde-worlde atmosphere which oozes from every nook and cranny of this picturesque Cornish fishing village.

Indeed, as the enormous car park fills up with scores of private cars and coaches (plus the odd motorhome), the people of Polperro look forward to welcoming the hordes of day trippers to their delightful and historic village. All these modern day invaders will spew out of their vehicles and stream down to the village where, despite the crowds of tourists at peak times, they will be transported to a bygone era largely free from the stress and strain of modern urban life. They will enjoy a lovely day out amongst superb scenery and be tempted by the many up-market gift shops, tea rooms, pubs and restaurants which, although tourist-traps in their way, don't rip off the visitors but gently entice them to part with their money.

All these establishments are quaint and cater for most price brackets ranging from the cheap(ish) and cheerful right up to the near top end of the market. I suppose there must be intense competition between all these similar businesses and it's difficult to imagine how they all manage to survive. However, it appears to be a friendly rivalry and, on the face of it, they all seem to make some sort of decent living.

At the end of the day when the day tripping hordes are homeward bound, Polperro must once again become the quiet peaceful place it was meant to be. Visitors lucky enough to be staying in a bed and breakfast or holiday cottage would be absolutely spoilt for choice in deciding where to eat their evening meal. If staying for a week, they could easily try a different venue each night and still not sample them all. They may put on a few pounds or two, but they could easily work it off the next day by walking along the spectacular coast path and, at the same time, work up an appetite for the next gastronomical feast.

We noticed numerous holiday cottages to let, and I couldn't help wondering whether they were owned by locals or affluent people from London and the Home Counties. It's a sad fact of life these days that young people brought up in out of the way villages like Polperro, Cadgwith and the rest have limited hope of finding work or owning a house and living there. Money talks and property prices are hiked so high that young locals are forced out of their villages to make a living elsewhere, whilst small cottages are snapped up by wealthy outsiders to be used as holiday lets or second homes.[26] Such second homers are not seen to contribute a great deal to the local economy and therefore many locals can feel hostile towards them. It's definitely a problem for which there is no simple answer, but somehow, despite all these difficulties, Polperro seems to prosper well enough.

I imagine that visitors who rent the olde-worlde holiday cottages actually spend most of their time in Polperro and end up splashing out a fair amount of money in the local shops, pubs and restaurants. After all, Polperro is such an idyllic spot for a relaxing break free from all the stresses of modern life, so why pay good money to rent a cottage there for a week and only use it as a base to tour the surrounding area?

There are no campsites or caravan parks in Polperro itself and I suppose that, other than the throngs of day trippers, it only attracts the more well-to-do holiday maker who can well afford to rent one of the more up-market cottages. Judging by the number of restaurants and eating places, I imagine that many such holidaymakers dine out in a different one each mealtime and feast on freshly caught fish dishes accompanied by the best wines or beers.

Unfortunately we were too early for lunch and would be home for dinner, so had to be content with studying all the mouth-watering menus on offer. In any case we couldn't have taken Monty into one of the poshest restaurants, although we did see several inviting pubs that were dog friendly. All the menus looked absolutely delicious and,

---

26 At the time of writing an internet search showed over thirty-five holiday cottages in Polperro, but I've no idea of how many second homes there are.

even though some of them were pretty pricey, we promised ourselves that we'd come back some other time and treat ourselves to a really special seafood meal. That is if we could actually decide which restaurant or pub to choose!

For now, we had to be content with a flying visit to refresh pleasant memories of previous trips to this fascinating place, and as we climbed the path between the higgledy-piggledy cottages we found ourselves looking at what many believe to be the prettiest harbour in the whole country. After the night's high tide and strong winds we half expected to see evidence of flood damage, but thankfully everything appeared to be normal. In any case, the tide was out and the inner harbour not much more than an expanse of thick oozing mud sucking on the bottom of boats that could go nowhere until the next high tide. Although still picturesque in its way, we both remarked how much prettier the same view appeared on a previous visit when the tide was up and the sun reflected off the clear blue sea water which completely filled the harbour.

We then decided to stroll up through the picturesque, narrow and traffic free streets in the area known as *The Warren*, which runs alongside the east side of the harbour and was the area where we first stepped into Polperro many years previously after walking up from Talland Bay. It's so named because in medieval times rabbits were caught there for meat, which probably made a welcome change from all the fish that would have been the main source of food. It's not too clear when this practice ceased, but there's still plenty of land behind the area where rabbits probably still thrive today.

An interesting, and much photographed, building in this part of the village is known as the *Shell House*. Indeed we have a several old photos of the girls standing in front of this strange, almost fairy tale like building which is completely covered in seashells. It was the creation of an ex-naval man who lived there in the 1950s, and during his days sailing the seven seas he amassed a huge collection of shells. I imagine that, having settled in Polperro, he wanted a retirement project which would display his collection to best effect, and came up with the unusual idea of rendering his cottage with fresh cement into which he embedded his shells in carefully thought out and intricate patterns, including the Eddyson Lighthouse, various yachts and the name *SHELL HOUSE* in large capital letters.

Just as I'd wondered about the Minack theatre, I cynically speculated as to whether the imaginative old seadog ever obtained planning permission for his original creativity which, even though it has given pleasure to thousands of tourists over the years, would probably contravene today's planning regulations. After all, Polperro is in a conservation area and I somehow doubt whether today's planning laws would allow such a dramatic change to the outside of an original centuries old fisherman's cottage. Nevertheless, it is a unique attraction and a fitting memorial to the retired seafarer, whose meticulous creation will continue to give pleasure to thousands more people of all ages for many years to come.

I noticed that it's now become one of the many holiday homes and is advertised as having a large kitchen/diner, lounge, two twin and one double bedroom, plus a large bathroom. There's also access to a roof top sun-deck, which would have fabulous views across the harbour, as must some of the other rooms.

With a host of mod cons, it certainly seems to be completely transformed from what it must have originally been like when it was built as a basic fisherman's cottage all those years ago. Indeed, if the seaman could come back today I imagine that, after standing outside and admiring his handiwork with the shells, once he'd stepped inside the front door he would hardly recognise the place where he lived in the 1950s. It certainly sounds appealing and, provided visitors are not disturbed by all the tourists standing outside taking photographs, it would be a great place to spend a relaxing holiday or weekend break.

After admiring the *Shell House*, we made our way over to the other side of the harbour where memories of a previous visit during one of our Tencreek holidays were triggered off. We'd bought Rowena a toy snake which she'd taken a particular liking to. It would have been made somewhere in the Far East from pieces of dark brown bamboo, which fitted together so they could move sideways about their vertical axis.[27] There would have been about fifteen pieces and the total length of the snake would have been about forty centimetres, or fifteen inches in old money. When this was held by its tail, the snake would wriggle from side to side in a realistic manner.

We'd all had great fun with that particular toy, especially when sneaking up behind somebody and wriggling it beside their face. Anyhow, young Rowena was so taken by her snake that she'd carried it with her all the way from Talland Bay to Polperro, where she accidently dropped it into the very shallow harbour water just beyond the *Chip Ahoy* fish and chip shop. The tide was out, just like it was now, and even though she was very upset at losing her favourite toy there was no way I could wade through the mud to retrieve it for her.

Since then, whenever Emm and I have been to Polperro we've always stood on the same spot and thought of Rowena and her snake. We've peered down into the water (or more often the mud) and pointlessly looked for any sign of her lost toy. No doubt it was carried out to sea with the tide long ago and is now lying on the bottom of the ocean wriggling realistically as the marine life drifts by. We looked once again and thought about our little girl with tears running down her sweet face because Daddy could not, or would not, wade out through the mud to rescue her favourite toy.

It's strange to think that, at that young age, both my daughters thought I knew virtually everything there was to know and was also capable of doing anything that needed to be done, which is why Rowena was so upset I didn't retrieve her toy snake from the mud. Consequently I find it rather bizarre that when she reached her terrible teenage years she suddenly thought she knew everything and Emm and I knew next to nothing!

Anyhow we carried on around the harbour towards the *Three Pilchards* pub and paused to take in the view. We marvelled at the three storey white washed stone buildings on the other side which rose up

---

27 These days they mostly seem to be made from yellow plastic.

out of the sea, or rather the mud, and I hoped they all had effective damp proof courses. They seemed surreal, almost as if they were the backdrop to some fantasy movie, and I thought that if Polperro wasn't the most picturesque place to live in the whole of the country then it couldn't be that far behind, especially when the tide was up and the buildings and boats were reflected in the water. However, Polperro has been prone to flooding with considerable damage caused to property, and bearing in mind the previous night's very high tide and strong winds, I imagine that residents would always be anxious about living so close to the untameable sea.

We'd both enjoyed revisiting this beautiful village but time was getting on, our car park ticket would soon be running out and we had a hundred mile drive ahead of us. Therefore we forced ourselves to head back to the car park, and as we paused to take a last look at the harbour I was dismayed to see the remains of a wooden bench. Only the rear legs and backrest were left, with the actual seating part and front legs nowhere to be seen

My initial thought was that it must have been vandalised which I could almost understand, but not condone, if it was in some inner city area. But surely it couldn't happen in this peaceful, litter free and virtually crime-less utopian Cornish fishing village – could it?

Looking over the adjacent wall into the harbour, I half expected to see the missing seat languishing in the shallow water below. But it was nowhere to be seen. I then noticed an oval shaped brass plaque screwed onto the back of the bench and on closer inspection saw that it was engraved with the following words in italic joined up writing:-

'In Loving Memory Of
Jean and Gren.
Will Always Be A Part Of Polperro.'

I assumed that Jean and Gren must have either lived in Polperro or were regular visitors, and wondered what sort of lives they led and what stories they could have told. I hoped their seat hadn't been vandalised, and that it had either been taken apart to be repaired or, if that wasn't feasible, that the original plaque would be removed and screwed onto a new seat so that Jean and Gren, whoever they were, would still be remembered for years to come.[28]

Whilst pondering over Jean and Gren we'd virtually forgotten our earlier experience with *Mr Jobsworth*, the car park attendant. Now we realised the time, we started to worry that he would be standing right next to our motorhome waiting to issue an excess parking ticket the moment our time was up and ruin our fine morning with a fine. Consequently we found ourselves stepping out as fast as we could in a determined effort to get back to the car park on time. We would have much preferred a leisurely stroll admiring all the quaint and interesting houses along the picturesque route known as *The Coome*, and it was a shame we had to rush. The River Pol, which is just a stream at that point, runs down along the side of the lane and the houses on that side all have to be reached by crossing small bridges. In the late summer sunshine, with the stream trickling gently down towards the harbour against a background of immaculately kept and colourful gardens, it all looked pretty idyllic. However, I couldn't help wondering what it would be like when it was pouring with rain and the water came rushing down off the surrounding hills between the valley and the sea.

Later on, I found out that there had been two serious floods in recent times, the first in September 1976 and then again in December 1993, which were both caused by high intensity rainfall and the inadequacy of the water course flowing through the village. The 1976 flood coincided with a high surge tide, unnervingly just like the previous few nights' high tides, and resulted in around eighty properties being flooded and one elderly man tragically drowning.

In 1993 ninety-nine residential and business properties suffered from extensive flood damage, but mercifully no loss of life. In both instances, torrents of rainwater cascaded down from the surrounding

---

28 We went back several years later and there was no sign of the seat or a replacement.

hills and caused the tiny stream-like River Pol, which seemed so harmless and picturesque as we walked beside it, to swell up way beyond my comprehension and transform itself into an overwhelming wall of water, which roared down towards the harbour causing misery and destruction along the whole of its course.

How the owners of the flood damaged properties coped, I can't possibly imagine. It must have been harrowing helplessly standing by whilst their precious homes, businesses and possessions were being destroyed by such an uncontrollable and destructive force. When such terrible things happen swarms of reporters and TV crews descend on such stricken communities to report and analyse every single tragic detail and it's front page news – for about a week. Then, once they've reported every devastating detail, they depart, seemingly no longer interested in old news and hardly another word is heard again by the general public who rapidly forget and assume everything must be back to normal.

Of course, it's not just a simple matter of mopping everything up. It must take months, or even years, for flood damaged properties to be dried out, cleaned up and rebuilt. It's not clean sterile water that has to be dealt with; it would be muddy, full of debris and contaminated with foul smelling sewage. Consequently carpets, soft furnishings, electrical goods and everything else that came into contact with the foul water would be beyond redemption. Such possessions are replaceable, but not precious one-off personal items such as family heirlooms and photographs or, of course, someone's very life…

Also, it's not just homes and belongings that are damaged. It's also peoples' livelihoods and businesses, such as shops, restaurants, pubs, tea rooms and suchlike. Even though most people would be covered by insurance, I'm sure it must take ages before claims are met and essential building work completed. So what do people do in the meantime? And where do they live? It must be absolutely horrendous, and when it's all finally sorted out insurance premiums will have rocketed. Or, even worse, their properties and businesses become uninsurable and unsaleable. So, how on earth do the unfortunate owners of such at-risk properties cope whilst it's all sorted out?

As far as Polperro was concerned, as a result of the 1993 flood the Environment Agency decided something had to be done and a flood relief scheme was formulated and constructed. Under normal conditions the river (which, as I said, is actually more like a stream) trickles peacefully down the existing channel through *The Coome*, on through the centre of Polperro and discharges into the sea, just like it was doing when we were there.

Nevertheless, near where we'd parked at the far end of the car park, a huge underground control structure was built. During times of heavy rain, it was designed to divert any increased water flow from the surrounding hills into a three metre diameter by one kilometre long concrete lined flood relief tunnel; its purpose being to direct all potentially devastating water from the control structure to a point above the high tide level to the west of the harbour, thereby bypassing the village and discharging it harmlessly into the sea.

Thankfully these defences were completed just prior to November 1997, just in time to deal with similar conditions that resulted in the 1976 and 1993 floods. It must have been a heart stopping moment for everyone in Polperro, but especially those who'd suffered the most during the previous devastation, as they waited to see if the new flood defence system would actually work. Thank goodness it did and has done so ever since, but one can't help wondering what effects climate change will have on such coastal communities in the future?[29]

Anyhow, by the time we arrived back at the car park entrance we were fifteen minutes overdue. Consequently I was in a bit of a panic and rushed on ahead before *Mr Jobsworth* could pay the motorhome a visit. Luckily I'd beaten him to it and I managed to relax once more. Once Emm and Monty had caught up, we decided to have a quick snack and a cup of tea before setting off for home. (Or rather Emm and I had the snack and cup of tea and Monty had a drink of water and a Bonio biscuit.)

Just in case *Mr Jobsworth* did decide to walk all the way down to

---

29 In 2010 massive power operated gates, which can be closed to keep out abnormal surge tides, were installed across the harbour entrance.

where we were parked, we kept a vigilant eye open and were fully prepared to drive off the moment we spotted him coming towards us. There being loads of spaces and no logical reason why we couldn't have parked much nearer the entrance in the first place, we wanted to get one over on him by gaining some extra free parking time.

On reflection, however, I thought it just as well we hadn't parked too close to the entrance where *Mr Jobsworth* could easily keep his beady eye on our vehicle. After our earlier experience with him, I reckoned that the minute our ticket expired he would have homed in on our motorhome and joyfully slapped an excess parking ticket on our windscreen. At least by parking down the far end of the huge car park, he had to make a fair bit of effort to walk all the way down to where it was parked and back again, which luckily he hadn't bothered to do.

Polperro is such a beautiful and unflustered place that once there, soaking up the atmosphere and discovering all there is to see, it's very hard to leave. Consequently many people could easily underestimate how long they were likely to stay and end up being late back to the car park. I could then imagine the zealous *Mr Jobsworth* eagerly issuing tickets to any vehicle that just happened to be a few minutes overdue.

In any case, a warning to future visitors, *do not under any circumstances try to drive into the village.*

Some motorists have been known to ignore the evidence of their own eyes and blindly follow sat nav directions with disastrous consequences. After getting well and truly trapped in the very narrow streets, which taper and get narrower the further one goes, highly embarrassed motorists have ended up losing wing mirrors, seriously damaging their bodywork or even burning out clutches in their futile efforts to reverse back out again!

A Tesco's delivery van (similar in size to our motorhome) famously got tightly jammed between two walls and was stuck for all of fourteen hours before being released. I can't imagine how the driver felt, but whilst waiting to cook their evening meals I don't suppose his customers thought that every little helps!

But seriously, it would be absolutely stupid to ignore the road signs – in Polperro *narrow* means *quite a bit less wide than your vehicle* and *steep* literally means *quite a bit steeper than your clutch can endure.*

So always park in the car park, make sure you pay for enough parking time and either walk or fork out a few pounds to ride down in a horse drawn or electric carriage. Doing what I did in Mevagissey doesn't bear thinking about – Polperro would be far, far worse!

28

HOME AGAIN & MEMORIES OF THE MISSING MOWER

Feeling rather smug at having staying parked up for almost an hour beyond our time and won a small victory against *Mr Jobsworth*, we finally left for home around one o'clock. Fully expecting to get snarled up in traffic near Plymouth, we were pleased that the road was almost empty and, compared with our experience on the way down, the journey was uneventful. It was a dry sunny afternoon, so no problems with windscreen wipers, and there were no traffic jams to slow us down and stress me out.

Also, of course, I felt far more relaxed about driving the motorhome, being quite happy to let all the speeding cars on the dual carriageways hurtle past in their manic impatience to get to wherever they were going in the fastest possible time. Indeed, during our holiday, whilst dawdling along the more minor roads with hardly ever having another vehicle in front of us, life in the slow lane had been much more enjoyable.

As we ate up the miles, just for a fleeting moment I thought that if I put my foot down we might get back in time for me to be able to watch the afternoon's big football match. Whilst we'd lived in Somerset, Yeovil Town had risen up from the relative obscurity of non-league football to the third tier of the English leagues, a significant footballing achievement and an exciting time to follow my local team.

During the same period, former English champions and two times European champions, Nottingham Forest, had fallen on hard times and were now competing at the same level as unsung Yeovil Town, who they were playing in a league match that very afternoon. A capacity crowd of around 9,500 was expected at Yeovil's compact stadium and I would have loved to be there for this historic fixture.

However, no sooner had the thought entered my head and no matter how much I would have liked to go, I had to accept it was a non-starter. Emm certainly wouldn't have been a happy bunny if I'd been selfish enough to have got back and just left her to sort everything out on her own. Her displeasure would have been acutely felt and completely ruined our good holiday. Even so, I was still tempted but, as the match was all ticket with none being sold on the day and I was ticket-less, the decision was made for me, which was probably just as well…

As our return journey didn't take nearly as long as we thought (and after I'd given up on going to the big match) we started to wish we'd stayed on in Polperro a bit longer or stopped off somewhere on route for a couple of hours. However it was too late now and when we found ourselves turning off the main road into Chiselborough, Monty immediately woke up and started to bark excitedly. This was no surprise as, every time he goes out in the car and we turn the corner to come back into the village, he always tells us we're virtually home by jumping up, barking loudly and wagging his tail. It's not as though he can see out of the car, or in this case the motorhome, so he must have some sort of doggy sixth sense. Either that, or there's something about the smell of the place – but somehow he *always* knows.

Anyhow, as we proceeded up our drive he was well away whilst, without saying a word to each other, Emm and I simultaneously cast our eyes in the direction of the two up-and-over doors on our double garage.

The last time we arrived home after a holiday (we'd been to Switzerland for two weeks on a coach tour) we were horrified to find that one of the doors was wide open. Emm immediately blamed me although I was certain it was closed and locked when we left home.

As far as I was concerned, the only explanation was that someone must have forced it open and got into the garage. If that were the case, they worryingly would have had access to all my tools, including a powerful circular saw which they could have plugged into a power point and, completely unobserved, cut through the adjoining door into the utility room to get themselves inside our bungalow.

Wondering what I would find, or rather what I'd find missing, it was with much trepidation that I went to investigate. Fully expecting to discover a ransacked garage with a large hole in the utility room door and all our valuables in our bungalow either missing or vandalised, I was much relieved that everything appeared to be just as we left it.

After closing the garage door, we checked every room in the bungalow and satisfied ourselves that we'd not been burgled. Having brought everything in from the car and loaded the first batch of dirty clothes into the washing machine, Emm was still muttering that it must have been my fault and that I needed to take more care in future. I was still mystified as to how we could have left an open invitation to any passing opportunist thief. But that was precisely what we appeared to have done.

Sometime later when we were sat in the conservatory drinking a cup of tea and still puzzling over the open door, I noticed how much the grass had grown whilst we'd been away and decided to cut it after finishing my tea. Then, when I went into the garage to get the mower, no matter how hard I looked, it was nowhere to be seen!

It was an expensive petrol driven mower which we bought from the bungalow's previous owner when we purchased the property. It was virtually brand new at that time and, as it was essential I had a powerful and reliable mower to keep virtually a third of an acre of grass under control, I was very pleased to be able to buy it for a reasonable price with the bungalow. Now it was gone, and I just couldn't believe it. Nor could I believe, let alone understand, how I hadn't noticed it was missing when I first looked around the garage immediately after finding the door wide open.

Before we went on that holiday, we'd put one of our cars in the garage and the mower was between the car and the back wall. I had a row of benches down the middle of the garage and, in order to get the mower out, the thieves would have had to squeeze between the car and the benches, lift the mower over the top of the car and out of the up-and-over door at the front. Luckily they hadn't damaged the car in any way which suggested that there must have been two quite hefty, but very careful villains, who even had the cheek to go back for my half full can of petrol.

I got on the phone to the local police who told me how easy it was to get inside these types of up-and-over garage doors. They explained that all that needs to be done is to poke a piece of hooked wire through the gap between the top of the door and the frame, and use it to pull on the thin wire cable which is stretched between the door handle and the locking mechanism. Then, hey presto, the catch is released and the door springs open.

They advised me to fit a couple of large bolts to the top of the door frame inside the garage, so that they locked down over the door itself and made it impossible to open without causing a heck of a lot of damage, which is something petty thieves are reluctant to do as it would draw attention to themselves. However, as the bolts can only be unlocked from the inside, this sound advice is only practicable if there's another lockable access door into the garage (such as our adjoining door from the utility room).

I was naive enough to think the police were about to send a squad car with sirens blaring and a finger print team to check for dabs, which must have surely been left all over the garage door and on the car roof. However, they weren't at all concerned and almost seemed bored with this heinous crime committed against our property. I realised that a major investigation wasn't going to take place to solve the mystery of our missing mower and, apart from giving me the useful tip about fitting security bolts, they just took a few details and gave me a crime number which they said I'd need when making an insurance claim. The saying 'closing the stable door after the horse has bolted' sprang to mind!

Having been brought up in the 1950s and early 1960s with the *Dixon of Dock Green* TV series where crime never paid and the villains always got caught, it was a bit of a shock to realise that the only thing the 21st century police were going to do was fill in a form with a yawn and file it away. Of course, as far as the police were concerned, this was just an everyday occurrence which, as there was hardly a hope in hell of ever catching the culprits, just didn't warrant any effort to follow up. Or if by some fluke they did get caught, they'd almost certainly only receive a slap on the wrist, plus a paltry fine they'd never pay.

I wondered what had happened to our society over the last fifty years, why crime did seem to pay these days and why we paid so much council tax towards a police force, which law abiding citizens hardly ever saw unless they were motorists driving at thirty-three miles an hour in a built up area. But it could have been much worse – at least we were insured and Emm finally let up about me being responsible for leaving the garage door wide open!

Mind you, every day for the next three weeks, we had to watch the grass grow visibly longer, whilst numerous telephone calls were made and various forms were posted back and forth to the insurance company, before the claim was finally settled and we got a replacement mower. By that time, there was five weeks growth of long, thick and very lush West Country grass to cut, which took a heck of a lot of hard work on my part to get under control again. Also, we were still out of pocket, as we had to pay some ridiculous excess towards our claim.

The other puzzling thing about the theft was that we never did find out when it actually occurred and, therefore, for how long the door had been open. Being screened by tall conifer hedges the garage wasn't visible from the lane, so I guess we could consider ourselves lucky that no passing opportunists took advantage by helping themselves to anything else from the garage or broke into the bungalow. I did ask the neighbours if they'd seen anything untoward or noticed when the door first appeared to be open, but none of them even realised it had been.

If the mower thieves ever get to read this — that's if they can read of course — have a personal message for them:

I'd like to thank you for taking that extra bit of care in lifting the mower well clear of the car and not bouncing it across the roof and causing hundreds, if not thousands of pounds worth of damage; also for not stealing anything else. However, I still hope there's some justice in the world and that you did get some comeuppance for breaking into my property in the first place. I hope something horrible happened to you, like dropping the mower on your feet and causing an extremely painful and long lasting injury. Or, if you didn't just sell it for beer or drug money and actually used it to cut grass, I'd love to think poetic justice was done and that you accidentally ran it over your foot and sliced off a toe or two!

Anyhow, when we arrived home this time from Cornwall in the motorhome, everything was just as we left it and we had plenty of time to unload all our stuff. Since the break-in we'd always told our next door neighbours when we were going away, and they'd been good enough to keep a general eye out for any suspicious activity. We also left a key with them so they could come in each day and move any post away from the glazed front door, where it could be seen and advertise the fact that the place was temporarily empty.

Whilst enjoying a cup of tea in the conservatory we ploughed through the huge pile of post that awaited us. It was just the usual stuff, junk mail, free newspapers, bills, letters from banks offering to lend loads of money, and nothing remotely exciting like premium bond winnings or letters from heir hunters informing us some long lost relative, we never knew about, had left us a huge inheritance.

One of the problems about going away in September is that most of the vegetables need harvesting around this time otherwise they bolt and go to seed. This was true of the lettuce and rocket we'd planted and the runner beans were virtually over, with all the remaining beans being tough and stringy. However, there was a superb crop of small cherry tomatoes, which we would be eating at every meal for the next month or so.

Whilst Emm piled the first load of dirty washing into the washing machine and sorted out the rest of the stuff, I took my aunt's old bicycle off the rack where, having travelled all the way down to Cornwall and back, it had remained for the whole trip without once being used. Emm had said all along that that would be the case and, although I hate to admit it, she was proved to be right. Even though I'd stubbornly insisted on taking it I had to agree it had just added to our weight. Also, having Monty with us and only having one bike between the two of us, it was unlikely it would ever be used. That is, unless we bought another one for Emm and Monty sat in the basket…

Anyhow, I then had the rest of the afternoon free to cut the grass front and back, whilst Emm got on with the washing and all her other jobs. At five o'clock I checked the football results and was disappointed to learn that Nottingham Forest had beaten Yeovil Town by one goal to nil. Mind you, a few years previously even in their wildest dreams nobody in Somerset would have imagined that their local football club would be playing such a big team in a league match, so it wasn't too bad. Similarly, in their wildest nightmare, no Nottingham Forest follower would have believed they would be playing in the same league as Yeovil Town and other such small town unfashionable teams.

We were sorry our first motorhome holiday was over but, after a week of having to make up the bed each night and then putting it all away again the next morning, it was good to sleep in our own bed again. It was also good to be able to have a hot bath, use our own toilet and put all our dirty dishes in the dishwasher. We went to bed pretty much exhausted and enjoyed a good night's sleep dreaming of our next motorhome trip, whenever and wherever that might be.

29

SHEPTON MALLET MOTORHOME SHOW

As soon as we woke up, Emm reminded me it was the last day of the motorhome show at Shepton Mallet, which was only a forty minute drive away. She'd cut a two-for-the-price-of-one entry voucher out of a motorhome magazine and suggested we go along and make it part of our holiday.

After our hectic week, I must admit I wasn't all that bothered and was hoping for a restful day before going back to work. Also, I was mindful of how much money we'd ended up spending the last time we looked at motorhomes. Emm said it would be a good opportunity to look around and buy some of the bits and pieces we'd need on future trips and, as a glorious sunny day was forecast, I didn't put up too much resistance.

I took Monty for a quick walk around the churchyard and he seemed exited to be back on familiar territory. All the while I kept my eyes peeled for the Golden Retriever who, given half a chance, he'd want to fight. Luckily he wasn't about, although judging by the way Monty kept sniffing everywhere in an agitated manner I'm sure he smelled where his adversary had been. Thankfully we returned home in one piece to find that Emm had made up a couple of ham and cheese baguettes for our lunch and we were all set to get the show on the road. Or should it have been, get on the road to the show?

As Emm stepped inside the passenger door, Monty seemed to be slightly confused. It was as though he thought it odd that, having returned home after being away in the motorhome all week, we were setting off in it once again. He paused for a moment, looked at both of us in turn then, appearing to give us the benefit of the doubt, leapt inside.

If I say so myself, I then rather expertly reversed out of our parking area, drove down our drive and out of the village. As we approached Shepton Mallet virtually every vehicle we saw on the road was a motorhome of some sort, all of which were either going to the showground or, having already spent a day or two there and camping overnight, were leaving. They ranged from the small camper vans to the huge American Winnebagos, and what with all the friendly hand waving to all these fellow motorhome drivers our arms soon began to ache. So much so, that after a while I just concentrated on driving, kept both hands on the steering wheel and let Emm wave for both of us.

When we arrived we were marshalled into a huge field where hundreds of motorhomes of all shapes and sizes were parked up, as well as a few cars. We supposed that the car drivers had come to look at all the motorhome models with a view to buying one and we felt rather smug that, after our tour of Cornwall, we now considered ourselves to be experienced old hands at this motorhome phenomenon.

Once we'd parked up, we meticulously looked around to pinpoint a landmark or two so that, when it was time to leave, we'd be able to find our motorhome again amongst all the others. More or less satisfied that we'd be able to find our way back by lining up with a large tree and a gap in the hedge, we set off towards the showground entrance, handed over our reduced entrance fees with our voucher and made our way inside.

There, spread out before us like some small town made up entirely of motorhomes, were hundreds, maybe thousands, of different sized models all gleaming in the sunshine, the like of which we'd never seen before. Not really knowing where to make for, we found ourselves wandering along an area where specialist traders were selling all sorts of accessories, gadgets and outdoor paraphernalia, most of which I had no idea motorhomers couldn't do without.

We planned to buy a few things we realised we'd need for future trips; like some ramps, to keep the van level when having to pitch on a slope; a reverse polarity adapter to use in France, where we hoped to go the following spring; and, of course, a selection of hose adapters, so we'd be able to top up with water without wasting any or spraying it all over ourselves. Everything we wanted was on sale in a number of stalls and rather than having to carry our purchases around with us for the rest of the day, I was reasonably happy to browse around, compare prices and buy everything we needed later in the day.

However, after a couple of hours following Emm in and out of all the stalls and sidestepping swarms of people in the hot autumn sunshine, my patience began to wear thin. I just wasn't interested in buying awnings, chairs, fly swatters, bicycles, satellite television equipment, outdoor clothing or most of the other merchandise on offer. It was hot; I was hungry, thirsty, tired and bored and felt as though I could collapse from fatigue at any moment. In fact I felt like I always do when I go shopping!

Emm, however, was in her element and there was no stopping her. She took no notice when I told her I needed a rest, and she always had just one more stall to look at. It had got much more crowded and was no longer possible to take Monty into the stalls lest he got trampled under peoples' feet. So I had to stand with him outside and wait, and wait, whilst Emm inspected everything on offer in each and every stall.

I'm afraid I started to get somewhat ratty as I virtually begged her to take a break, but she took no notice and carried on with her relentless tour of all the retail outlets. Eventually, having walked in and out of the crowds in the mid-day sun Monty visibly flagged, and at long last Emm agreed we should find somewhere to sit down so he could have a rest and a drink of water. I thought it was a good job Monty was with us – otherwise I would have been on my feet all day!

Luckily we found an unoccupied bench to sit on, and with immense relief I finally took the weight off my aching feet. Monty flopped down under the bench in the shade and we gave him his midday Bonio biscuit and a bowl of water, which he gratefully slurped up in next to no time, before curling up to have a siesta. Whilst eating our packed lunch, we noticed a couple coming towards us with a young Border Terrier which was frantically pulling on its lead and making a beeline for Monty. As it approached to have a sniff, Monty stirred and sniffed back in a slightly aloof fashion, but took hardly any notice as the young dog playfully jumped up all over him. Being a much more mature dog, Monty couldn't be bothered to join in with any games. He just wanted to snooze, so lay still and glared at his potential, much younger playmate, whose owners immediately pulled him away.

Border Terrier owners are a very friendly breed and we chatted about our special dogs, all of which have a mind of their own as well as hearing problems. No matter how well trained they are, even though they fully understand each and every command to heel, stay, leave, come or whatever they all have selective hearing, and if their owner's commands are not to their immediate liking, they will ignore them. Even so, we've never met another Border Terrier owner who regretted their choice of dog.

After bidding our new friends farewell, Emm was raring to go once more and wanted to look at all the motorhomes, hundreds of which were on display. I had to admit that that was more appealing than traipsing round all the stalls again, and now that I'd had a rest I was ready to set off once again. Despite being quite happy where he was, Monty trustingly made no protest as Emm showed us a clean pair of heels and sped off towards the multitude of motorhomes, seemingly determined to look inside each and every one of them.

Every motorhome manufacturer was there and the choice of sizes, layouts and styles seemed endless. Emm darted from motorhome to motorhome inspecting every nook and cranny, but as I had Monty to look after and couldn't take him inside, all I could mostly do was stand on the steps and poke my head in.

However, when Emm (or I) really liked a particular model I was able to extend Monty's flexi-lead to its maximum length and, whilst leaving him happily sitting under the vehicle in the shade, step inside for a closer look. At first it was interesting looking around all the various makes and models, but after about the tenth, twelfth or twentieth, my head started to spin. I couldn't help thinking that having only just bought our motorhome, for what appeared to be a very reasonable price, we certainly weren't in the market to buy another – especially at those prices!

I mean, some of them cost anything between ten, twenty or even fifty thousand pounds more than we paid for ours, and there was no way I could even think about spending so much more money. Not unless we won the lottery that is, and as our respective work syndicates had never had a sniff at a big prize I didn't think we could rely on that vain hope to fund a new motorhome. Mind you, for people who were seriously looking to buy their first motorhome or upgrade their existing model, this was the place to come to. The dealers were keen to unload their previous year's models before the new season started, and there seemed to be plenty of genuinely discounted vehicles on offer.

Occasionally, a salesman would appear out of nowhere and engage us in conversation, no doubt checking to see if we were serious buyers, casual browsers or total time wasters. They'd obviously all attended the same motorhome salesman's school, as they waited until we were both inside, then pounced and positioned themselves by the door so we couldn't get out and escape their sales pitch.

First of all they'd ask if we had a motorhome. Then, when we told them we'd only just bought one and returned from our very first trip the previous day, they would further ask whether we were considered upgrading to a later model. Before Emm could give them the wrong impression, I'd quickly say we were perfectly happy with ours at present and weren't in the market for a new one just yet, which to their credit they understood and made no attempt at a hard sell.

However, it was good to look at the various motorhomes and discuss the pros and cons of all the different types with the experts, as if at some point in the future we did decide to change we'd have a much better idea what to look for. Also, having carefully scrutinised the countless motorhomes we saw, we were more than pleased with the one we'd so hastily bought. It certainly fitted our current requirements, and for the price we paid we were happy we wouldn't have got a better deal at the show. Neither of us had any regrets regarding our choice, let alone a serious desire to part exchange it and spend out loads more money on a different model. Well, at least not for a couple of years…

Nevertheless, now that we were no longer complete motorhome novices, it was interesting to inspect all the different models and layouts with a more critical eye. For example, bearing in mind we'd driven down loads of narrow country lanes, we wouldn't have wanted anything bigger. Nor would we really have needed one with a bed over the top of the cabin like many of the popular models have. As well as creating more drag and being more thirsty on fuel than ours, having to climb up and down a ladder to go to the toilet in the middle of the night could have been a bit of a problem.

Emm particularly liked the ones with a permanently made up bed that wouldn't have to be made up each night and put away again in the morning. Although I thought such models would be fantastic passion wagons, I certainly couldn't justify the extra expense. In any case, separate bedrooms and permanently made up beds were only possible on the longer vehicles, which inevitably ended up with a relatively smaller lounge and dining area for daytime use. To my mind, the bedroom took up too much space and a larger living area was more beneficial. After all, unless there's an incredible upturn in our love life, we only need the bed at night, and ours only took a few minutes to make up or put away again leaving a reasonably spacious seating area for daytime use.

We were both impressed with the continental models which were all of an ultra-high standard, although that extra quality was more than reflected in their prices. However, one thing we noticed that wouldn't have suited us was that they mostly came fitted with microwaves and not conventional ovens.

Although we'd used electric hook-ups during our Cornish holiday and could have used a microwave, we didn't intend to rely so much on electricity in future. We ·these microwaves also worked off 12 volts. If so, I suspected they'd either drain the leisure battery or be so low powered they'd take too long to cook anything. (I would have asked a salesman, but didn't want to get drawn into a sales pitch.) We supposed these oven-less motorhomes were designed for the Mediterranean climate where people mainly ate al fresco and cooked on barbecues. But to us, a conventional oven was an essential item. After all, microwaved pasties and pizzas are never quite the same as oven cooked ones.

Some of the British built van conversions also caught our eye. They were of excellent design, with every possible nook and cranny made use of in some ingenious and practical way. They weren't as tall or wide as ours and could possibly be used as an everyday vehicle, thereby dispensing with the need to run a car as well. However, the downside was that they didn't have so much living space and felt ·a bit cramped. Also, their prices were way above what we paid. Even so, we were both impressed by them and agreed that, if we ever won the lottery, we could be sorely tempted…

No matter what, everything about a motorhome has to be a compromise and it's impossible to get everything on one's wish list. For me, the perfect motorhome would be small enough to be used as an everyday vehicle, narrow enough to go down the smallest country lane and low enough to go under any barrier. It would have a good sized kitchen with ample workspace, a fridge freezer and, it goes without saying, a conventional gas oven. (I wouldn't be that bothered about a microwave but, if one could be fitted in, I suppose it could prove useful at times.)

There would be a spacious washroom and WC with a separate shower cubicle and, to satisfy Emm, a separate bedroom with a permanently made up bed, plus plenty of hanging and storage space for clothes and shoes. I would want a large lounge, a comfortable dining area with a permanently made up table, plus at least four seats with seat belts. Also, a large garage area to store all the chairs, tables, bicycles, skis, barbecues and all the other paraphernalia we could be tempted to buy in the motorhome show stalls to take with us. Oh yes, it would be nice to have a dishwasher, a fuel consumption in excess of fifty mpg, the very latest built in Satellite Navigation system and cost not much more than the trade in value of our motorhome to boot!

Unfortunately, even amongst the countless models we saw that day there was nothing that remotely ticked *all* those boxes. When I talked to a salesman about it, he gave me a funny look and asked me what planet I was on. He said he'd only heard of one vehicle which remotely fitted my specification, but it was a 'one-off' and wasn't for sale. He implied it was so hi-tech that it was out-of-this-world and, if it ever did come on the market, its cost would be 'astronomic'. He went on to say it was owned by a doctor who constantly toured in it and was called a *Tardis!*

Anyhow, having finally looked around virtually every single motorhome of all shapes and sizes I, for one, felt completely shattered. However, we couldn't go home just yet, as we had to go back to the stalls to get the levelling ramps, the reverse polarity adapter and water hose adapters, which were the essential items we'd specifically come to buy. So, off we went back to the stalls.

I thought we knew exactly what we wanted and more or less where to get them from, and I naively thought we could just stop off on our way back to the exit, buy them and go home. But nothing is ever that simple with us, for when we got back to the market place Emm started to browse and get distracted again.

We came across the *Camping and Caravanning Club* stall, where they had loads of information on spending the winter motorhoming in Spain or the South of France. This was something we both want to do in the future, and for motorhome newcomers like us it seemed a good idea to arrange it through a club. We were both impressed by the friendliness of the representatives, after all it is known as *the friendly club*, and came away with loads of information on their sites and continental winter breaks.

If we hadn't already belonged to the rival organisation, *The Caravan Club,* we would have almost certainly taken advantage of their discounted introductory offer and signed up on the spot. However, we didn't really see the point of belonging to both organisations at that time, but thought we probably would do so after we'd both retired and had more time on our hands to go away more often.[30]

We spent far more time with *the friendly club* than I wanted to, but they were so friendly it seemed rude to walk away. However, it was getting late and I wanted to get home, have dinner and prepare for work the next day. So, insisting we got a move on, I more or less dragged Emm away and led her to one of the largest accessory stalls where I told her to hold Monty whilst I went in to buy everything we needed.

I straight away picked up a reverse polarity adapter, which I knew would be required in France where I'd read that campsite electrical hook up supplies can be opposite to the UK standard. Without being too technical, it means that the live and neutral wires could be crossed over, and if we British holiday makers just connected our motorhomes and caravans to the French supplies a great deal of very expensive damage could be caused to our electrical systems. Mind you, the polarity is sometimes the same as ours, and if that were the case it would be disastrous to use an adapter to reverse it!

All very disconcerting to a novice like me, and it almost sounds like a devilish plot by the French to gain revenge for defeating them at Waterloo and Trafalgar! So, how does one know whether the supply is safe to plug into? Well, I found out that a reverse polarity tester is required to ascertain whether the adapter is needed or not. All very confusing, and I just hoped it would become much clearer when we actually went to France. Anyhow, I picked up a reverse polarity adapter and the all-important polarity tester, thought the prices for these essential items for French campsites were reasonable and decided to buy them.

---

30 Now we are both retired, we belong to both excellent organisations.

Next on the list were some levelling ramps and there were plenty of them in the same stall. Now that the crowds had died down somewhat, Emm came in with Monty to join me and, despite sucking in our breath when we saw how much they were, we picked out a pair of bright yellow plastic ramps which looked as though they'd do the job.

Emm then saw some similarly coloured plastic runners that were meant to be used if the vehicle got stuck in mud. The idea was to stick one under the front wheels where they'd allegedly provide grip for the tyres and enable the vehicle to effortlessly move forward out of a sticky situation. I wasn't entirely convinced we really needed these, as on the odd occasion my car has got stuck in mud I've always found an old bit of carpet always did the job. However, not wanting to get into a long and protracted discussion and be later than ever getting home, I succumbed and picked up a pair to add to our other purchases.

I thought that was it and was just about to pay when Emm homed in on an enormous selection of plastic drinking glasses, which came in all shapes and sizes. When we were away we drank our wine from plastic throw away cups, which I had to admit didn't taste the same as wine from proper glasses. Also, every time we picked up one of the flimsy cups, we had to take great care not to hold it with too tight a grip lest it collapsed in on itself and caused the wine to spill out over the top – which did happen on more than one occasion.

On the other hand, we were a bit nervous about travelling around with real glass, and I had to concur that plastic wine glasses seemed like a good idea. I would have just grabbed a couple, paid for everything and left, but we had to weigh up all the pros and cons of every style of wine drinking vessel they had on offer. By that time, I couldn't have cared less whether I drank my wine out of a short stemmed glass or long stemmed glass, or whether they were large, medium or small. Well, maybe I drew the line with the small ones! Eventually, Emm chose a couple of medium short stems which, before we could waste any more time, I snatched from her, paid for everything and led her away.

We were almost in striking distance of the exit, when we passed yet another stall which immediately mesmerised Emm. They were selling cleaning materials, and just as we walked past were demonstrating a long handled brush attached to the end of a hose pipe. It looked like a broom with a telescopic handle which could be extended to about twice its normal length, thus enabling it to easily reach the highest point on a caravan or motorhome where the water flowing out of the brush would effortlessly wash it down. We stood with the small crowd that was gathered there and listened to the cockney salesman giving his pitch, and in no time at all had parted with some more cash, convinced that cleaning the motorhome in future was going to be a doddle.[31]

Wanting to get back home before midnight and determined not to spend any more money, I then made Emm stride out back to the car park as fast as I dared. Ours was one of the few motorhomes left, so we had no trouble locating it and all our efforts pinpointing where we'd parked proved to be a waste of time. Monty was just as pleased as me to get back, and as soon as I opened the door he jumped aboard, settled down and immediately fell asleep. I also felt absolutely shattered and wished I could have done the same. Instead, I started the engine and, much later than anticipated, headed for home, waving to the exhausted drivers of all the other motorhomes that were clogging up the roads radiating from Shepton Mallet.

Although I'd moaned and groaned about trekking around the motorhome show, it had been pretty interesting in its way. It was just that it was very hot, I was tired after our holiday and it was all too much to see in one day. These shows, several of which are held all over the country, last several days and I promised Emm we'd definitely go again, but that next time we'd stay overnight and stay at least two full days and have a more leisurely look at everything. We would also take advantage of some of the free evening entertainment on offer

---

31 This proved to be a total waste of money, as I've never been able to find a suitable hose connector that screwed into the end of the handle!

and, as we wouldn't have to drive anywhere, be able to enjoy a drink or two.

When we eventually turned off into our village, Monty was immediately alerted by his mysterious sixth sense and woke up, barked loudly and wagged his tail. I also seemed to wake up at that point, as I realised we'd forgotten to buy the most important items we needed before going away in the motorhome again. That is, the special hose adapters we desperately needed to simplify the job of filling up our fresh water tank. I'd seen the very ones in the very same stall where we bought everything else, but had been distracted looking at all the glasses. Anyway, it was too late now. We were home and had to adjust ourselves to work mode in preparation for the following day.

★ ★ ★

Even though we'd got off to a terrible start in the rain and the grand finale at Shepton Mallet had been exhausting, our first motorhome holiday had been a great success. We'd been to loads of fascinating places, some for the first time and others we'd been pleased to revisit, reminisce and revive happy memories.

Being motorhome newcomers, we'd made a few mistakes and had a few hairy moments, but everything had worked out well in the end. We'd had the freedom of the road, and realised that if we didn't like somewhere we could always move on to pastures new. Conversely, if we particularly liked a place we could stay on and see more of it. We couldn't wait until we retired when we'd have much more time on our hands to take to the road for longer periods, as well as go further afield.

When I told a grumpy old work colleague we'd bought a motorhome, he thought I was mad and said he preferred hotels. Well, maybe some people do prefer hotels, but now we'd had a taste of staying on the move in our motorhome, we fully appreciated the freedom it offered and were looking forward to many more adventures.

There were so many interesting places in the UK we'd never been to, and we wanted to explore much more of our own country. Now that Joscelin had settled in Cumbria we'd have lots of trips up there, and I certainly wanted to tour around the north of England and see places like Iron Bridge, Hadrian's Wall and the Beamish Museum. Even though we are apprehensive about the Scottish midges, we also wanted to tour Scotland and especially climb Ben Nevis. After all, in the past we'd made our way to the summits of the highest peaks in England and Wales and just had to complete the set.

Also, we wanted to travel abroad and follow the sun, especially during our cold winter months. We were already planning a trip to France the following year and were going to get Monty a pet passport. After all, he's getting on a bit now, and we're sure he thinks that coming on holiday with us in the motorhome would be far better than being left behind in kennels not knowing how long it will be before we come back to collect him.

So, having survived our first motorhome tour around Cornwall, we no longer felt quite like motorhome novices and were sure we'd enjoy many more holidays on the move in our truly mobile holiday home.

Appendix 1

THINGS TO TAKE ON FUTURE TRIPS

Essentials

1. Basic Tool Kit
2. Ordnance Survey Maps
3. Flip Flops to Wear in Shower
4. Plugs for Campsite Wash Basins
5. Old Gloves for Winding Up Wet and Muddy Electric Cable
6. Selection of Hose Connectors
7. Old Washing Machine Hose for Emptying Grey Water
8. Flexible Plastic Container for Muddy Boots
9. Levelling Blocks

Desirables

10. Television with Built in DVD Player & Selection of DVDs
11. Extra Tinned Food and Dried Foods, e.g. Beanfeasts
12. Electric Kettle (To Save Gas When Connected to Electric Hook-up)
13. SatNav
14. Reversing Camera

And most importantly, a SENSE OF HUMOUR!!!

Appendix 2

LIST OF PLACES TO VISIT (OR REVISIT) IN FUTURE

1. St Michaels Mount
2. St Ives Tate Gallery
3. Barbara Hepworth Museum and Sculpture Garden
4. Coast Path at Zennor including *The Devil's Frying Pan*
5. Geever Tin Mine
6. Levant Beam Engine
7. Complete coast path walk from Land's End to Sennen Cove
8. Porthcurno Telegraph Museum
9. Minack Theatre for a Performance
10. Charleston (When the Tall Ships are in the Harbour)
11. Eden Project
12. Lost Gardens of Heligan
13. Looe Island
14. Polperro Museum of Smuggling and Fishing
15. Posh restaurant in Polperro for special sea food meal

Nigel Rowland Hicks worked man and boy for the Ministry of Defence in a number of aeronautical engineering jobs. He has always enjoyed reading, especially biographies – he likes to know what makes people tick – as well as nostalgia, travel and humour, and always has a book on the go. Sometimes when he's been disappointed with a certain book, he's thought he could have written a better one himself, but never found the time to do anything about it. Whilst a senior manager at Yeovilton, he often thought that embellishing annual staff reports and bonus reviews to be excellent practice for writing fiction! So, when he and his wife bought their motorhome and everything started to go wrong, he decided to record everything that happened and then write it up. Although not fiction – it couldn't possibly have been made up – *Some People Prefer Hotels* is the result.'

ACKNOWLEDGEMENTS

There are a number of people I'd like to thank for their immense help in producing this book: Penny Stent for painstakingly poof reading and rooting out all the silly mistakes I couldn't see for myself; Jimbob Issacs for miraculously metamorphosing the images in my mind to that on the cover illustration; my wife, Emm, for her years of patience and encouragement – well most of the time anyway! – whilst I locked myself away in my study writing and researching; all the staff at Matador for making it possible, and finally to Ray, my grumpy old work colleague, for inadvertently giving me the title *Some People Prefer Hotels*.

If you have enjoyed this book, why not write a review at

www.troubador.co.uk

or the author's own website,

somepeoplepreferhotels.co.uk (where you can see loads more photos of our trip)